LABOUR
WELFARE ADMINISTRATION

Labour Welfare Administration

Theories & Legal Provisions

Edited by
Jagdish

AKANSHA PUBLISHING HOUSE
NEW DELHI - 110 059 (INDIA)

AKANSHA PUBLISHING HOUSE
R-37B, Vani Vihar, Uttam Nagar
New Delhi - 110 059
E-mail: ektabooks@yahoo.com

Show Room
4649/21, Ansari Road
Daryaganj, New Delhi - 110 002

Labour Welfare Administration

First Published, 2004

ISBN 81-87606-64-9

PRINTED IN INDIA

Published by M.P. Misra for Akansha Publishing House,
New Delhi - 110 059 and Printed at Tarun Offset Press, Delhi.

Contents

Preface

Labour welfare is a generic concept, subsuming several fields of development that fall under economic development, industrial growth, social justice and democratic growth. Amidst the several books on the subject, the present volume spells out the significant factors that the organisers, administrator, employer, planner and trade union activist has to take care of and be sensitive in understanding workers, their needs and working with them for their welfare and advancement.

Though exploitation of labour has been a universal phenomenon, before the advent of welfare and other legislation in India, the conditions of labour were very pathetic. Exploitation of child labour long and tedius working hours, bad sanitation, lack of safety measures etc. were the regular features of labour life. The movement to improve the working conditions of Indian labour started with the passing of first Factories Act in 1881. Thus emerged the institution of Labour Welfare Administration.

This book encompasses twelve chapters pertaining to labour welfare administration. The material is based on secondary sources—abstracts, reports, articles in journals and books. We owe a deep sense of indebtedness to all whose work are cited or borrowed. Entire credit goes to them. And no claim for originality.

The employers, administrators, organisers and field activists, teaching and training community, concerned with and working in the field of labour welfare administration will find this book useful and informative.

—Editor

1

Labour Welfare: A Historical Account

Before the advent of welfare and other legislation in India, the conditions of labour were miserable. Exploitation of child labour, long working hours, bad sanitation, absence of safety measures, etc., were the regular features of factory life. The earliest legislative approach could be traced back to the passing of the Apprentices Act of 1850. This Act was enacted with the objective of helping poor and orphaned children to learn various trades and crafts. The next Act was the Fatal Accidents Act of 1853 which aimed at providing compensation to the families of workmen who lost their life as a result of "actionable wrong". Next came the Merchants Shipping Act of 1859, which regulated the employment of seamen and provided for their health, accommodation, etc. Earlier attempts at legislation in this country were mainly aimed at regulation of employment.

Meausre during Pre-independence Era

The movement to improve the working conditions of Indian labour started with the passing of the first Indian Factories Act in 1881. The pathetic conditions in which labour worked in the textile mills in Mumbai during those days, as testified by the Factory Commission of 1875 was the immediate cause for the passing of the Act. The Act applied to factories employing not less than 100 persons and using power. Under this Act, the employment of children below the age of 7 years was prohibited, while those between 7 and 12 years were not to work for more than 9 hours a day. An hours' daily rest and 4 holidays in a month were prescribed for children. Adult labour, however, was not protected in any manner. It was found inadequate in many respects. Anyhow, it recognized the right of the government to safeguard the interests of the workers by means of suitable legislation. The Mulock Commission was appointed by the Government of Bombay in 1884 to review the working of the Factories Act of 1881. N.M. Lokhande, founder of the Bombay Mill Hands' Association brought the workmen together on two different occasions in 1884 and presented on their behalf a charter of demands to the Commission. Under pressure from labour, the Bombay Milliowners' Association conceded the demand for a weekly holiday.

The Factories (Amendment) Act 1891 was passed as a result of the recommendations of the Bombay Factory Commission of 1884 and the Factory Labour Commission of 1890. It applied to all factories employing 50 persons or more. The lower and upper age limits for children were raised to 9 and 14 respectively and their hours of work were limited to 7 and between 5.00 a.m. and 8.00 p.m. Employment of women between 7.00 p.m. and 5 a.m. was prohibited. Women were allowed to work for 11 hours in a day with 1½ hours' rest. Provisions relating to better ventilation, cleanliness and for preventing overcrowding overcrowding in factories were also made.

The Government of India appointed a Commission in 1907 to study the working conditions of labour in industry and make recommendations. A more comprehensive Act was introduced in 1911 on the basis of the recommendations of this Commission. The Indian Factories Act of 1911 was made applicable also to seasonal factories working for less that 4 months in a year. The hours of work for children were reduced to 6 per day. The hours of work of an adult male worker were specified for the first time to 12 hours a day. Certain provisions were also made for the health and safety of the industrial workers.

In the meanwhile, voluntary action in the field of labour welfare also made considerable progress. Group efforts came to the forefront. The Amalgamated Society of Railway Servants of India and Burma (1897) started a number of friendly benefit schemes. The Printers Union, Calcutta (1905) and the Bombay Postal Union (1907), introduced mutual insurance schemes, night schools, educational spends, funeral allowances, etc. In 1910, the Kamgar Hitvardhak Sabha was established which helped variously the workers.

The outbreak of the World War-I in 1914 led to a number of new developments. The Russian Revolution had a tremendous impact on the attitudes of government and society towards labour. During the war years (1914-18) the number of factories and the number of persons employed therein increased. Wages did not keep pace with the rising prices and profits. The working class became more conscious as a result of the general unrest following the war. The establishment of the International Labour Organization in 1919 was another important landmark in the history of labour welfare movement in our country. The I.L.O. declared that universal peace can be established only if it is based upon social justice. The formation of AITUC (1920), the first central trade union organization in our country, also helped in furthering the cause of welfare movement.

As a result of all these developments, the importance of labour in economic and social reconstruction of the world was recognized. All these factors created the background for a new factory law. Following industrial unrest in 1919 and 1920, the Government of India passed the Indian Factories (Amendment) Act, 1922 which was made applicable to all the factories using power and employing not less than 20 persons. Children below 12 years of age were not to work in factories and those between the years of 12 and 14 were not to work for more than 6 hours a day. Children and women were not to be employed between 7.00 p.m. and 5.30 a.m.

The hours of work for adults were limited to 60 in a week, and 11 in a day. Factory inspection was improved by the appointment of full time factory inspectors possessing technical qualifications.

The Royal Commission on Labour under the chairmanship of J.H. Whitley was appointed in 1929 to enquire into and report on the then existing conditions of labour in industrial undertakings, plantations, etc., in British India. The Commission made an indepth survey of different aspects of health, efficiency, welfare, standard of living, conditions of work and relations between employers and employees and submitted its monumental report on March 14, 1931. It recommended the enactment of a number of legislations relating to payment of wages in time, minimum wages, need for health insurance for industrial workers, improvement of working conditions of plantation workers, etc. Most of the recommendations of this Commission were accepted by the government and they constituted the powerful influence that led to the enactment of the Factories Act of 1934.

Apart from amending and consolidating all the previous enactments, the Factories Act, 1934 introduced a number of important changes. It drew a distinction between perennial and seasonal factories. The hours of work for children between 12 and 15 were reduced from 6 to 5 per day, while those for women from 11 to 10 in all kinds of factories. The Act also made provision for the improvement of working conditions within a factory. For the first time in factories' legislation, welfare measures were also thought of and provision was made to provide rest sheds and creches by big factories.

A number of committees also were set up by the provincial governments to enquire into the working conditions of labour including the provision of housing facilities. Some of these committees were : Bombay Textile Labour Enquiry Committee (1937), the Kanpur Labour Enquiry Committee (1937), the Central Provinces Textile Labour Enquiry Committee (1938) and the Bihar Labour Enquiry Committee (1938). These Committees conducted detailed investigations regarding housing facilities available in various industries and drew pointed attention of the government towards inadequate and unsatisfactory housing conditions of industrial workers.

One more milestone in the field of labour welfare was reached with the appointment of Labour Investigation Committee (Rege Committee) in 1944. The Committee was asked to investigate the problems relating to wages and earnings, employment, housing and social conditions of workers. The Committee went into details of the working conditions, including welfare measures available, for workers employed in a large number of industries. The Committee covered different areas in labour welfare such as housing policy, rest and recreation, occupational diseases, relief in the case of old age and death, creches, canteens, medical aid, washing and bathing facilities, educational facilities, etc. For the first time in India, this Committee highlighted the importance of welfare measures for workers in improving their social and economic life. it also emphasised the need for strengthening the enforcement machinery for effective implementation of various laws.

In May 1944, the grand Charter of Labour, popularly known as the Declaration of Philadelphia, was adopted by the member states of the I.L.O. Amongst its aims and objects, the Declaration said that labour is not a commodity and that it is entitled to a fair deal as an active participant in any programme of economic development or social reconstruction.

The World War-II brought about far-reaching consequence in all fields of activities. The need for sustained and increased production gave a filip to Indian industry. The number of factories and factory employees increased enormously. The government took the intiative and actively promoted various welfare activities among the industrial employees. A number of legislations were also enacted for the welfare of the working classes.

Post-Independence Era Scenario

After Independence, the labour welfare movement acquired new dimensions. It was realized that labour welfare had a positive role to play in increasing productivity and reducing industrial tensions. The state began to realize its social responsibilities towards weaker sections of the society. The emergence of different central trade union organizations—INTUC (1947), HMS (1943), UTUC (1949), BMS (1955) CITU (1970), NLO, etc. — gave a further filip to the growth of labour welfare movement.

Mainly on the basis of the recommendations of the Rege Committee, the Government of India enacted the Factories Act, 1948. To draft this important piece of legislation, the services of Sir Wilfried Garrett, (who was Chief Inspector of Factories in the United Kingdom before he came to India) were utilised. He drafted the legislation in detail using his wide experience of Factories' Law. The Factories Act of 1943 came into effect from 1st April, 1949. It is a comprehensive piece of legislation. The Act applies to all establishments employing 10 or more workers where power is used and 20 or more workers where power is not used, and where a manufacturing process is being carried on. However, Section 85 of the Act empowers the state governments to extend all or any provisions of the Act to any premise. It contains many important provisions regarding health, safety, welfare, employment of young persons and children, hours of work for adults and children, holidays, leave with wages, etc.

The responsibility for administration of the Act rests with the state governments who administer it through their own Factory Inspectorates. The onus for compliance with the provisions of the Act wholly rests on the occupier of the factory, though certain obligations are also imposed on workers. The Directorate-General of Factory Advice Service and Labour Institutes coordinate the work of enforcement of the Factories Act throughout the country, frame Model Rules and suggest amendments to the Act and the Rules in consultation with the State Chief Inspectors of Factories.

The Constitution of India enshrined a list of Fundamental Rights and Directive Principles of State Policy for the achievement of a social order based on Justice, Liberty, Equality and Fraternity. It is stated in the chapter embodying the Directive Principles that "the State, shall strive to promote the welfare of the people by securing and protecting as effectively as it may a social order in which justice, social economic and political, shall inform all the institutions of national life."

Many labour welfare activities were incorporated in different five year plans. The First Five Year Plan (1951-56) paid considerable attention to the welfare of the working classes. It laid emphasis on the development of welfare of the working classes. It laid emphasis on the development of welfare facilities, for avoidance of industrial disputes and for creating mutual good-will and understanding. During this period, the Plantations Labour Act, 1951, the Mines Act, 1951, the Employees' Provident Fund Act, 1952, were enacted. A subsidised housing scheme for industrial workers was evolved in 1952. The state governments passed various laws regarding housing for industrial labour, e.g., the Bombay Housing Board Act, 1948.

During the Second Five Year Plan (1956-61) the importance of better working conditions had been progressively recognized. Greater stress was laid on the creation of an industrial democracy. The Second Five Year Plan saw further developments in the field of labour welfare. New enactments were made to cover seamen and motor transport workers. The coverage of the Employees' State Insurance Scheme was also extended bringing in its fold more workers. A comprehensive scheme known as Dock Workers (Safety, health and Welfare) Scheme was drawn up in 1951. In 1959, the

Government of Assam passed an Act called the Assam Tea Plantations Employees' Welfare Fund Act. In April 1956, a New Plantation Labour Housing Scheme was envolved which envisages a certain amount of loan for construction of houses for workers. Various state enacted legislation to regulate the working conditions in shops and establishments. The Second Five Year Plan period also saw a number of enactments in the field of industrial housing by various state governments.

The Third Five Year Plan (1961-66) stressed the need for more effective implementation of various statutory welfare provisions. It recommended improvement in working conditions and emphasised greater productivity and more efficiency on the part of workers. It called upon the state governments to strengthen the factory inspectorates for effective implementation of various labour enactment. The Plan also recommended setting up of co-operative credit societies and consumers' stores for industrial workers, and emphasised the role of trade union and voluntary organizations in administering such co-operative. Some of the legislative measures during this period include the Maternity Benefit Act, 1961, Apprentices Act, 1961, Iron-Ore Mines Labour Welfare Cess Act, 1961 and the Payment of Bonus Act, 1965. Some of the state governments have also providing for passed labour welfare funds.

The Fourth Five Year Plan (1969-74) provided for the expansion of the Employees' State Insurance Scheme to cover medical facilities to the families of insured persons, and to cover shops and commercial establishments in selected centres. During the Fourth Plan period, the Contract Labour (Regulation and Abolition) Act, 1970, the Payment of Gratuity Act, 1972, Employees' Family Pension Scheme were passed. The Plan directed that programmes for welfare centres, holiday homes, and recreational centres should be included under the state plan, and stress be laid on strengthening labour administration machinery for effective enforcement of labour laws. For labour welfare programmes, a provision of Rs. 37.11 crore was made in the Plan.

The Draft Fifth Five Year Plan (1974-79) also laid down programmes for labour welfare. For promoting industrial safety in increasing measure, the Plan provided for setting up of safety cells in various states. An amount of Rs. 57 crores was provided for labour welfare including craftsmen training and employment service.

In the Sixth Plan (1980-85) according to the Planning Commission, "the thrust of the programmes should be on implementing effectively the measures contemplated in different legislative enactments and in extending the coverage of the employees state insurance scheme, the employees provident fund and family pension scheme. Special programmes would also need to be undertaken by the state governments for the benefit of agricultural labour, artisans handiloom weavers, fishermen, leather workers and other unorganized workers in the rural and urban areas". An outlay of Rs. 161.9 crores is proposed for Labour and Labour Welfare Programmes for the period 1980-85. Of this, the Central outlay would be of the order of Rs. 78.5 crores and the remaining Rs. 83.4 crores being accounted for by states and union territories.

The Committee on Labour Welfare (1966-69), set up by the Government of India under the chairmanship of Shri R.K. Malviya reviewed at length the functioning of various statutory and non-statutory welfare schemes in industrial establishments, both in the public and private sector, including mines, plantations, railways, etc., and made comprehensive recommendations for their improvement. The National Commission on Labour (1966-69) also covered several aspects of welfare services in different establishments and made useful suggestions for their improvement.

The above survey of the labour welfare movement shows

that there are schemes of two types in the development of labour welfare—Firstly, a movement through voluntary effort by some of the employers and secondly, the legislative movement. In the field of labour welfare, the government is now playing a triple role—that of a legislator, administrator and promoter. In spite of all these efforts, the welfare work in India is still considerably below the standard set up in other countries. However, it has come to stay as an accepted feature of employment conditions and is bound to make rapid progress in the years to come, especially when the Indian Republic is wedded to the ideal of a welfare state with socialistic objectives.

2

Philosophy of Labour Welfare

Labour welfare includes both the social and economic contents of welfare. Social welfare is primarily concerned with the solution of various problems of the weaker sections of society like prevention of destitution, poverty, etc. It aims at social development by such means as social legislation, social reform, social services, social work, social action, etc. The object of economic welfare is to promote economic development by increasing production and productivity and through equitable distribution. Labour welfare is a part of social welfare, conceptually and operationally. It covers a broad field and connotes a state of well-being, happiness, satisfaction, conservation and development of human resources.

The Concept

Labour welfare can be viewed as a *total concept*, as a *social concept* and an a relative concept. The total concept is a desirable state of existence involving the physical, mental, moral and emotional well-being. These four elements together constitute the structure of welfare, on which its totality is based. The social concept of welfare implies the welfare of man, his family and his community. All these three aspects are inter-related and work together in a three-dimensional approach. The relative concept of welfare implies that welfare is relative in times and place. It is a dynamic and flexible concept and hence its meaning and content differ from time to time, region to region, industry to industry and country to country, depending upon the value system, level of education, social customs, degree of industrialization and general standard of the socio-economic development of the people.

Labour welfare implies the setting up of minimum desirable standard and the provides of facilities like health, food, clothing, housing, medical assistance, education, insurance, job security, recreation, etc. Such facilities enable the worker and his family to lead a good work life, family life and social life. Labour welfare also operates to neutralise the harmful effects of large-scale industrialization and urbanization.

Definitions

The *Oxford Dictionary* defines labour welfare as "efforts to make life worth living for workmen". *Chamber's Dictionary* defines welfare as a state of faring or doing well; freedom from calamity, enjoyment of health, prosperity, etc. The *Encyclopaedia of Social Sciences* defines it as "the voluntary efforts of the employers to establish, within the existing industrial system, working and sometimes living and cultural conditions of employees beyond what is required by law, the customs of the industry and the conditions of market" In the words of R.R. Hopkins, "Welfare is fundamentally an attitude of mind on the part of management, influencing the method by which management activities are undertaken "Obviously the emphasis here is on the "attitude of mind". Arthur James Todd defines welfare work at "anything done for the comfort and improvement, intellectual and social, of the employers over and above the waves paid, which is not a necessity of the industry." E.S. Proud defines welfare works as "Voluntary efforts on the part of the employers to improve the existing industrial system and the conditions of employment in their own factories." In the Report II of the ILO Asian Regional Conference, it has been stated that worker's welfare may be understood to mean "such services, facilities and amenities, which may be established outside or in the vicinity of undertakings, to enable the persons employed therein to perform their work in healthy and congenial surroundings and to provide them with amenities conducive top good health and high morale." The Labour Investigation Committee (1944-46), includes under labour welfare activities anything done for the intellectual, physical, moral and economic betterment of the workers, whether by employers, by government or by other agencies, over and above what is laid down by law or what it normally expected as part of the contractual benefits for which the workers may have bargained." The Report of the Committee on Labour Welfare (1969) includes under it "such services facilities and amenities as adequate canteens, rest and recreation facilities, sanitary and medical facilities, arrangements for travel to and from work and for the accommodation of workers employed at a distance from their homes, and such other services, amenities and facilities including social security measures as contribute to improve the conditions under which workers are employed."

The entire field of welfare is said to be one "in which much can be done to combat the sense of frustration of the industrial workers, to relieve them of personal and family worries, to improve their health, to afford them means of self expression, to offer them some sphere in which they can excel others and to help them to a wider conception of life". It promotes the well-being of workers in a variety of ways. Welfare work 'covers all the efforts which employers make for the benefit of their employees over and above the minimum standards of working condition fixed by the Factories Act and over the above the provisions of the social legislations providing against accident, old age, unemployment and sickness," opines N.M. Joshi.

Scope of Social Welfare

It is somewhat difficult to accurately lay down the scope of labour welfare work, especially because on the fact that labour is composed of dynamic individuals with complex needs. Its scope has been described by writers and institutions of different shades in different ways. The scope of labour welfare can be interpreted in different ways by different countries, with varying stages of economic development, political outlook and social philosophy. While expressing its interpretation regarding the scope of labour welfare, the ILO has observed: "the term is one which lends itself to various inter-pretations and it has not always the same significance in different countries. Sometimes the concept is a very wide one and is more or less synonymous with conditions of work as a whole. It may include not only the minimum standard of hygiene and safety laid down in general labour legislation, but also such aspects of working life as social insurance schemes, measures for the protection of women and young workers, limitation of hours of work, paid vacations etc. In other cases, the definition is much more limited, and welfare, in addition to general physical working conditions, is mainly concerned with the day-to-day problems of the workers and the social relationships at the place of work. In some countries the use of welfare facilities provided is confined to the workers employed in the undertaking concerned, while in others the workers' families are allowed to share in many of the benefit which are made available." wide field of amenities and activities, limits cannot be rigidly laid down regarding its scope for all industries and for all times. In the final analysis, labour welfare services should include all extra-mural and intra-mural welfare work, statutory and non-statutory welfare facilities undertaken by the employers, government, trade unions or voluntary organizations and also social security measures which contribute to workers' welfare such as industrial health, insurance, provident fund, gratuity, maternity benefits, workmen's compensations, retirement benefits, etc. More specifically, we may examine the ways in which labour welfare is classified in order to obtain a clearer understanding of its scope. Labour welfare work can be broadly divided into two categories (*i*) statutory, and (*ii*) non-statutory or voluntary. Statutory welfare consists of those provisions of welfare work which depend for their implementation on the corrosive power of the government. The government enacts certain rules of labour welfare to enforce the minimum standards of health and safety of workers. The employers are required by law to fulfill their statutory obligations on welfare. Every country is increasing gradually its statutory control over labour welfare. Non-statutory welfare measures include all those activities which employers undertake for the welfare of their workers on a voluntary basis. There are some social welfare organizations which undertake voluntary welfare services, for instance, Y.M.C.A. Some of the trade unions also undertake voluntary welfare work for the benefit of their members.

The Committee of Experts on Welfare Facilities for Industrial Workers constituted by the ILO in 1963 had divided the welfare services in two groups: (a) Welfare amenities within the precincts of the establishment (intra-mural): latrines and urinals, washing and bathing facilities, creches, rest shelter and canteens, arrangements for drinking water, arrangements for prevention of fatigue, health services including occupational safety, administrative arrangements within a plant to look after welfare, uniforms and protective clothing and shift allowance; (b) Welfare amenities outside the establishment (extra-mural): maternity benefit, social insurance measures including sports, cultural activities, library and reading room, holiday homes and leave travel facilities, workers; cooperatives including consumers' cooperative stores, fair price shops and co-operative thrift and credit societies, vocational training for dependants of workers, other programmes for the welfare of women, youth and children, and transport to and from the place of work. Thus, labour welfare is very comprehensive and embraces a multitude of activities of employees, state, trade unions and other agencies to help workers and their families.

Aims and Objectives

The aim of welfare activities is partly humanitarian—to

enable workers to enjoy a fuller and richer life—and partly economic—to improve the efficiency of the workers—and also partly civic-to develop among them a sense of responsibility and dignity and thus make them worthy citizens of the nation. Another object of labour welfare is to fulfill the future needs and aspirations of labour.

The following motives and considerations have prompted employers to provide welfare measures: (1) Some of the early philanthropic and paternalistic employers tried to ameliorate the working and living conditions of their workers by providing various welfare measures; (2) Some of them took recourse to welfare work to win over their employees' loyalty and to combat trade unionism and socialist ideas. The devotion to welfare work by many American employers during the twenties could be attributed to their anti-unionism. However, such a motive did not succeed in checking the spread of trade unionism; (3) Some employers provided labour welfare services to built up a stable labour force, to reduce labour turnover and absenteeism and to promote better relations with their employees; (4) At present, labour welfare has been conceived of by some employers as an incentive and good investment to secure, preserve and develop greater efficiency and output from workers. Anyhow, time is no direct relationship between welfare work on the on hand and efficiency and productivity on the other. Apart from this, it is very difficult to quantify the additional contribution of welfare measures to the increased productivity. However, some studies have shown a positive link between labour welfare and productivity; (5) The purpose behind provision of welfare amenities by some companies is to enhance their image and to create an atmosphere of good-will between labour and management and also between management and the public; (6) One of the objects for provision of welfare activities in recent times by certain employers is to save themselves from heavy taxes on surplus.

The aims and objectives of labour welfare have progressively changed during the last few decades. From the primitive policing and placating philosophy of labour welfare, it gradually moved to the era:

1. The employer should not bargain labour welfare as a substitute for wages or monetary incentives. In other words, the workers have a right to adequate wages in addition to welfare measures.
2. The labour welfare work of an organization must be administratively viable and essentially development oriented.
3. The labour welfare activities should pervade the entire hierarchy of an organization. Management should be welfare-oriented at every level.
4. There should be proper co-ordination, harmony and integration of all labour welfare services in an undertaking.
5. The management should ensure co-operation and active participation of unions and workers in formulating and implementing labour welfare programmes.
6. There should be periodical assessment or evaluation of welfare measures and necessary timely improvements on the basic of feed-back.

Financing for the Welfare

1. The capacity of the economy puts the ultimate limit to the extent of welfare measures to be provided to the workers or to any other section of society.
2. If is difficult to specify who bears the costs of welfare services. Even where employers finance the welfare activities, either voluntarily or under the requirements of law, no body can say who meets the ultimate costs; the employers, the consumers or the workers. The employers do strive to pass on the burden to the consumes by raising prices or to the workers by delaying wage increases.
3. It is really difficult to make the employers pay for the welfare amenities out of their profits. It is the community which pays for the welfare services and the employer is

merely an agency for collecting the cost from the community and spending it on the welfare of workers.

Though numerically small, the industrial workers in India today constitute functionally a very significance vulnerable element of the country's population. They also contribute substantially to the nation's economy. This group faces certain unique problems in their work life like long hours of work in unhealthy surroundings, drudgery, of factory work, rural attachment, uncogenial factory environment etc. They fall an easy prey to various evils such as indebtedness, alcoholism, gambling and other vices which naturally demoralise them and sometimes completely ruin their family life. The high rate of labour absenteeism in Indian industries is indicative of the lack of commitment on the part of the workers. Absenteeism can be reduced to a great extent by provision of good housing, health and family care, canteens, educational and training facilities. Provision of welfare amenities enables the workers to live a richer and more satisfactory life and contributes to the productivity of labour, efficiency of the enterprise, and helps in maintaining industrial peace.

REFERENCES

1. I.L.O., *Asian Regional Conference Report—II*, 1947.
2. *ILO Report II*—Provision of facilities for the promotion of workers' welfare—Asian Regional Conference—Nuware Eliva, Ceylon. Page 3.
3. *Report of the Labour Investigation Committee*, 1946.
4. *Report of the Committee on Labour Welfare*, Govt. of India, 1969.
5. *Industry and Society: A Sociological Appraisal of Modern Industrializ*ation, p. 250.
6. N.M. Joshi, *Trade Union Movement in India*, 1927.

3

Theories and Philosophy of Labour Welfare

Generally speaking, philosophy is concerned with the problems of primordial emergence, with phenomenal continuance and final destiny of life, with experience, and the "things" we see, yet, it could be stated that there could be a philosophy of anything or "nothing"! Philosophy is a rational system of beliefs. It is a theory or complex of theories relating to existence, being, purpose, activity or behaviour, etc. It is necessary for every one to have a philosophy,—his own or derived from others. For, it is one's philosophy that determines one's values of life. It is one's patterns of behaviour, influences one's reactions and relations to others, moulds attitudes and thinking, inspires ambition or anxiety, compromise or cunning.

In nutshell, philosophy lays the path for the way of life. Further, it provides one with an approach, an outlook which shines through one's thinking and activities, making them meaningful. Though philosophy is so very important for a way of life and approach to problems, very few have a philosophy of their own or one which they have inherited or derived. Quite often, what one holds as a philosophy, is found, on probing and analysis, to be a bundle of unreasonable beliefs and incoherent superstitions,—which perhaps, cannot be the basis of a progressively evolving individual or of social life.

The following seven approaches to a philosophy or theory of labour welfare can be identified:

1. The Policing Theory of Labour Welfare.

2. The Religious Theory of Labour Welfare. This has two aspects: (*a*) the atonement and (*b*) the investment aspects.
3. The Philanthropic Theory of Labour Welfare.
4. The Paternalistic Theory of Labour Welfare or the Trusteeship Theory.
5. The Placating Theory of Labour Welfare.
6. The Public Relations Theory of Labour Welfare.
7. The Functional Theory of Labour Welfare.

THE POLICING THEORY OF LABOUR WELFARE

According to this theory, a majority of people tend to do evil. Very few persons are inclined by nature to be virtuous or be helpful. Man is full of self interests; and does not hesitate to further his own ends, if necessary, at the cost of other's welfare—particularly if he is placed in an advantageous position, by reason of wealth or authority, there is every likelihood of his using his authority and wealth for (what he considers to be) his own welfare, exploiting those under him. It, is perhaps, to express this view that the Bible says: "It is easier for a camel to go through the eye of a needle, than for a rich man to enter into the Kingdom of God." (St. Mark. 25). It is with a similar apprehension of exploitation of the poor by the rich, our constitution proposes that the means of production will not be concentrated in the hands of a few.

The factory and other industrial work-places, provide ample opportunities for owners and managers of capital to exploit workers in an unfair manner. This could be done by making labour work long hours, paying workers low wages, keeping the workplaces in an unhygeinie condition, by neglecting safety and health provisions and by ignoring the provision of elementary human amenities such as, drinking water, latrines, rest rooms, canteen, etc. Clearly, a welfare state cannot allow this state of affairs to continue as it cannot permit theft and disorder to persist in the interests of its own (the State's) survival and progress. Low wages, long hours of work, bad working conditions, lack of social security would lead to impoverishment, pauperisation, enfeeblement of the working population and a great measure of explosive disgruntlement. This, if left unchecked would certainly undermine the foundation of State-security and prosperity. Hence, laws or enactments to compel the managements to provide minimum wages and better working conditions and amenities become imperative. Further, these laws need enforcement. Since employers could possibly evade these provisions, vigilance of, and constant or at least, periodical supervision by a properly constituted inspectorate becomes necessary. Thus (1) passing of the laws requiring employers to provide for the welfare of the workers, (2) and periodical supervision to ascertain that these welfare measure *are* provident, and (3) punishment of employers in cases of neglect or disobedience of the law are the outcome of this Policing Theory of Labour Welfare.

Advantages and Disadvantages

This theory was its own advantages as well as disadvantages. It is true that human nature has not yet fully and universally evolved into helpful attitudes and behaviour. There are many in society who are wicked to others, many who take advantage of others' weaknesses and misfortunes. There are several good managements; but an equal number of them, if not more, are bad. Labour welfare laws are necessary to restrain the bad employers from evil and constrain him to do good. At least, out of state compulsion and fear of exposure and punishment, employers would attend to improvement of working conditions, and institute creches, cloakrooms, canteens, safety measures, etc. It could be contended that welfare programmes could be spontaneously provided and planned and not compelled; for what is wrung out from the employer is grudgingly given by him. What is done out of fear or force may *"do"* or *work* for a time but will not fully correspond with the spirit of welfare. When employers are forced by law even to do good works, they may feel a sense of resentment and endeavour to find loopholes in the law and constantly look out for ways and means of escaping from the provisions. This "attitude of dodging" on the part of employers will entail the creation and maintenance of a costly inspectorate.

Secondly it could be argued that enforcement of welfare provisions, while they may not accord with the spirit of welfare, do result in a measure of benefit to workers. Employers may resent compulsion. But some there are who, after they get over their initial resentment, may get accustomed to the provision of welfare activities, may come to like them, and indeed, may later be converted into enthusiasts and protagonists of welfare. Though this is a consummation devoultly to be wished, is not utterly in the realms of impossibility. There are factories' inspectors who disclaim police responsibilities and outlook, and claim that they have been able to achieve the implementation of labour welfare measures through pursuation of the employer. Pursuation is a good technique of getting the employer to institute and observe labour welfare programmes. But as long as behind the factory inspector there is legal sanction and the threat of enforcement and punishment of the employer for his non-observance of provisions, welfare cannot be said to be wholly devoid of police authority and outlook. Under the circumstance, the employer may tend to provide only as much of welfare as is enforced; and also, if possible, to discover loop-holes in the enactments for escaping from his liabilities whenever he can; and finally, not to institute welfare programmes not required by law such as housing, recreation, employees' counselling, etc.

RELIGIOUS THEORY OF LABOUR WELFARE

Though every one may not have a philosophy of life, man could still be described as essentially a religious animal. Religion consists of sentiments and practices, beliefs and superstitions, hopes and behaviour patterns—in regard to matters of this life as well as in regard to affairs of the next life—all these generally developed in individuals in accordance with the culture and discipline of the land. Employers as well as employees as human beings, do subscribe to religious sentiments and beliefs. In India concepts of Dharma and Karma and rebirth influence man's conduct. The generally held belief is that if one does a good or charitable deed here, one will reap the benefits of such deed, if not now in this life, most certainly in some future life. As you sow, so you reap. It is in the expectation of future benefit, several take to a path of piety and charity. Charitable houses for travellers, schools, scholarships, endowments, hospitals, feeding of the poor, distribution of clothing, etc., are all manifestations of such sentiments and belief. Any good work is thus looked upon as "an investment". He who feeds the poor will be sumptuously fed in his next life; he who clothes the naked will be amply clothed; and he who shelters the houseless will be adequately sheltered. Indeed, come or many of our unfulfilled wants are believed to be due to our neglect of good works in a former life. Thus King Sudraka in Bana's *Kadambari* tells his queen who is sorrowing for want of an offspring. "Why do you weep for a state over which we have no immediate control. We did not do good and pure deeds in our former life to deserve children now."

This can be that inspired with this sentiment and hope, some employers plan and organize canteens, and creches. And closely allied to this investment theory which is religious, we could also recognize the atonement theory. According to his view, present disabilities of a person are the result of the sins committed by him previously. He should undertake to do good deeds now to atone or compensate for his sins. Thus persons who have leprosy, heart diseases, blood pressure, digestive disorders, defective limbs, and other deformities, or who have children with these or mental disabilities, believe that they are due to their previous bad *Karma*, and could be remedied to some extent, if not completely removed, by penance and virtuous and charitable acts here and now.

Thus labour welfare work, as well as welfare work in other fields, is taken up in a spirit of atonement and contrition. In India several forms of penance and charity could be traced to this prevailing religious sentiment, i.e., a kindly and benevolent act being treated either as an investment or an atonement.

Advantages and Defects

Obviously welfare activities inspired by such religious sentiments are based on personal, private and selfish ends. They cannot form a rational foundation for welfare work. What a benefactor or an employer seeks here is his own welfare primarily, and the welfare of others secondarily. Welfare work in this view is treated as a means for the regeneration of oneself and promotion of one's own ends. Moreover, as all may not for all time hold to the sentiments of investment and atonement, welfare works may not be universal and continuous. In spite of all these disadvantages, workers do benefit by welfare work done under this theory. As said earlier, the religious sentiments of alonement and investment are live forces and constitute a part of our culture, thinking and behaviour. Moreover, compared to the policing theory, the religious theory has this advantage that welfare activities in the former are forced while in the latter they are voluntary. Also under the latter view, more than what is required by legal enactments could be undertaken.

PHILANTHROPIC THEORY OF LABOUR WELFARE

The word "philanthropic" is significant. *Philos* is Greek means loving, and *anthropos* means man. Therefore philanthropic implies "loving mankind". According to the philanthropic theory, it could be stated that man generally loves man. He does not like any one of the species to which he belongs suffer and lack human amenities. Man is overcome by feelings of pity even at the sight of suffering animals, and more so in the presence of human misery. He has a spontaneous urge to better be lot of his fellow-beings. Compassion compels him to remove suffering and promote and well-being of mankind. This is and instinctive urge which man, perhaps, does not fully understand. In the working of this instinct or urge, there may be deeper and inscrutable laws of affinity sustaining and preserving human society. The philanthropic force is a powerful drive which not only engages man to good and kindly works, but calls forth from him acts of the noblest sacrifice.

Labour welfare work, such as the improvement of working conditions, the institution of the creche and the canteen, etc., could be acts of pity on the part of employers who want to remove the disabilities of workers. Indeed, originally some part of the welfare activities were purely philanthropic. This is true not only in the field of labour welfare but also in the areas of child and women welfare, welfare work amongst the crippled and work with the diseased. Robert Owen of England was philanthropic employer who worked for the welfare of his workers. In our own country Shapoorji Bengalee, Lokhande, B.P. Wadia and Mahatma Gandhi, though not employers of labour, yet were well known Philanthropists who strived in several ways to bring about workers' welfare. Buddha, Jesus, Mahatma Gandhi are amongst the most eminent names of philanthropists. Love of man is the essence of their teaching, serving suffering humanity was their constant endeavour.

Advantages and Defects

The Philanthropic theory of welfare work depends much on the kindly intincts of man. Whether man's love of man is instinctive and natural or cultivated in a given environment has yet to be proved. Further, the philanthropic sentiment may not be a universal and continuous one. Welfare work based on such sentiments, though voluntary, would be precarious. However, wherever such philanthropic sentiments are found to be in employers, there is much to be gained by utilising them for welfare works. In doing so we would be appealing only to the employers' nobler sentiments.

Paternalistic or Trusteeship Theory

According to the Paternalistic Theory of Labour Welfare, the industrialist or the employer holds the total industrial estate, properties and profits accruing from them in trust. The property which he can use of abuse as he likes is not entirely his own. He holds them for his use no doubt, but also for the benefit of his workers, if not of the whole society. For several reasons such as low wages, lack of education, etc., the workers are at present unable to take care of themselves fully. They are, therefore, in the nature of minors, and the employers should provide for their well-being out of the funds in their current control. This trusteeship is not actual and legal but it is moral and therefore not less real. The relations between employers and employees should be somewhat of the type found between fathers and children in joint families; or of the kind subsisting between the elder brother and the younger ones in the same familial set up. Under this pattern of relationships, the elderspends—or rather should spend for the behoof of the younger ones who are too tender and in experienced to know their own interests or manage their own budget. This theory may also be designated "the Fraternalistic Theory of Labour Welfare", the contents and purport and arguments remaining the same as explained above. The workers and employers belong to the same human and industrial family. their interest are identical. The role of the elder member of the family as administrator of the welfare of the younger ones, is one which is rooted in morals and in history. It could be mentioned here that Mahatma Gandhi was a protagonist of the Trusteeship Theory of the industrial estate. It is essentially an ancient and continuing Hindus idea that those who have the superior advantage economically, physically, intellectually and socially, have the moral obligation to work for the improvement of those who do not have similar advantages. The possession of any power of advantage is justified only to the extent such advantage and power are utilised for the well-being of others. The words of Lord Sri

Krishna: "You should act having in view only the unity and well-being of society", though addressed to all, applies with particular emphasis to those in positions of trust and powers. Indeed, power should be trust, and trust should have power. On the basis of this view the king in the State, the leader in the community, the administrator in office, the teacher in the school, the father in the family, the merchant in business, and the capitalist in industry, were endowed with power and trust in the Indian society of old, so that a common purpose running through individuals and reaching through institutions, could provides for the progress of all. It is in this spirit that Kalidasa described his ideal Prince as the "king", the "father" and the "guru"—words which are loaded with immense significance. The trusteeship ideals of property, profit, position, power, run throughout the Hindu systems of throught and social organization.

Advantages and Defects

The theory, as the previous, one, appeals in the nobler sentiments of the employers, and to that extent it is good. Moreover, it encourages voluntary provision of welfare activities, and may lead to good-will between labour and management. The trusteeship idea could, perhaps, appeal to Indian management and also to labour, as the theory is nearer to one social concept and experiences. The strength of the theory lies in its ethical spirits and outlook which it seeks to inculcate in the employer. Mahatma Gandhi is said to have converted a few great industrialists to this view to some extent, at least. While the Paternalistic Theory of Labour Welfare is attractive, it is not without its several defects. Like the earlier theories, it makes labour welfare and special responsibility of top management who alone can take the initiative. It does not explain how the capitalists came to be trustee of the properties to be used for the benefit of the workers. Trustees are temporary guardians who relinquish their tutelage when their charges or wards come of age and become majors. In this case, however, workers are conceived to he perpetual minors and industrilists eternal guardians! Since there is no legal sanction behind this trusteeship idea and arrangement, the entire terminology wears and aspect of deceptive rhetoric! However, the theory does amphasise the moral element in the employers" role so far as welfare is concerned. It also draws attention to labour's interest in the properties and profits of the concern, thus tempering in some measure, the rigorous of claimant proprietorial claims with soft sympathy for the labourers.

PLACATING THEORY OF LABOUR WELFARE

This theory could be said to hold the following views: Workers are becoming conscious of their rights and privileges. They are welding themselves into powerful groups. The times are changing. The workers' claims to higher wages and better standard of living can no long be ignored. It these are withheld, the leviathan, i.e., the brute working masses will inflict signal injury not only on management but on the entire scheme of capitalism. Therefore it is prudent to appease the workers, while appeasement avails. This could be done by timely and periodical acts of grace and welfare. Workers are like children who are intelligent, but not fully so. As crying children are placified by sweets, so workers should be pleased by welfare works. This is a necessary show of kindness and friendly gesture. This is also the best means of securing the workers' cooperation. Even as a barking dog is bought off by a piece of bone, so too workers could be contented by welfare porgrammes.

Advantages and Defects

This opinion makes of labour welfare activity a matter of policy. It is a prudent course of action to buy off discontent. This theory is based on fear on the part of management—fear of labour becoming conscious of its rights and putting forward its claims. Hence, there is likely to be lack of sincerity in programmes of welfare initiated with a view to placating labour. It is true that workers will be pleased by welfare works; and their discontent in a certain extent could be allayed. Especially amongst ignorant group of workers who do not perceive their permanent interests, this theory may succeed for a while.

PUBLIC RELATIONS THEORY OF LABOUR WELFARE

As per the Public Relations Theory of Labour Welfare, welfare programmes by employers are necessary for the creation of goodwill between labour and management, and between management and the public. Industry exists in the society. To the extent that goodwill is created amongst the members of society, to that extent industry flourishes. And employees too of an industrial organization are the organization's first primary group of the public, welfare programmes become necessary. Clean and safe working conditions, a good canteen, creche and other amenities, never fail to make a good impression on the workers, visitors and the public. Indeed, certain managements in India are proud to advertise their welfare activities, and show them to distinguished visitors. The employers want the public to know the good work the company is doing. Moreover, some of the welfare activities afford excellent opportunities for advertising the name of the company. Thus, for instance, the creche could be used for the best child exhibition with a prize or award. Several companies do have expensive sports activities and maintain and train sports teams, such as teams in hututu, volley ball, cricket, football, hockey, etc. These teams and their periodical competitions at city, state or inter-state or even international levels, which are supported by the companies concerned, help publish the names of the companies in the country's popular newspapers. It is believed that such frequent presentation before the public, of the company's name in victorious situations, creates a favourable image of the company in the public mind. It is also possible that the company's image so created may tend to increase the sale of the firm's products and also improve industrial relations. Thus welfare activities become part of sales technique and perhaps also of industrial relations art.

Advantages and Defects

This theory has its own merits and defects. Employers easily perceive the value and advantages of public reactions. It is a matter of pride and satisfaction that the company's best activities in the field of welfare are witnessed by the public and reported in the newspapers. This satisfies the go of the management. Welfare programmes which do advertise the company's name would be voluntarily undertaken by the employer. But this merit could itself be the defect of this theory; for there is every possibility of the company neglecting welfare programmes which could be really useful to the employees but have no advertisment value. Also, welfare work undertaken in this spirit may lack sincerity and reality and could easily degenerate into mere show and window-dressing-a pure make-believe.

FUNCTIONAL THEORY OF LABOUR WELFARE

In this theory of Efficiency Theory of Labour Welfare, workers are described as operatives. They are the productive groups in industry. They handle and prepare raw material for manufacturing, they man the machines, process the products, haul, pack and ship the commodities. They work strenously in difficult environments Really speaking, it is the workers who deliver the goods. Just as machines should be kept in good condition for smooth operation, the operatives too should he maintained in satisfactory physical, emotional mental and moral condition for unbroken and increasing production. If workers are fed properly, clothed adequately and treated kindly, and if the conditions of work are congenial, they will work efficiently. Welfare work is a means of securing, preserving and increasing the efficiency of labour. A wise owns of a bull or a horse takes good care of the animal according to the use he puts it do. Napoleon said that armies march on their stomachs by which he meant that soldiers fight better if they are properly fed and taken care of. Similarly, since labour constitutes the working groups, they should be well cared for by a wise employer. Thus proper maintenance of personnel leads to greater efficiency, and efficiency, results in increased production. Ultimately the employer, the worker and the country will benefit by the profits of the industry thus secured.

Advantages and Disadvantages

This Functional or Efficiency theory has several merits, which could make the theory an excellent basis for planning welfare programmes. It easily appeals to the employer as it promises to make the workers efficient and thereby assure more production and better industrial relations. The employers who accept the arguments of this theory would recognize their own interests and voluntarily provide for the welfare of their workers. Further, they would be sincere in their attempts as they are interested in achieving the objective which is the efficiency of the workers, and through it more production.

The criticism that could be raised against this theory is that the main or ultimate object of providing for the welfare of workers is the realization of higher levels of production by securing the efficiency of the employees. Welfare provisions are here used as means for selfish ends of employers. This is neither a valid criticism nor argument. For, the workers efficiency, and greater production that flows from it, are gains as much to the workers as to employers. Through higher production he can secure higher wages and even claim a share in profits. An efficient worker is an aspect to himself, to his family, to the community, and the country and not merely an asset to the employer.

The fact that welfare is treated as a means to securing workers' efficiency is not obnoxious or mean. Welfare is not an end in itself. As a desirable conditions if existence it must express itself in some form of useful action—useful to oneself and useful to community. Efficiency is only a functional aspect of welfare. Welfare expresses its dynamic content by securing efficient worker from those who are enjoying a state of welfare. Efficiency is an expressive and eloquent mode of welfare. Indeed, efficiency is welfare at work.

We have outlined above seven approaches to the building up of a philosophy of labour welfare. It is not suggested that any one approach is exclusive of other approaches. It is possible that in the policies of an employer or a management, two or three or even more approaches can be discovered to be combined. There is an instance of a big Jain employer who firmly held that providing for welfare of workers was outside the duties of management. Whatever he did provide was under government compulsion and supervision. It happened that the children born to him died as soon as they were born. Later, his own health suffered. He felt that as compensation, or expitation or even as an investment in a good deed he should liberally contribute to the creche in the factory and also to the medical services for his workers; consequently in this particular factory there came to exist an excellent creche and a well organized dispensary. We may recognize in this instance how, what in the beginning started in answer to the policing approach developed into an atonement and investment approach based on the religious sentiments and superstitions of the Jain employer. In such instances it is not possible for us not to read traces of the philanthropic approach too,—though in very faint colours. This observation suggests the thought that some of the approaches to a philosophy of labour welfare may be found combined or even that one approach may lead on to, or be substituted by another approach according to the changeable circumstances as well as sentiments of the management or employers.

One should not assume that the possession of a philosophy of labour welfare is the sole privilege or monopoly of the employer. Labour may, and *should* also subscribe to a philosophy of welfare as such philosophy concerns labour equally, if not more. For later research we may propose here without discussion that when labour and management subscribe to an identical and worthwhile approach too a philosophy of welfare, the administration of welfare would be smoother and richer. In such circumstances participation by labour in labour welfare activities would tend to be more intense. In our view this observation would apply only to the trusteeship theory and the functional theory of labour welfare as explained above. In the present circumstances, labour in India largely clings to a paternalistic approach, while some managements held to a policing theory,—two irresconcilable approaches! This, perhaps, is a reason for labour's too high expectations from the employers, and for half-hearted measures of welfare on the part of the employers. In consequence, welfare presents an unsatisfactory and poor picture. How good would it otherwise be if both labour and management subscribed sincerely to the functional approach! Employers would then plan constructively for labour welfare, and workers would participate willingly and intelligently. The scope and effectiveness of welfare would be fuller and richer. Other approaches may not inspire equally comprehensive schemes of welfare and a like intensity of workers' participation.

4

Welfare Measures at a Glance

There are certain employers especially in the organized sector of industry, who have provided a wide variety of welfare amenities and services to their employees. A brief account of such welfare measures is given below:

Educational Facilities

Education plays a very important part in motivating and enabling the working population for changes necessary for accelerated progress and for their mental and physical development. This has been recognized in our social and economic planning and a suitable financial outlay on education has been made in the different five-year plans. Improvement in the quality of the industrial work force demands accelerated peace of economic development for which education of workers, their families and their children is very essential. The need for imparting necessary education to workers in India had been emphasised by the Indian Industrial Commission (1918) and Royal Commission on Labour (1931). The Indian Industrial Commission observed that "a factor which has tended in the past to delay the progress of Indian industrial development has been the ignorance and conservatism of the uneducated workmen." The Royal Commission on Labour stated that "in India nearly the whole mass of industrial labour is illiterate, a state of affairs which is unknown in any other country of industrial importance."

Though considerable improvement has been made since then, the overall position regarding removal of illiteracy amongst the working population still continues. No exact data are available as to the extent of illiteracy among the industrial workers. Efforts have been made by some of the employers to provide adult education facilities to their employees but so far so tangible all-round efforts are being made to eradicate illiteracy amongst industrial workers. Hence, necessary financial and non-financial incentives should be provided for effective implementation of various adult education programmes. An attempt should also be made to make it compulsory under law.

It is also important that the children of the workers should be provided with educational facilities. It is statutorily binding on the plantation employers under the Plantations Labour Act (1951). It is the joint responsibility of the state governments and employers to set up primary schools, secondary schools, high schools and colleges in predominantly industrial areas. Some of the public sector and private sector establishments and departmental undertakings, corporations and municipalities have provided educational amenities to the workers' children. Some of the well-to-do employers in private sector like TISCO have provided educational facilities to the children of their employees in the form of provision of schools, reading rooms, libraries, financial assistance, etc. Railways occupy the first place in extending educational facilities to their employees' children. Educational facilities to the children of the workers are fairly widespread in all the public sector enterprises, particularly in iron and steel industries and in heavy engineering. The ordinance factories have made arrangements for education of the children of their employees. This includes provision of primary, junior and higher secondary schools. In the different units of Bharat Heavy Electricals, there are a total of about 75 educational institutions with a students community of over 50,000 and teaching force of about 1,400. Education is imparted to the children of the employees in English and in local languages.

Medical Facilities

Employers, whether in private or in public sectors have been providing medical facilities for their workers and their families, even before the introduction of E.S.I. Scheme. The workers in departmental undertakings are more or less governed by the medical rules applicable to government servants, or such other facilities, both indoor and outdoor. In the case of public sector undertakings, it has been a matter of rule that the provision of adequate indoor and outdoor medical facilities should form an integral part of the project plan itself. These undertakings have provided, by the large, suitably equipped first-aid centres, ambulance rooms and even regular hospitals either in the factory premises or inside the township. Besides general medical treatment and health-care, separate arrangement for specialist treatment for diseases like T.B., Cancer, Leprosy, Mental diseases have also been made in many hospitals. The expenditure on medical and health facilities differs from one public sector undertaking to another. Private sector companies, such as TISCO, TELCO, Philips, DCM, Hindustan Lever, Godrej, J.K. (Kanpur), Larsen and Toubro, Indian Dye Stuffs (Bombay), Mafatlal Group of Concerns and many others have extended medical amenities to their employees. Many of the large plantations have extended hospital and dispensary facilities for the treatment of workers and their families. They have also made arrangements for the treatment of their workers at government hospitals at their own cost. The problem is in the case of small-sized units. The Committee on Labour Welfare has recommended that in the case of smaller units, medical facilities should be provided on joint basis by a group of employers in scattered areas. The institutions like industrial co-operatives, industrial estates can play an important role in providing medical facilities to the workers by a joint drive. It has also recommended to popularise other systems of medicine, namely, Ayurvedic, Sidda, Unani and Homeopathy, by setting up dispensaries run on these systems in areas of concentration of industrial workers.

Transport Facilities

In all countries of the world, mobility and accessibility is made possible by modern transportation. It is amongst the key factors for attainment of industrial development. Recently, road and rail transport have acquired considerable significance because of their role in socio-economic development of the country. The provision of transport facilities to industrial workers forms an integral part of the general transport facility and is, by and large, the responsibility of the public authorities like the local bodies, transport corporations, state governments etc. In some of the big cities, the industrial workers make use of the local trains run by the railways.

Transport facilities to workers residing at a long distance are essential to relieve them from strain and anxiety. Such facilities also provide greater opportunity for relaxation and recreation, and help in reducing the rate of absenteeism. The practice followed with regard to transport facilities varies from country to country. In developed countries of both Western and Eastern Europe, transport facilities generally form a part of the civic and community amenities within the limits of local authorities. The legal imposition to provide these facilities has been rare and limited to certain special circumstances. In certain countries there are agreements with the local transport authorities to set up new services or to improve the existing ones. In certain cases where industries are established in isolated or distant places, the undertakings either provide their own transport services or pay conveyance allowance to workers in lieu thereof. In some of the developing countries there are statutory measures requiring employers to provide transport facilities to their employees. In certain developing countries transport facilities are also provided through collective agreements. In certain parts of Mexico, where public transport facilities are inadequate, the employees themselves have formed transport co-operatives. In Japan, many undertakings provide transport facilities for their workers including "commutation tickets". Thus, the necessity of ensuring transport facilities to enable workers to attend to their work without undue delay and physical strain has been recognized in a majority of the countries. The International Labour Organization has also stressed the importance of extending this facility to the industrial employees.

The International Labour Conferences while adopting "Utilisation of Spare Time Recommendation" urged its member countries that "by means of a well-conceived transport system and by affording special facilities in regard to fares and time-tables, workers should be enabled to reduce to the minimum the time spent in travelling between their homes and their work." This Recommendation urged upon the public transport authorities to consult workers' and employers organizations in matters of planning for transport facilities. Specific principles with regard to transport for industrial workers were, however, laid down in Welfare Facilities Recommendations (No. 102) adopted in 1956.

Unlike many industrially developed countries, the public transport systems in our country have not yet been fully developed. Certain improvements are needed in this regard keeping in view the existing situation of our country. This problem can be tackled on a joint basis by the state, local bodies, public and private transport organizations and employers. The Committee on Labour Welfare recommended the provision of adequate transport facilities to workers to enable them to reach their work place without loss of much time and without fatigue. Whatever may be the agency for the provision of this facility, it is essential that the workers should not be unduly put to avoidable strain due to inadequate transport facility. In all places of industrial concentration the state governments and local authorities should streamline, increase and improve the functioning of the local transport services, so as to give maximum possible assistance to industrial workers to reach their place of work in time. In industrial undertakings where transport services are not provided, some conveyance allowance, as may be mutually agreed to between the employers and employees, should be paid by the employers. To encourage the workers to have their own conveyance, the employers should advance loans liberally to the workers for the purchase of bicycles, etc. The smaller industrial establishments located in contiguous areas should undertake to provide transport services on a joint basis. The cost of providing these services can be shared by the participating establishments on the basis of number of workers employed. The Committee also recommended staggering of working hours wherever feasible.

Transport facilities have been provided to the employees by some of the undertakings in private sectors like Larsen and Toubro, Godrej, Sandoz, Pfizer, Siemens, Chemicals and Fibres, Voltas, Philips, etc. Similar facilities have also been extended to their employers by certain public sector enterprises.

Recreational Facilities

Recreation is commonly taken to be the opposite of work. It has an important bearing on the individual's personality as well as his capacity to contribute to social development. It affords the workers an opportunity to develop his sense of physical and mental discipline. Music, dance, drama, games and sports, paintings, carvings, etc., are different forms of recreation.

The importance of recreation in creating a healthy climate for industrial peace and progress has been emphasised by several Study Teams, Committees and Commissions, which have surveyed the working and living conditions of labour in India during the last four decades. The Labour Investigation Committee (Rege Committee) had stated: "The average industrial workers works in an atmosphere of dust, noise and heat, and lives in terrible overcrowded and insanitary dwellings which are generally no better than dark dungeons, with the consequence that many workers fall prey to vice."

The process of industrialisation itself has accelerated the need for recreational amenities. In many of the developing countries the need to provide adequate recreational facilities for workers employed in medium-sized and smaller undertakings has been widely felt. In East European countries, the problem of leisure activities for the working population as a whole is the concern of trade unions.

The I.L.O. Recommendations on Welfare Facilities adopted in 1956 urged upon the member countries to take appropriate measures "to encourage the provision of recreational facilities for the workers in or near the undertaking in which they are employed, where suitable facilities organized by special bodies or by community action are not already available, and where there is a real need for such facilities as indicated by the representatives of the workers concerned." The I.L.O. further recommended that "such measures, where necessary, should be taken by works committees or other bodies established by national laws or regulations if these have a responsibility in this field, or by voluntary action of the employers or workers concerned after consultation with each other. These measures should preferably, be taken in such a way as to stimulate and support action by the public authorities so that the community is able to meet the demand for recreation facilities."

In India, a variety or recreational facilities have been provided in more than one way, statutorily, voluntarily and also by different social welfare agencies, and to some extent by trade unions as well. Broadly speaking, these can be divided into two parts, namely, (i) recreational amenities provided by the industrial organizations inside or near the work place, and (ii) amenities provided on community basis.

Provision of recreational facilities has been made obligatory on employers in plantations. In most of the plantations, there are facilities for indoor and outdoor games. In mining industries the efforts of the employers are supplemented by different labour welfare funds. In factory establishments, the employers have made a considerable improvement by providing avenues for recreational facilities on their own. Their efforts, in some places, have been supplemented by state governments, labour welfare centres or by the statutory labour welfare boards. The need for providing these amenities on a desired scale has been accepted without reservation by the public sector and departmentally run undertakings. There are a number of recreational schemes operating in defence establishments, railways, posts and telegraphs and in some other central government undertakings through a system of contribution by the employees and the government.

Necessary lead in this regard was given by some of the progressive employers in private sector like TISCO, TELCO, Indian Aluminium Co., Hindustan Lever, the Mill Owners' Association the most of the public sector undertakings such as Steel Authority of India, Hindustan Aeronautics, Air India, Heavy Engineering Corporation, Bharat Heavy Electricals, Indian Telephone Industries, Hindustan Machine Tools, Life Insurance Corporation, Indian Railways, etc. In almost all the public sector undertakings, provision of indoor and outdoor games has been made part and parcel of the project plan itself. Even some of the large private sector undertakings have made definite provisions in their budget for recreational and cultural activities. The affiliate textile mills of the Bombay Millowners Association have set up sports clubs, cultural clubs, reading rooms and extended other recreational facilities like film shows, radio sets, etc. The jute mills affiliated to the Indian Jute Mills Association maintained welfare centres which catered to the recreational, social and cultural needs of the jute mill workers.

Some of the recommendations made by the Committee on Labour Welfare for improvement of recreational facilities are given follows:

(i) The Committee recommended the need for providing recreational facilities to the industrial employers on a regular and sustained basis. Particularly the medium and small-sized industries should pay sufficient attention towards provision of some basic minimum recreational facilities for their workers.

(ii) As the capacity to bear additional financial burden varies from industry to industry, the state has to intervene in some cases and lend a helping hand by way of suitable grants to the employers or by arranging joint-recreational facilities for a group of small-scale units. The cost of these amenities can be shared by the state and by the employers.

(iii) Recreational centres should be established outside the place of work, preferably in working class localities or in industrial housing colonies. They should be well-equipped to attract sufficient number of workers.

(iv) Statutory labour welfare boards are to be constituted in states where they are not existing, and they should be provided with adequate funds to carry out their duties effectively.

(v) Trade unions should also actively associate themselves with the management in popularising various social and cultural activities amongst the workers.

(vi) Industrial tours and excursions should be organized for the members of different industrial units with a view in sharing of ideas and experiences on common problems to their mutual benefit. This will also help in the process of social and national integration. Such tours should be properly organized on regular basis in co-operation with central and state governments, employers' and workers' organizations. The expenses for these tours should be shared by the state, the employers and the workers.

(vii) The Committee also felt that various measures such as boys clubs and youth clubs in working class areas, holiday homes for industrial workers and their dependents, encouragement to sportsmen, artists and writers amongst industrial workers, etc. should receive sufficient attention by all concerned as a measure to promote recreational facilities.

Housing Facilities

Some of the industrial employers both in public and private sectors have provided housing facilities to their employees. In Greater Bombay, out of 48 members mills of the Bombay Millowners' Association, only 14 mills have provided tenements to their workers. The tenements consist of single as well as double rooms. There are a few two-room self-contained tenements also. In some of the remaining centres of the industry, viz., Calcutta, Delhi, Gwalior, Nagpur, Kanpur, Madras, Bangalore, Madurai, the employers have provided housing colonies comprising self-contained units for some of their workers. Larger units of the engineering industry have their own housing colonies with different types of quarters for different categories of workers. In this connection, it is worth mentioning the housing colonies that have sprung up in TELCO (Jamshedpur and Poona), Larsen and Toubro, Godrej, Hindustan Machine Tools. The Tata Iron and Steel Company had built about 18,000 residential quarters till the end of 1979. The Company also encourages its employees to construct their own houses by allotting them land at nominal rent on certain conditions. The Company also renders assistance to the co-operative housing societies formed by in employees. The Mysore Iron and Steel Company Ltd., Bhadravati, has also provided housing accommodation to some of its employers.

Almost all the public sector enterprises have either provided or are in the process of providing housing facilities to their employees. At Chittaranjan most of the workers in need of housing have been provided with self-contained houses with two rooms, a kitchen, a back verandah and a court yard with city sanitation and water supply. Hindustan Aeronautics Ltd. has a colony for housing its employees. Bharat Electronics has also provided houses for its low-income groups employees. For providing accommodation to its employees, the management of Bharat Heavy Electricals at its different factory locations have constructed townships with all modern amenities. A total population of over 2 lakhs is estimated to be residing in these townships located at Trichi, Bhopal, Hardwar and Hyderabad. The total number of houses constructed in these townships in around 25,000. Indian Telephone Industries and Hindustan Machine Tools have also provided good housing facilities to their employees. The public sector steel plants at Rourkela, Durgapur, Bhilai and Bokaro have provided standard housing facilities to their employees. The township of Rourkela Steel Plant spread over into 20 sectors, has around 24,000 quarters provided with modern amenities. About 60 per cent of the employees have been allotted quarters. Those who are not provided accommodation are entitled to house rent allowance at a rate fixed by the company. Townships having all facilities have been developed at each of the units of Rashtriya Chemicals and Fertilisers Ltd. The employees who are not provided corporations' quarters are paid house rent allowance at some of the places. The community centres that have developed around the public sector townships are the focus of recreational, cultural, sports, literary and many other activities.

Consumer Co-operative Societies

According to the Co-operative Planning Committee (1966), "Co-operation is a form of organization in which persons voluntarily associate together on the basis of equality for the promotion of their economic interest." It is based on definite rules which are as follows: (i) No one is compelled to join a co-operative society, not is its membership closed afterwards; (ii) the management of a co-operative society is democratic—"one man one vote" is the ruling principle; (iii) the members combine to promote the economic interest of themselves and not of anybody else—"self help through mutual help" in their guiding principle; (iv) co-operative association is not an association of selfish individuals. There prevails a co-operative instead of competitive spirit; and (v) lastly, co-operation is not simply a movement for economic betterment. It leads to the development of higher values of life, *i.e.*, honesty and unselfishness. It is a spirit of service which evokes loyalty, fellowship and a corporate feeling. It has, in this way, a greater moral and social element in it than merely economic. It entails "the acceptance of new ideas, new standards of conduct, new habits of thought and behaviour."

Aristole, while discussing the constitution of Athens in 329 B.C., had made provision for such things which we find today in a co-operative society. In those days there were Market Commissioners whose main function was to check all articles offered for sale in the market. In India, the co-operative idea goes back to ancient times. But the present phase of the co-operative movement could be traced to the recommendation of the Rural Credit Survey Committee in 1954 which laid down the basic guidelines for the co-operative movement in our country. The co-operative movement has a significant role to play in the promotion of economic development of the weaker sections of our society.

Apart from the economic benefits, the consumer co-operatives have some important social benefits which have salutary moral and social effects on the members. In the co-operatives, members are not looked upon as individual entities struggling against one another in seeking individual self-interest but are looked upon as a group, pursuing the interest jointly and in fairness. They develop in themselves the habits of mutual aid, intimate knowledge, honesty in dealing, etc.

The institutions of co-operative stores/fair price shops has a definite role to play in providing workers with essential items of need. The objectives of the consumers' co-operative stores are: (i) to provide to the members good quality foodgrains, cloth and all necessary articles of daily consumption and to keep the prices at a fair and reasonable level, lower than the market rate; (ii) to protect the consumers from the vagaries of market and middlemen and from rising prices and adulteration of food products; (iii) to protect factory workers from the clutches of the money-lenders and to inculcate in them the habit of thrift and saving; (iv) to develop habits of mutual aid, intimate knowledge and honesty in dealing; (v) to inculcate and pursue group interest jointly rather than individual self-interest; (vi) to strengthen the public distributing system to ensure availability to scarce-commodities and help bring down their prices in the open market.

The importance of opening consumer co-operative societies/fair price shops for the working class was first realized during the Second World War when a large number of consumer co-operative societies were organized by the Government for distribution of controlled commodities. The impetus gained by this movement had a temporary set-back with the lifting of control on foodgrains in 1948. Its importance was again recognized when the country embarked upon planned economic development. A review of its impact was made in 1961 when a Committee was set up (under the Chairmanship of Dr. P. Natesan, General Secretary, Tamil Nadu Cooperative Union Ltd. Madras) by the National Co-operative Development and the Warehousing Board to suggest measures for the development of the co-operative movement. The Committee recommended a pattern of organization and structure, finances, business techniques and operation, democratic control and management, etc. It also recommended the setting up of consumers' cooperative stores in factories and colonies in a planned way. The Committee also felt that this should be made obligatory on employers. The matter was discussed in the 20th session of the Indian Labour Conference held in August 1962. The Conference adopted a scheme for setting up of consumers' co-operative stores in all industrial establishments, including plantations and mines, employing 300 or more workers. Under the scheme, the employer was called upon to give financial assistance in the shape of share participation, working capital loan, managerial subsidy, etc. They were also expected to provide accommodation free of rent or at nominal rent, free furniture and free supply of water and electricity. The matter assumed further importance in the wake of Chinese aggression. In order to improve production, articles of daily need were made available to workers at reasonable prices. An integral part of the Industrial Truce Resolution, 1962, was to keep the prices of essential commodities as low as possible and to ensure that sufficient number of fair price shops/consumer co-operative stores were opened in industrial undertakings as decided by the Indian Labour Conference in its 20th session. The functioning of the scheme of co-operative consumer stores and fair price shops was reviewed a year later by the Standing Committee on Industrial Truce Resolution. It expressed its dissatisfaction with the progress in the setting up of cooperative consumer stores. It noted that there were a number of reasons for slow progress of the movement, such as delays in registration of societies, adoption of bye-laws, election of managing committees, etc. The Standing Committee also decided that the industrial units which had not already set-up co-operative stores, should open fair price shops and distribute through them rice, wheat, sugar, etc., at the same prices and scales as supplied by government in the Conference and Indian Labour Conference held in New Delhi in 1966 again took stock of the progress in the matter. They were dissatisfied with the implementation of the programme, particularly in the case or private undertakings and plantations. The overall coverage was 71 per cent of an March 1, 1968 (300 or more).

The following are some of the suggestions of the Committee on Labour Welfare for improvement of consumer co-operative stores and fair price shops:

1. The employers should encourage the formation of co-operative credit societies in such establishments by way of granting advances at the initial stage, at nominal rates of interest for long periods.
2. To popularise fair price shops/consumers' co-operative stores, state governments should take effective steps

including taking assistance from central government to ensure regular and adequate supplies of essential articles of foodgrains to these institutions.

3. The central and state governments should propagate amongst industrial workers the utility and need for not only forming such societies, but also running them well. This could be achieved in a number of ways, namely, by bringing out suitable literature on the subject, by holding seminars and also by arranging study tours of workers drawn from good co-operative credit societies functioning in different parts of the country.
4. Instead of opening fair price shops/co-operative stores in the precincts of industrial establishments, they may be opened in the residential areas, if workers so desire. Where large workers housing colonies have come up and which are away from the main urban settings, fair price shops may be set up by individual establishments or by a number of establishments jointly where workers of these establishments reside in a colony.
5. Though trade unions have made extreme use of co-operative facilities in some cases, the labour movement as a whole has not taken to co-operation. The trade unions should play an active role in the co-operative movement.

The importance of education for the success of co-operation has been acknowledged from the very start of the movement. Rochdale Pioneers included it in his famous principles. According to the Commission on Co-operative Principles, all co-operative societies should make provision for the education of their members, officers, and employees and of the general public in the principles and techniques.

Welfare Work by Workers' Organizations

Labour welfare work of workers' organizations refer to the services or programmes developed by union for the benefit of their members. Obviously, these are provided out of their own resources and are administrated by them. Though limited in extent and scope, certain trade unions have taken interest in different social welfare programmes. They have organized adult literacy and leadership training programmes. Trade union colleges have been set up by INTUC and AITUC. In addition, they have undertaken publications and research activities and also established libraries. A brief review of welfare work undertaken by some of the unions is as follows:

Textile Labour Association (Majoor Mahajan)

Mahatma Gandhi established the Textile Labour Association (TLA) in 1916 and considered it to be his "laboratory to make experiments in the sensitive labour field through truth, non-violence, and welfare activities." In 1941 Gandhiji wrote: "The Ahmedabad Labour Union is a model for all India to copy. Its basis is non-violence, purity and simplicity. It has never had a set-back in its career. It has grown from strength to strength, without fuss and without show. It has its hospitals, schools for the children, of mill-hands, classes for adults, its own printing press and khadi depot, and its own residential quarters. Almost all the hands are voters and decide the fate of elections. They came on the voters list at the instance of the Provincial Congress Committee. The organization has now taken part in the party politics of the Congress. It influences the municipal policy of the city. It has to its credit, very successful strikes which were wholly non-violent. Mill-owners and labourers have governed their relations largely through voluntary arbitration. "If I had my way, I would regulate all the labour organizations of India after the Ahmedabad Model." (R.N. Bose, Gandhian Technique and Tradition in I.R).

Gandhiji formulated a "constructive programme" and called upon all organizations including trade unions to adopt and implement the same. The programmes included activities to promote communal unity, removal of untouchability, prohibition, education, health and hygiene, upliftment of women, harijans and the tribal communities, etc. He called upon trade unions to take up adult literacy work. In 1918, when the organized a strike in the textile mills in Ahmedabad he told the striking workers that "they should who are literate should spend time in reading books and increasing their knowledge. They can also teach the illiterate." The Hindustan Mazdoor Sangh which was formed in 1938 by Gandhian trade unionist, made it obligatory for the affiliated trade unions to undertake adult literacy work.

Over the years the TLA has evolved its own norms of trade unionism which go beyond negotiating and agitating for workers' rights. Its programmes are all comprehensive and aim at all round development of workers and their families. Apart from their cultural enrichment, they offer to the workers the possibility to get together, enjoy things together and thus to develop a feeling of social identity within their trade unions that adds value to their life.

Gandhi's concept of all-round development of the workers and their families led the TLA to the establishment of a number of social welfare institutions, one of which is the girls' hostel, popularly known as J.B. Kanyagrih. It was founded in 1927 to promote secondary and higher education among the girls of the backward communities. Mrs. Anasuyaben Sarabhai, first president of the TLA, looked after the institution until her death. Two boys' hostels were also established in the same year. There is provision of scholarships in the engineering and medical institutions for talented or specially gifted students whose parents are members of TLA.

Among the developmental activities undertaken by the TLA, education and training play a major part. In fact, they can be found everywhere, involving every one from children to those who have already retired from work. It offers required education or training through a wide variety of different schemes to enlighten the working masses and their families. It has also set-up a vocational training centre for textile workers to create opportunities for alternative jobs for which skills are needed e.g., radio repair, motor rewinding, training as-wiremen, shorthand and typing classes, sewing classes etc. Since 1937, the TLA operates a regular educational programme to train its office bearers for the various functions within the organization.

The Textile Labour Association has celebrated its Diamond Jubilee after 60 years of its existence on December 4, 1976. The following are the services offered by the Association:

(1) Pre-natal and maternal care through a maternity home and dispensary at Khanpur; (2) Creche for children of working mothers at Dairapur; (3) 35 pre-nursery schools in hired buildings and even orphans in labour localities; (5) 25 game centres for school-going children conducted by trained personnel; (6) 5 gymnasiums for workers and their children under the guidance of trained physical culturists; (7) Tuition class for workers' children before examination; (8) 2 hostels for students for staying and studying; (9) One girls' hostel for backward communities with 60 inmates; (10) Volunteer Corps of 500 disciplined workers for serving the community needs, particularly of textile workers; (11) Educational help worth Rs. 300 to each medical and engineering students coming from workers' families; (12) Encouragement of cultural and religious activities such as bhajan, kirtan, musical training, satyanarayan katha, mushairas, etc.; (13) Celebration of national festival with the help of the cultural centres; (14) Vocational training like typewriting, radio repairing and wiremen classes; (15) Sewing classes numbering 30 for girls and women folk of workers and special classes for knitting and embroidery; (16) Formation of mahila mandals and training in homecraft and good house-keeping; (17) Workers' education in mills as well as residential localities including adult education; (18) 25 libraries and 120 reading centres in working class areas; (19) Legal aid to members in civil as well as criminal matters; (20) Aid to village level problems of members in their native places; (21) Special cell to organize the unorganized and agricultural workers; (22) Attending to civil and municipal problems; (23) Doing social and educational work among socially and educationally backward communities through

their own organizations; (24) Formation of community development centres with accent on cleanliness, literacy, thrift, prohibition and healthy living; (25) Arrangement for treatment of sick people in dispensaries and hospitals; (26) Blood bank and blood donation camps; (27) Propagating family welfare schemes; (28) Providing service to heirs of workers in getting the various benefits; (29) Aid to the family members of deceased workers from Rs. 100 to Rs. 300 under the Khandubhai Desai Parivar Sahayak Yojna; (30) Conducting consumer stores, credit and housing societies; (31) A workers' co-operative bank with 43,000 members and working capital of about one crore of rupees; (32) Encouraging rural employment through production centres of khadi in villages and propagating use of khadi cloth among workers.

The Majoor Mahajan has set up the Gujarat Khet Majoor Mahajan which started its work in villages near Ahmedabad. Its scope and activities are confined to farm workers and to such vital activities as enforcement of minimum wages, relief from indebtedness and creation of supplementary occupation to raise the income level of such workers.

The TLA is Mahatma Gandhi's gift to the nation. It has grown up to be an association of 12 departmental unions representing more than 90 per cent of the total textile work force (135,000 cut of 150,000 in 1981) in the state. It has an annual budget in excess of 2.5 million rupees, collected individually from the members at shop level. Some 4,000 shop stewards are elected every four years. In addition, it maintains a staff of 400 full-time/part-time social workers to implement its programmes of social activities. In this sense, the TLA has become a living monument of Gandhi's doctrines, and his spirit has left its imprint on this particular union, especially in its social, economic and educational ventures.

Mill Mazdoor Union

The Mill Mazdoor Union, Indore, has established welfare

centres to provide cultural, recreational and other amenities to its members. It organizes music, dance, and social get-togethers. It has a Balmandir where educational facilities and games are offered to the children of the employees. Similarly, in the Kanyamandir (Girls' Section), elementary education, tailoring, knitting, training in hygiene and care of children, etc., are organized. In its Mahila Mandir, it has made necessary arrangements to provide educational amenities and craft training to women employees. Night classes a library, a reading room and facilities for indoor and outdoor games are also provided for the benefit of workers.

Welfare facilities are provided for the workers by certain unions like the Mazdoor Sabha of Kanpur, the Railwaymen's Union, the Indian Federation of Labour in U.P. and the Assam Branch of the INTUC. The Railwaymen's Union has allotted funds to meet unforeseen contingencies like retirement, unemployment, sickness, death, etc. They also provide for legal defence and life insurance. Further, they have also organized co-operative societies for the benefit of its members.

The social welfare activities organized by certain trade unions in Bombay are enumerated below:

Rashtriya Mill Mazdoor Sangh (RMMS)

It was founded by late G.D. Ambekar and was registered on August 26, 1941, under the Trade Unions Act, 1926, in the name of Rashtriya Kamgar Sangh. It changed its name to Rashtriya Mill Mazdoor Sangh in September 1947 and got itself affiliated to the INTUC. The Girni Kamgar Union affiliated to AITUC was the representative union for the textile mills in Bombay prior to 1945. In 1945, RMMS was given the status of an approved Union. In 1941, the Union applied for registration as a representative union under the B.I.R. Act and was recognized as a sole bargaining agent for all the textile workers in Bombay. Since then it continues to enjoy its representative status. Its activities primarily consists of:

(a) representation of individual grievances; (b) handling of industrial disputes and (c) provision of welfare amenities to its members. The following are some of the welfare activities undertaken by the union.

(1) It has a Workers' Education Centre at Khandala with an investment of Rs. 5 lakhs; (2) It provides merit-cum-need based scholarships and text books for needy students; (3) It has a reference library with 8,400 books and a Research Cell; (4) It has made arrangements for sewing and tailoring classes for family members of the employees; (5) It provides medical facilities to the union members in its allopathic and homeopathic clinics; (6) From its printing press it publishes a weekly known as "Kamgar" and other booklets of interest to its members; (7) In its auditorium dramas are staged and films are screened; (8) It has a holiday home at Khandala known as "Ambekar Smriti"; (9) It has also a housing co-operative society for the benefit of its members.

The Ambekar Institute for Labour Studies, jointly sponsored by the INTUC and the RMMS, Bombay, was established in 1976. It is registered under the Societies Registration Act, 1860. It has been set up to meet the felt need of Indian workers in general and the textile workers in particular for a better understanding of labour problems in the broader context of their aspirations as set out in the national plans.

Mill Mazdoor Sabha

It was established in 1947 as an organization for textile workers. It is affiliated to Hind Mazdoor Sabha. It is a representative union under the B.I.R. Act for silk, cotton processing and hosiery mills in Bombay. Some of its welfare activities are listed below:

(1) The union runs credit co-operative societies for the members belonging to small factories which have no such facilities. (2) It grants scholarships to the members' children

studying in 8th, 9th and 10th standards on the basis of merit. The amount varies from Rs. 15 to Rs. 20 p.m. (3) It also issues books to the needy students on the condition of their return at the end of the year. (4) In the event of the death of a member, the union gives Rs. 200 to the family of the deceased to meet the immediate expenses. (5) It has a holiday home at Khandala for its members. (6) It conducts workers' education programmes for its members in collaboration with the Central Board for Workers Education. (7) It has its own research wing which feeds enough data to its representatives in collective bargaining process.

Transport and Dock Workers' Union

It was established in 1932 by P. D'Mello, a clerk in Bombay Port Trust. In 1958 it became a Federation of Dock and Transport Workers under the able guidance of D'Mello. Its total membership is 35,000 out of 70,000 port and dock workers. Its welfare activities consist of housing, free medical treatment for family and dependents, schooling for children, etc. Workers get 150 rupees per year towards outdoor treatment. The union has a holiday home at Khandala. It has a credit co-operative society with branches in residential localities. It grants scholarships to some of the needy students. It maintains a co-operative credit society to provide loans to its members on easy terms. Consumers' goods and other articles are provided at a cheaper rate to its members through its consumer co-operative stores. Employees' children are given scholarships and in certain cases free education from D'Mello Trust.

In addition to the welfare facilities provided by the above mentioned unions, there are also some other unions of workers doing more or less similar labour welfare work for the benefit of their members, both in private and public sectors, in various parts of the country. In recent years they have undertaken different social, recreational, educational and developmental activities for the benefit of their members.

5

Structural Adjustment and Labour Standards

INTERNATIONAL LABOUR STANDARDS

The word labour standard is used in two ways, descriptively and normatively. Used descriptively, it tells us the actual terms of employment, quality of work and the well-being of workers at any specific time and place. Used normatively, labour standards specify rights and stipulate normative rules. Basically, they represent the common understanding or agreement between employers and labour. International labour standards, generally expressed as conventions or recommendations, are adopted by the International Labour Conference following an elaborate procedure for standard setting and their translation into conventions and recommendations.

Conventions are the basic instruments of setting standards. Recommendations provide guidance for national action. The ILO has so far adopted 172 conventions and 179 recommendations. A member country which ratifies a convention binds itself to its observance. Not all conventions are ratified by all members. India, for instance, has ratified only 35 of the 172 conventions adopted by the ILO—by no means an enviable record. We shall soon see that ratification is not the end.

Types of Standards

Labour standards have been classified in many ways. The following typology is attributed to Sengenberger (1994a).

Standards of Protection

These include ILO conventions and recommendations relating go (i) regulation of duration and scheduling of working time, (ii) standards ensuring occupational health and safety, (iii) protection against loss of job, employment and income, (iv) protection of income through minimum wage regulation, (v) protection of equality and treatment, (vi) protection of particular groups of workers, and (vii) protection from forced labour and bonded labour.

Standards of Participation

Standards of participation provide the rights and the means required for the joint setting and implementation of labour standards by employers, workers and the government, and for the active involvement of workers in the process of restructuring. The owners of capital exercise the managerial prerogatives but the extent of unilateral control differs from country to country. Rights of workers to condetermine and be consulted limit the managerial prerogatives on the Continent but not in the U.S. and the U.K. Participation in decision-making may be at the level of the board of directors or at the workplace.

Participatory labour standards imply collective organizations of the actors, employers, workers and the governments. Collective organizations to be effective need to be legally guaranteed. ILO Convention No. 87 provides for (i) freedom of association and protection of the right to organize, (ii) protection of organized workers from employer interference, (iii) protection of workers' and employers' organizations against acts of interference by each other, and (iv) the promotion of voluntary collective bargaining. Genuine participation emerges when workers' and employers' organizations are independent of the state and are financially and organizationally strong enough to play an autonomous role. The level of participation may range from the level of the workplace to the national economy. It is needed at both levels because the costs of decisions often affect the managers and the managed unequally. It increases the chance of a fairer distribution of resources. Besides, participation may, and often does, increase the size of the cake and transforms a zero-sum game into a positive-sum game.

Standards of Promotion

Standards of promotion are defined as those which further the productivity of labour, promote creation of employment, combat unemployment and under-employment and finance functioning of the labour market. Standards of promotion that are internationally recognised include:

(a) improvement of qualifications of labour through education, vocational training, and on-the-job training (ILO Convention No. 142),

(b) the active promotion of full, productive and freely chosen employment (ILO Convention No. 122),

(c) provision of public services to promote employment and improve the functioning of the labour market information systems, vocational guidance, placement and training (ILO Conventions No. 160, 142 and 88),

(d) active policies of vocational rehabilitation (ILO Convention No. 159), and

(e) the establishment of an effective labour administration with the participation of the employers and workers and their organizations.

Sengenberger (1994) emphasises the "package" role of labour standards, each standard being complementary to the others. No wonder, he deprecates the practice of considering the effects of one standard in isolation of others.

Case Against Labour Standards

Neo-classical economists regard labour standards as 'rigidities' which hinder the employer from adjusting his output and employment to changes in demand and technology. They show that the rigidities distort the allocation of resources and reduce employment, investment and growth below what they would be under conditions of competition. Competition equalises terms and conditions of employment in the long run without the distorting effects of labour standards. Therefore, they conclude that labour standards are redundant at best and harmful at worst. Though the neo-classical paradigm rejects most labour market regulations as distortions, in practice, a few concerned with minimum wage protection, employment security and severance pay and hiring and firing have borne the major brunt of the paradigm's attack. Trade unions, collective bargaining and labour standards are anathema in so far as they raise the terms and conditions of employment above what would be under competition. The paradigm is antithetical to ILO philosophy and ignores the value of labour standards as instruments of social justice. The neo-classical economists have been criticised by neo-institutionalists who defend labour standards and institutions on the basis of their contributions to productive efficiency and social justice (Plant, 1994).

Neo-classical economists from developing countries express fears that internationally imposed labour standards will be a veil for protectionism, and will close off export opportunities for developing countries. Neo-institutionalists fear that the insufficient regulation of labour standards in the international economy will lock some firms and countries into low productivity methods of production that not only deprive workers of their basic rights but also produce poor economic outcomes. The neo-classical view implies that policy maker should avoid imposing regulation on firms. The neo-institutional perspective advocates finding the appropriate level and kind of regulations to facilitate the operation of economically dynamic and socially acceptable national and international labour markets (Plant, 1994). As Plant observe, the basic disagreement between different economic schools of thought is not a normative one. They agree on desirable outcomes but disagree on the means for achieving these outcomes.

Sengenberger raises two general objections against the neo-classical criticisms of labour standards. He argues first that "they (criticisms) are derived from deductive economic theory built on few abstract axioms, with poor empirical content and not proven in reality" (Sengenberger, 1994, p. 5). He points out that labour standards are founded on vast practical experience and the common perceptions of workers, employers and governments in many countries. They arise from the desire of the three participants in the labour market to avoid the undesirable consequences of market failures. Based on a consensus, they require no theory to justify them.' However, to criticise neo-classical theory for lack of empirical support in one breath and then to assert in the next that labour standards need no theory and hence, no empirical verification to justify them because they are based on consensus is, to say the least, odd indeed. History of science is full of many corpses of consensus such as that the earth is stationary and the sun moves round it or that it is flat and if one walked far enough in one direction one was sure to fall off the edge.

The World Bank has undertaken considerable research on the relationship between adjustment measures and labour market institutions. Its country case studies have been challenging the traditional perceptions that labour market institutions in different developing regions are obstacles to effective adjustment. These studies conclude that labour markets do not appear to have impeded stabilization efforts, and that real wages show remarkable flexibility (Horton et al., 1991). Perhaps, no generalization can be offered and the extent of flexibility prevailing in a market needs to be verified empirically in each specific market as and when required.

Sengenberger's second general observation that the enterprise being the unit of analysis in neo-classical theory, its conclusion cannot take into account the negative social externalities of the profit maximizing behaviour, is unassailable.

No neo-classical writer has denied the proposition that markets fail when there are externalities. However, they assert that, though market failure justifies regulation, it does not guarantee its success. Market imperfections, like market failures, are often advanced as justifications for labour standards. It is argued that, labour markets are less competitive today than they were in early days of industrial revolution. This appears to be a very specious argument when we consider the enormous increase in the number and diversity of products, many of them close substitutes of one another, integration of world economies into a global village and, lowering of trade barriers, mobility of goods, factors of production, information, largely a consequence of application of new micro-electronics technology to production, transport and communication. As far as social pollution is concerned, virtue does not seem to lie necessarily with either the large producers (MNCs) or the small ones. The latter may produce greater physical and social pollution because their numbers being large relative to the inspectors who monitor them, their chances of being detected are very low.

Labour standards are justified as a compromise solution to the conflict between private and collective and economic and social interests is the LDCs. The precise level at which the compromise is struck will differ from time to time and place to place. Times change and require a change in the labour standards. There are no permanent states of over-regulation and under-regulation. A set of regulations deemed adequate in one period may be over or under regulated in another. For example, the great consensus of the Keynesian era when economic and social development was mutually reinforcing and could be reconciled easily fell apart after the mid-seventies as the economic, demographic and technological conditions changed. Welfare states which appeared to be well regulated so far suddenly came to be regarded as over-regulated. The words, consensus and compromise, used above raise problems in dualistic economies. Consensus among whom? And compromise between whom? Employers, unions and governments in dual economies may all agree and pitch up labour standards higher than the levels implied in the Lewis model. This would slow down the pace of absorption of labour from the traditional to the modern sector. High labour standards may thus reconcile efficiency in the formal sector but only at the cost of justice to the informal sector.

The relationship between labour standards and economic development has generated much controversy with some scholars giving primacy to growth (Fields, 1990) and others maintaining that if the goal were development rather than growth the conflict disappears and the two become mutually reinforcing. Economic development emphasises the quality of life, enlargement of the opportunity set, development of capabilities, participation in decision making, sustainable improvements in standard of living—attributes which directly or indirectly are related to protective, participatory and promotional role of labour standards. Sengenberger (1994) refers to studies in the USA which relate competitiveness to observance of labour standards.

In such a debate, it is easy to get carried away by idealism, emotion and intellectual hair-splitting. What one is concerned with here is not the abstract concept of standards but a time and space specific, contextual, minimum or the maximum as the case may be. The industrialised countries of today developed without let or hindrance of standards in their early stages of development (Caire, 1977). The NICs suppressed the freedom of association substantially and China is unlikely to score any better than the NICs and may do even worse. These instances show that the ILO Convention on freedom of association, considered the basic standard, is often the first to be sacrificed at the altar of growth. It is argued in the LDCs that labour standards are required to stop the race to the bottom which would take place in their absence. This role of standards in the LDC is limited by the existence of large unorganized sector. It enables a firm to bypass or evade the standards. The Indian government has enacted the minimum wage for scheduled industries but it could claim some success in its implementation only in the larger informal establishments in glass, bidi and powerloom industries.

Labour standards, if applied successfully to the organized sector, would widen the dualism in the labour market, due initially to the efficiency wage, even further. Though the insider-outsider dualism based on efficiency wage does not distort the allocation of resources, it may increase inequalities and poverty. According to some, a high wage policy in the organized sector does not represent efficiency wage but quasi-rents, the reduction of which should not reduce output in theory but it would in practice through fall in worker morale and increase in industrial conflict. There is also the possibility that a higher minimum wage may not increase the efficiency of the workforce employed in the organized sector because the restricted employment would increase the burden of unemployed dependents on the employed population and prevent the transformation of higher wages into benefits in terms of better health and improved nutrition of the employed. *In other words, labour standards cannot succeed without an appropriate development strategy that maximizes savings as well as the efficiency with which they are invested.*

STRUCTURAL ADJUSTMENT AND ITS CHALLENGES

The World Bank's definition of structural adjustment implies the following objectives:

(i) stabilising the macro-economic environment,
(ii) promoting economic growth and alleviating poverty,
(iii) promoting openness of the economy.
(iv) improving transparency in the incentive system,
(v) improving efficiency in the resource allocation,
(vi) improving scope for private sector development,
(vii) strengthening institutions and capacity for policy analysis.

The world economy is undergoing structural changes of a long term nature. They include:

(a) sectoral shifts from industry to services, the decline of old industries such as mining, steel, shipbuilding, footwear, textiles and the rise of new sectors such as telecommunications, bio-technology, software engineering etc.; and within each industrial sector the increase of producer and commercial services at the expense of divert manufacturing,

(b) the decline of mass production in the industrialised world and its replacement by a combination of flexible specialization, lean production or Neo-Fordism,

(c) as international division of labour with more traditional, low value added consumer goods and industries moving to the NICs and the older industrialised countries concentrating on high value added production and services,

(d) rather contradictory developments of globalization of the economy and rising number of international trading blocks,

(e) changes in the size distribution of businesses involving the de-centralisation of production within big companies and contracting out production and employment to medium and small enterprises.

These trends carry with them risks and opportunities for labour and labour institutions, risks of greater dependencies, disparity and marginalization, and also opportunities for more balanced development. They reduce the reliance on vulnerable business structures and offer opportunities for new frontiers based on redesign, skill enhancement and competence etc. (ILO, 1991).

These changes have posed many challenges to employers' association and trade unions. Both have lost members, unions loosing then much faster than employers' associations. The increase of small and micro-enterprises poses problems for the collective representation just as it does for the organization of workers in trade unions. The welfare state provides a social net to protect the workers against the risks of loss of job and income making a trade union redundant. A worker in a developed country is well protected against the hazards of occupational health and safety. Being educated he is able to defend himself and prefers to be treated as an individual. The general conditions for collective organization and action are less favourable today then they were a hundred years back. This analysis led Sengenber (1994) to question whether by helping to improve the lot of workers, the trade unions had not become victims of their own success. The answer, as he says, may be 'yes' or 'no' at the same time. Yes, because the setting for labour policy is different today, thanks to the spread of labour standards. No, because this progress is not a once and for all progress, but one that is constantly called into question by the emerging unregulated business environment and hazards and risks, requiring new collective action for containing them. The new problems include the widening gap of development in the first, second and third worlds growing economic disparities and rising levels of poverty, the spread of stress at work of growing economic disparities and rising levels of poverty, the spread of stress at work of decay in the labour force, increased numbers of school dropouts, alcoholism, drug abuse etc. Some of these evils would be related at least partly to unemployment, under-employment and unsatisfactory working conditions. They cannot be tackled by the individual on his own and would require collective action.

Labour Standards and Restructuring

Labour standards are essential to the high road approach to restructuring. This approach may not be possible without the enabling framework of labour standards. Stories of successful development in the last two decades have brought out the crucial role of quality of labour. The second critical element in the performance of the productive system is cooperation among workers, among managers, between workers and management and between firms. Work has become more systemic. Tasks, functions, jobs, and firms have become interdependent because they are an integral part of an extended division of labour that needs co-ordination. Co-operation on an increasing scale can be observed among large companies where strategic alliances and joint ventures are formed to pool resources. Success depends on this high road approach of productivity improvement, innovatioin, and development through intra—and inter-firm co-operation. Whereas some firms may show the foresight to follow this approach many may not if the easier road of wage competition were available. Hence it is necessary to ban downward directed wage competition by setting an effective floor to wage rates and other conditions of employment. With the downward adjustment blocked, the firm is compelled to improve productivity, offer better or new products and look for new markets. *The labour standards provide this dynamic and innovative thrust.*

To develop co-operation among workers, management and firms, one needs to develop trust, defined as the stable expectation of two or more parties that each will behave co-operatively if the other does so. Labour standards can play a role in reaching such mutual understanding and co-operative relationships. Because of the systemic nature of modern manufacturing, its actual outcome is a collective product and depends on the joint efforts of the workforce. Performance depends more on human resource management than wage rates. The firm has to generate competence, skill, motivation, adaptability, creativity, the capacity for problem solving, good social relations at work and co-operative industrial relations. This implies that the firm must provide continuous education, specific and general, to its workforce. Labour standards aimed at promoting equality of opportunity and treatment in respect of occupation and employment could be an incentive for making the best use of human resources. There is some evidence to show that countries pursuing active labour market policies have a better record of employment generation. Besides an appropriate macro-economic policy one also needs measures to prevent social pollution.

Like technology, international trade is an instrument of economic development. But it does not produce desirable outcomes automatically. To reap the benefits of trade certain rules of the game need to be established. The observation of labour standards is one of them. But, as we shall see later, there is no justification for introducing the controversial social clause in trade.

After reviewing many ILO policy documents on labour standards and structural adjustments Plant (1994) concludes that the social issues arising from structural adjustment have been among the highest concerns of ILO. Efforts have been undertaken to seek closer collaboration with international financial institutions and influence their activities by reference to ILO concerns. However, the themes of ILO standards and structural adjustment have not been conceptually linked. Exception apart, there has been no effort to examine how structural adjustment could affect the application of particular ILO standards, or conversely how ILO standards might affect the design and implementation of structural adjustment programmes. Collaborations and discussions with Bretton Woods institutions have not focussed on specific ILO standards.

LABOUR STANDARDS AND STRUCTURAL ADJUSTMENT IN INDIA

Economic liberalization and globalization have had a chequered course in India. The reforms started with a bang in 1991 but since 1994 their pace slowed down and they have come almost to a halt. Industry, trade and finance have been liberalised considerably. The rupee is convertible on the trade account but not on the capital account. Both the FDI and the portfolio capital are welcomed in industry but not in insurance. Political uncertainty and the deceleration of growth in general and industrial growth in particular have reduced the inflows of foreign investments to a trickle. Public investments have fallen to a new low level and failed to compensate for the slow-down in private investment. The foreign exchange reserves are predicted to fall to the critical levels of 1991 very soon if the economy does not come out of its doldrums. This has an important bearing on the reforms process. The economy, which had recovered from the shock of stabilisation quickly, has gone deep into deflation and prolonged the pain of structural adjustment and increased its costs.

In effect the promise of structural adjustment with a human face has been belied. India exemplifies a country where high labour standards have been legislated and implemented for workers in the modern sector but where the number of workers covered is barely eight per cent of the workforce. The high labour standards and the privileged position of the trade unions in the modern sector have been strongly criticised for slowing down the growth of organized employment. The private sector has been able to achieve some measure of flexibility and reduce employment, albeit much too slowly (Deshpande, et al. 1997). Despite much talk about privatization there is little or nothing to report in practice. The public sector on the other hand continues to protect its employees and increase their emoluments even when the losses in some of the enterprises have wiped off their net worth many times more.

The data available from the National Sample Survey Organization (NSSO) for 1993-94 disproved most of the doomsday predictions of liberalization. Work force participation increased and unemployment declined. Most wage differentials, particularly male-female, casual-regular and between less and more educated narrowed relative to their levels before liberalization (Deshpande and Deshpande, 1998). It is now feared that there is a net loss of employment in the organized sector due to down-sizing, closures and VRS. The informal sector is likely to have been swollen by the influx of fresh additions to the labour force unable to find a place in the organized sector and the excess baggage unloaded by it. Till 1993-94 there was evidence of a decline in poverty. The trend is unlikely to have continued.

Labour Standards in India

Labour standards, as we saw earlier, have been divided into three types: standards of protection, standards of participation and standards of promotion. Among the standards of protection ratified by India are: Convention 1, (hours of work); Convention 4, (night work for women); Convention 5, (minimum age in industry); Convention 6, (night work of young persons in industry); Convention 14, (weekly rests in industry); Convention 15, (minimum age of trimmers and stokers); Convention 16, (medical examination of young persons as sea); Convention 18, (workmen's compensation occupational diseases); Convention 19, (equality of treatment in accident compensation); Convention 21, (inspection of emigrants); Convention 26, (minimum wage fixing machinery); Convention 29, (forced labour); Convention 32, (protection against accidents (dockers); Convention 41, (night work by women revised); Convention 42, (workmen's compensation for occupational diseases revised); Convention 45, (underground work by women); Convention 89, (night work by women revised); Convention 90, (night work by young persons in industry revised); Convention 100, (equal remuneration); Convention 107, indigenous and tribal population; Convention 111, (discrimination in employment and occupation); Convention 115, (radiation protection); Convention 118, (equality of treatment in respect of social security); and Convention 123, (minimum age for underground work).

India has not ratified conventions on occupational safety and health and conventions on social security (Tripathi, 1993). The main difficulty in doing so has been the existence of a large unorganized sector beyond the pale of law and its enforcement. The burden of ratifying the convention on social security would be too large to bear in the present socio-economic conditions. The Constitution of India provides for the right to work, to education and to public assistance in cases of unemployment, old age, sickness, disablement and undeserved want. Accordingly the union and the state governments have initiated a few schemes to serve the purpose and the spirit of relevant ILO conventions. Standards of participation include the most important standards such as basic human rights and freedom of association. Of the first, India has ratified Five out of the 11 ILO conventions, the include rights of association (agriculture) convention 11; forced labour (convention 29); equal remuneration (Convention 100); discrimination (employment and occupation (Convention 111); rural workers' organization (Convention 141). India has not ratified the remaining Six conventions in this group because the principles enunciated in these conventions are enshrined in the Indian Constitution and there are laws to protect them. Freedom of association and protection of right to organize and right to organize and collective bargaining (Convention 98), have not been ratified because they include some categories of government servants subject to code of conduct rules. India was one of the first Asian countries to ratify Convention 144 relating to tripartite consultations. There are a number of tripartite bodies with the Indian Labour Conference and the Standing Labour Committee at the apex; which in the opinion of Ratnam (1997) seem to be more symbolic than real. They have failed to produce a consensus on issues relating to industrial relations.

Standards Not Adequate

The above discussion shows that the labour standards ratified so far are not adequate to help India face up to the challenge of structural adjustment. This judgement would hold even when one includes the provision of National Renewal Fund to complement the labour standards. The enormity of the challenge would be all the greater if the threat of the social clause or linking of standards to trade materialises. The Government of India have questioned WTO's basic competence in taking on board new issues as also the propriety of doing so. They have urged the Committee of the WTO members to consider that international trade is the means of exchange of goods and services produced within a country with goods and services produced in other countries, and as such should not encroach on the production system itself in any country. Any attempt by the WTO to overstep the legitimate boundaries of trade and invade the jurisdiction of domestic production systems is bound to create serious problems and raise basic questions about WTO's competence and credibility. The director general of the ILO has suggested three principles for the linkage of standards to international trade:

(i) it must be multilateral and exclude any individual initiative by a state and group of states; and

(ii) it must be intended to supplement economic development.

Summing Up

Although labour standards are both descriptive and normative it is their normative role that has attracted greater attention. They protect workers against many hazards of an industrial society including loss of job and income. They promote participation in decision making and give the workers a say in deciding their future. Participation makes the system just and fair and requires organizations to represent the participants and encourage freedom of association with full autonomy. Labour standards play a promotional role. The firms adopting the standards are encouraged to improve the quality of the human resource they employ. The standards also encourage public authorities to adopt an active labour market policy which often increases the access of people to employment.

Despite these seemingly beneficial role the standards play, neo-classical economic theory looks upon them as distortions which reduce employment, allocative efficiency, investments and growth. Neo-institutionalists, on the other hand, see in labour standards a means to improve efficiency and equity. According to them, the problem is to find an appropriate and right kind of interventions to reconcile efficiency and equity. However, of a the view that, being based on consensus, labour standards require neither theory nor empirical validation appears dogmatic. Labour standards can be justified whenever there are market failures or market imperfections. However market failure is no guarantee that interventions would succeed.

Under-regulation and over-regulation of labour markets are relative terms and their extent differs over time. The labour market in most LDCs tend to be dualistic with the formal segment being the smaller of the two segments. This limits the application, coverage and benefits of labour standards to a small share of the working population.

The world today is undergoing substantial structural changes with far-reaching implications for the lives of people in the workplace and at home. These changes have led many economies to adjust their structure of production and life to global changes. The adjustment has created opportunities as well as risks. Labour standards are on test to protect the workers, block the race to the bottom and guide it on the high road to the top. However, the very organizations and labour market institutions that are to achieve this task are themselves threatened with extinction. A redeeming feature is that, success in making adjustment depends on development of human capital, co-operation and avoidance of conflict.

Globalization, which means integration of the domestic economy into world economy through trade does not necessarily confer benefits on all participants. There is a need for labour standards to prevent the adverse-effects of trade. There are moves to introduce a social clause in trade to prevent the relocation of industry from DCs to LDCs. The move is patently unfair to LDCs as it would deny them the opportunity to develop. All in all, questions are being asked whether the ILO has succeeded in relating labour standards to structural adjustment.

India now suffers from the ill effects of both liberalization and regulation. The promise of structural adjustment with a human face has been belied. As it is the labour standards have relevance only to a small segment of the Indian economy. As elsewhere so in India labour standards fall short of the responsibilities thrust on them by the structural adjustment process.

REFERENCES

Deshpande, Sudha, Guy Standing and Lalit Deshpande (1997), *Labour Flexibility in a Third World Metropolis: A Case Study of Bombay*, Commonwealth, New Delhi.

Fields, G. (1990), "Labour Standards, Economic Development and International Trade" as cited in Sengenberger (1994).

Horton, Susan, Ravi Kanbur and Dipak Kanbur (1991), "Labour Markets in an Era of Adjustment: Evidence from 12 Developing Countries", *International Labour Review*, Vol. 130, No. 5-6, ILO, Geneva.

International Labour Office (1991), *On Business and Work: Towards New Frontiers*, International Symposium on Work Life in Transition, ILO, Geneva.

Sengenberger, Werner (1994), "Labour Standards: An Institutional Framework for Restructuring and Development", in Sengenberger, Werner and Duncan Campbell (eds.), *Creating Economic Opportunities: The Role of Labour Standards in Industrial Restructuring*. International Institute for Labour Studies, Geneva.

Tripathi, K.M. (1993), "Background Paper on ILO Standards", *International Labour Standards*, Report of National Tripartite Seminar, National Labour Institute, Noida, Gazhiabad, U.P.

Venkataratnam, C.S. (1997), "Adjustment and Privatization in India" in Hoeven Rolph Van der and Gyorgy (eds.), *Lessons from Privatization: Labour Issues in Developing and Transitional Countries*, ILO, Geneva.

6

Social Security and Labour Welfare

'Social security', is one of the dynamic and progressive concepts of the modern age which is influencing social as well as economic policy. It is the security that the State furnishes against the risks which an individual of small means can not, today. Stand up to by himself or even in private combination with his fellows. The concept of social security is essentially related to the high ideals of human dignity and social justice. In a welfare State, comprehensive social security schemes take care of persons from 'womb to tomb.' It is one of the main pillars on which the structure of the welfare State rests. Article 38 of the Indian Constitution directs the State to secure a social order for the promotion of the welfare of the people. The Forty-fourth Amendment Act, 1978 has widened the scope of the Article 38, and it provided further that in particular, the State shall strive to minimise the inequalities in income, and endeavour to eliminate inequalities in status, facilities and opportunities, not only amongst individuals, but also amongst groups of persons residing in different parts of the country or engaged in different occupations.

Many Articles in the Directive Principles of State Policy as enshrined in Part IV of the Indian Constitution which have plethora of provisions bearing on social security directives and also promoting labour Welfarism are—Articles 23, 24, 32, 38, 39, 39-A, 41, 42, 43, 43-A, and 47.

While enacting social security legislation, certain basic principles of policy to be followed by the States which shall in particular, direct its policy towards securing:

(i) That the citizens, men and women equally, have the right to an adequate means of livelihood (Article 39-(a)).

(ii) That the operation of economic system does not result in the concentration of wealth and the means of production to the common determinate (Article 39(c)).

(iii) That there is equal pay for equal work for both men and women (Article 39(d)).

(iv) That the health and strength of workers, men and women and tender age of children are not abused and the citizens are not forced by economic necessity to enter a vocation unsuited to their age or strength (Article 39(e)).

(v) That the State shall within the limits of its economic capacity and development, make effective provisions for securing the right to work, to education and to public assistance in cases of unemployment, old age sickness and, disablement, and in other cases of undeserved wants (Article 41).

(vi) That the State shall make provision for securing just and humane conditions for work and maternity relief (Article 42).

(vii) That the State shall endeavour to secure to all workers, a living wage etc. (Article 43).

These measures have introduced an element of stability and protection in the midst of the stress and strains of modern life. Thus, it is a major aspect to public policy today of every developed and developing countries. The extent and coverage of its prevalence is a measure of progress made by a country towards the ideal of a Welfare State.

Inclusion of Social Security

Social Security as defined by Lord William Beveridge "is an attack on five giants, viz., disease, want, ignorance, squalor and idleness."

To understand the proper meaning of the above named five giants of Lord Beveridge, it is worthwhile to explain them in detail.

(a) *Disease*—Disease plagues every one. It plagues the workers in variety of ways due to use of sophisticated machinery and other hazardous chemicals in the modern industry including inhumane and insanitary conditions of work. Therefore, adequate provisions must be made for the purpose.

(b) *Want*—A worker always faces the rigours of the demon of *want*-Relief against means, ensuring that every citizen in return for service, has sufficient subsistence and that of his immediate dependents while he is working and when he cannot work. The state should strive to provide him living wage.

(c) *Ignorance*—A well informed, constructive and responsible minded industrial labour force is capable to look into the matters of health, welfare, safety, collective bargaining, rights and duties of workers etc. Ignorance of workers has given rise to various social problems including bondage, bad habits such as liquor consumption and addiction etc. A such, ignorance can be attacked by workers education, programmes, vocational training programmes etc.

(d) *Squalor*—Industrial pollution and insanitary conditions of work pose a threat to the workers as well as to the general public nearby industrial areas and cause disease, ill-health and even sometime deaths. It means all those evils which come through the unplanned growth of industries, cities, bad housing, dumping of effluents in rivers, destruction of forests etc. Thus, a remedial measures against squalor means planned industrial growth and population and revolution in housing. Article 48-A (as inserted by 42nd Amendment) provided that the State shall endeavour to protect and improve the environment, and to safeguard the forests of the country.

(e) *Idleness*—Idleness is the largest and fiercest of the five giants and the most important to attack. It is said that "empty mind is the house of all sins." The Indian Constitution also provides equality of opportunity for all citizens in matters relating to employment or appointment to any office under the State.

According to Weber and Cohen, "Social Security is a controversial and dynamic subject with various facets-

philosophical, theoretical, humanitarian, financial, administrative, social, economic political, statistical, acturial, medical and legal." W.A. Robson defines social security as follows—

"Social security is a way of ensuring freedom from want or poverty which is one of the formidable obstacles in the way of progress. Social security implies insurance against though misfortunes to which an individual remains exposed even the condition of society as a whole improves. It does not include the various measures for improving the conditions of society-full employment, minimum wage, factory laws, public health, education and so forth.

Fridlender also expressed the view that social security as a programme of protection provided by society against the contingencies of modern life-sickness, unemployment, old age, dependency, industrial accidents and invalidism against which the individual can not be exported to protect himself and his family by his own ability or foresight."

It has been defined by the ILO as "The security that society furnishes, through appropriate organization, against certain risks to which its members are exposed." These risks are essentially contingencies against which the individuals of small means and meagure resources can not effectively provide by his own ability or foresight alone or even with private combination with his fellows. According to it while all State policy has some bearing on social security, it is convenient to regard as social security services as provided the citizens with benefits designed to prevent and cure disease, to support when unable to earn; and to restore him gainful activity."

Under the Philadelphia declaration (1944), the International Labour Organization define the social security as "the extention of social and security measures to provide a basic income to all in need of such protection and comprehensive medical care."

The ILO further observed among others, adequate protection for the life and health of workers in all occupations, provision for child welfare and maternity protection and provision of adequate nutrition, housing and facilities for recreation and culture should be included in the national policy programmes.

It further emphasised the importance of comprehensive social security measures in the permeable to its Constitution, in which it proclaimed 'protection of the worker against sickness, disease and injury arising out of his employment, the protection of the children, young persons and woken; provision for old age and injury, the prevention of unemployment.

Thus, the above definitions lays stress on one or other aspect of social security. These aspects include income security, medical care, employment injury and other various contingencies and risks. The benefits covered by social security schemes, as described in above mentioned definitions.

The comprehensive objectives of all social security schemes is three-fold: compensation, restoration and prevention. Compensation goes to income security and is based upon the idea that during spells of risks, the individual and his family should not be subjected to a double calamity involving both destitution and loss of health, limb, life or work. Restoration implies cure from the disease and the invalid, re-employment and rehabilitation. Prevention is designated to avoid the loss of productive capacity due to sickness, unemployment or invalidity and to render the available resources which are used up by voidable disease and idleness and this increase the material, intellectual and moral well-being of the community. In modern times, there are two main currents in the movement towards social security, e.g. social insurance and social assistance. They are said to be two sides of the same coin and form an integral part of the social security of a country.

Social insurance is a modern idea, in which the persons concerned, their employers and the State make contributions, and mainly out of these contributions are benefits necessary to prevent want during unemployment, sickness, old age and other contingencies given as a right, subject to certain qualifying conditions. Thus in the words of William Beveridge, 'social insurance can be described as the "giving in return for contribution, benefits up to subsistence level, as of right and without means tests, so that an individual may build freely upon it." Thus, social insurance implies that it is compulsory and that men stand together with their fellows. Hence it is based upon the principle of compulsory mutual and or cooperative devise. Social assistance represents an unilateral obligations of the society towards its dependent groups. In this method, there are generally no contributory conditions. Social assistance is provided by the society or the Government to the poor and needy individuals. This assistance is provided voluntarily to all those persons of small means out of the general revenues of the State, to enable them to live at a minimum standard of needs directly or through some appropriate agencies as of right and subject to means test. However, the social assistance approach is the outcome of the poor laws which developed in most of the welfare States. It means in case of social assistance, the beneficiaries are not required to contribute towards the fund out of which reliefs such as workmen's compensation, maternity benefits, old age pension, unemployment assistance, medical assistance etc., are provided. However, in case of social insurance schemes, they are mainly financed through contributions by employers, employees and the State. The benefits to insured persons are linked to their contributions. The most important social insurance schemes at present in our country are the Employee's State Insurance Scheme and Employees Provident Fund and Miscellaneous Schemes.

Although all the social risks can be covered either by social insurance or social assistance, in practice, certain risks are usually covered by insurance and others are generally regarded as the special province of assistance. But now-a-days, it seems that both are moving closer to one another towards the common goal of a national system of social security. The ILO has precisely summarised the development of the two approaches in the following words:

"Social assistance is a progression from poor relief in the direction of social insurance, while social insurance is a progression from private insurance in the direction of social assistance."

Social Security Scheme in India

In our country, social security schemes have been in existence since times immemorial and joint families. Panchayats (Guilds), religious and charitable institutions, giving of alms have continued to provide assistance to the needy for various common risks, misfortunes, calamities etc. Kautilaya's *Arthashastra, Manusmriti* etc. bear testimony to the fact that social structure in those days was so evolved as affording protection to persons without means and without capacity to work as simultaneously designated to provide security to all the people. The Joint Hindu Family was the original cell of security and first line of defence which could cope only with limited misfortunes. In cases of natural calamities, i.e., flood drought, plague etc., an appeal was made to the neighbours or the guilts. References to such guilds are found in *Rigveda, Upanishads* and in other ancient Indian literatures. Their main purpose was collective security of life and property and security against common risks. But with the western impact and industrial development in the country, these institutions have fallen into decay and are no longer remain to meet the situation effectively and adequately. Hence it is now regarded the duty of the State itself to provide for social security.

However, it is true that idea of social security as at

present understood, is not quite new to India. A few employers have for instance been giving their employees such benefits as pension, provident fund and gratuity for many years, and have been providing some welfare measures.

As far back, the Workmens Compensation Act was passed in 1923, and the Maternity Benefits Act have been in force in various States since 1947. Even the Royal Commission on Labour (1931) did not stress for any national system of insurance as feasible in India, due to the absence of permanent labour force and migratory character of work force. Thus for a long time, the problem of social security was viewed in India merely as an academic discussion, and whatever thought was bestowed by various Committees, Commissions and Officials, was confined mainly to a few branches of social security. But organized social security measures in statutory form are only a recent origin with the coming of national Government.

Social security legislation in India for industrial workers consists of the following enactments-(i) The Workmen Compensation Act, 1923; (ii) The Employees' State Insurance Act, 1948; (iii) The Employees' Provident Funds and Miscellaneous Provisions Act, 1952; (iv) The Maternity Benefits Act, 1961; (v) The Payment of Gratuity Act, 1972. Each legislative enactment prescribes for the social security benefit in order to meet or combat against a social risk to which a worker is exposed. Let us discuss over all perspectives of all social security enactments one by one.

The Workmen's Compensation Act, 1923

Industrialization, expansion or modification of existing factories, and setting up of new industries as well as the use of sophisticated machinery and plants in industry have given rise to industrial hazards and accidents. Workers need protection against industrial accidents which occur in every country. Accidents are enormously costly, causing loss directly or indirectly and the losses are both visible and invisible. The invisible losses are immensurable and can not be valued in terms of money. Apart from this; fatal injury and permanent disablement cause agony and hardship to the family members. Due to the death or permanent disablement of the bread winner, the family sometimes is reduced to a state of penury. While technological progress in industry has made it possible to eliminate certain physically enacting jobs, it has also made work in industry more risky. Worker's safety has thus assumed more importance in recent years.

Prior to passing of the Workmen's Compensation Act, 1923 it was almost impossible on the part of an injured workman to recover any compensation for any injury which he has sustained in the course of his employment. Of course in few cases the employer was liable under common law for his own personal negligence and the dependents of a deceased workman in rare cases could claim damages under the Indian Fatal Accidents Act, 1885 if the accident occurred due to the wrongful act of the person who caused the death. In 1921, a Committee was appointed by the Government of India consisting of members of legislatures, medical profession, employers, Insurance experts to examine the ILO Convention on Employment Injury of 1921. Though the Committee resolved that the Convention could not be ratified by India in the original form, yet the public opinion in favour of protection against employment injury received strong support, as a result the Workmen's Compensation Act 1923 was passed in March 1923, and came into force on July 1, 1924. Subsequently, there were a number of amendments to the Act.

The object of the Act is to impose an obligation upon employers to pay compensation to workers or their families for accidents (including certain occupational diseases), arising out of and in the course of employment and resulting in death or disablement for a period exceeding 3 days.

The Act applies to all railway servants (other than those employed in administration work) and persons employed in any such capacity as specified in Schedule II to the Act. The schedule II includes persons employed in factories, mines, plantations, mechanically propelled vehicles, construction works and certain other hazardous occupations. Initially the limit for coverage under the Act was Rs. 500 p.m. The Act was amended by the Amending Act of 1976 on May 21, 1976 enhancing the wage limit from Rs. 500 to Rs. 1000 p.m. The Act was further amended by the Act of 1984 abolishing the condition of wage limit of Rs. 1000/- for coverage under the Act with effect from July 1, 1984. The benefits provided under the Act are not available to those persons who are covered under the E.S.I. Act, 1948. Under sub-section (3) of Section 2 of the Act, the State Governments are empower to add to schedule II any class of persons employed in any occupation which is hazardous occupation and to any occupational disease in Schedule III, after giving the three months notice in official Gazette.

Benefits

The amount of compensation payable depends on the nature of the injury and the average monthly wage of the worker concerned, also on whether he is an adult or a minor. The Act provides for payment of compensation to the workmen in case of temporary/permanent disablement and to his dependent in case of death. The minimum amount of compensation for death is Rs. 20,000 and for permanent disablement Rs. 24,000. The maximum amount for disablement can go up to Rs. 1,14,000 while that for death it can go up to Rs. 91,000 depending on the wages and age of the workmen at the time of his death. In case of temporary disablement, compensation at the rate of 50 per cent of wages is payable for a maximum period of 5 years. But no compensation is however, payable if the injury, not resulting in death is caused by the fault of the worker, e.g. due to influence of drunkness, wilful disobedience of an order/rule for the purpose of safety. Besides compensation is payable in the case of workers who contract certain occupational diseases.

The Compensation under Section 4 must be paid as soon as it falls due. And in cases where the employer does not accept the liability for compensation to the extent claimed, he was to make provisional payment based on the extent of liability which he accept, and such payment must be deposited with the Commissioner or made to the workman as the case may be. The amount deposited with the Commissioner is payable to the dependents as defined in the definition of the dependent, who amongst others include widow, minor, legitimate son, an unmarried legitimate daughter, a son or a daughter wholly dependent on the earnings of the workman and has attained the age of 18 years and infirm, a widower or a widowed mother. The employer if so desires can pay a maximum advance of Rs. 100 to any dependant of the deceased. The Commissioner can deduct from the compensation amount the actual cost of workmen's funeral expenses but not exceeding Rs. 50 and pay the same to the person by whom such expenses incurred. No claim for compensation shall be entertained by a Commissioner unless notice of the accident has been given to him and the claim is preferred before him within 2 years of the occurrence of the accident or in case of death within 2 years from the date of death. The claim filed beyond this period can also be considered if sufficient cause exists. In case of occupational diseases, the compensation will be payable only if the workman has been in service of the employer for more than six months. The Act does not permit contracting out i.e. a contract whereby the workman relinquishes his right of compensation for injury in the course of employment is null and void to such extent. The compensation payable to the workman or to his dependants can not be assigned, attached or changed.

If the compensation is not paid by the employer, the workman concerned or his dependants can claim the same by filling an application before the Commissioner for the purpose. An appeal will lie to the High Court within 60 days against certain orders of the Commissioners if a substantial question of law is involved and amount of dispute is more than Rs. 300/-. The Act is administered by respective State Governments/Union Territory administration.

The number of compensated injuries and amount of compensation paid under the workmen's Compensation Act, 1923 during previous years.

Employees' State Insurance Act, 1948

The Employees' State Insurance Act, 1948 is a pioneering measure in the field of social insurance in the country. The question formulating a health insurance scheme received the attention of the Government of India in 1927, when the subject of health insurance for industrial workers was first discussed by the Indian legislature in light of two Conventions (No. 24 and 25) which were adopted by the International Labour Conference in its 10th Session. The Royal Commission on Labour (1931) in its report also stressed the need for health insurance for industrial workers in India. The problem of health insurance was also discussed by the Bombay Textile Labour Enquiry Committee (1937) and by Kanpur and Bihar Labour Enquiry Committees of 1937 and 1938 and the Labour Ministers Conference in 1940, 1941 and 1942. The Government of India at that time, was not in favour of any such scheme, due to reasons of migratory character of workers and financial difficulties etc.

During the war period, the Government had under its consideration a compulsory health insurance scheme, for which funds were to be collected from both employers and employees, the Government taking the responsibility for the administration of the scheme. In pursuance thereof the work of preparing details of the compulsory health insurance for industrial workers was entrusted in March 1943 to Prof. B.P. Adarkar, an officer on special duty. He submitted his report in December 1944. The recommendations of Prof. Adarkar were based on compulsory contributory principles, contributions by the workers depending upon their earnings in slabs. In 1945, the Government of India appointed two ILO experts namely Mr. M. Stack and Mr. R. Rao to give their expert opinion on Adarkar's scheme. The experts expressed their view in favour of Adarkar's scheme and recommended its application. Adarkar's report was considered by the Government of India, in consultation with the State Governments and other interested concerned, which gave birth to the Workmen's State Insurance Bill, 1946. The Bill was further referred to a Select Committee on November 12, 1947. The Select Committee modified certain provisions making it applicable to all the employees in the factory and changed the name of Bill from "Workmen's State Insurance Bill" to "Employees' State Insurance Bill." Finally, the Employees' State Insurance Act was passed in 1948.

It was felt that the scheme could not be introduced at one stage through out the country, therefore a phased programme was chalked out and the scheme was put in operation on February 24, 1952 in Kanpur and Delhi to begin with.

The ESI Act, 1948 provides for certain benefits to employees in case of sickness, maternity and employment injury and to make provisions for certain other matters in relation thereto.

Coverage: The Act extends to the whole of India and applies to all factories, other than seasonal factories, run with the aid of power and employing 20 or more persons. The appropriate Governments are, however, authorised to extend it partially or wholly to any establishment or class of establishments industrial, commercial, agricultural or otherwise. The State Governments in exercise of the powers vested in them under Section 1(5) of the Act, extended the purview of the Act to new classes of establishments, viz., power using factories employing 10-19 workers and non-power using factories employing 20 or more workers and shops, theatres, cinemas, hotels, restaurants, roadmotor transport and news-paper establishments employing 20 or more persons.

The ESI Act was first amended in 1966 to enlarge the scope of the scheme and streamline and simplify the procedure relating to recovery of contribution and payment of benefits. The Act was again amended in 1975 with a view to enhance wage limit for coverage of employees under the scheme from Rs. 500 to Rs. 1000 p.m. along with revision of rates of contribution etc. The Act was further amended in 1984 with a view to raise the wage limit for coverage under the scheme from Rs. 1000 to Rs. 1600 p.m. with effect from January 27, 1985. The progress made during the period 1985 was as shown in Table 1.

TABLE 1

S. No.	*Item*	*As on 31.12.83*	*As on 31.12.84*	*Net increase/ Decrease*
1.	No. of Centres	486	513	+27
2.	No. of employees (in lakhs)	63.06	61.34	–1.72
3.	No. of insured persons (in lakhs)	72.29	69.90	–2.39
4.	No. of beneficiaries (in lakhs)	280.49	261.20	–9.29

Source: Annual Report (1984-85) Vol. I; Ministry of Labour, Government of India, p. 6.

The decrease in the number of employees, insured persons and beneficiaries as on 31.12.1984 as shown in table 2 is mainly attributable to the decoverage of employees due to the rise of wages beyond Rs. 1000 p.m.

Benefits: Freedom from economic fear is a great freedom and all social security legislation attack this fear and seek to annhilare it. The benefits conferred by the revisions of the Act attack this fear and seek to remove it. The benefits proposed for insured persons by this scheme are: (i) Sickness benefit;

(ii) Maternity benefit; (iii) Disablement benefit; (iv) Maternity benefit; (v) Disablement benefit; (vi) Dependants benefit; and (vii) Medical benefit. An insured person who is entitled to benefits under the scheme is not eligible to claim similar benefits under the Workmen's Compensation Act, 1923 or the State Acts relating to the maternity benefits.

(i) Sickness Benefit

For sickness occurring during any benefit period, an insured person is entitled to receive periodical cash payments in respect of such days of his sickness as are certified by the duly appointed medical practitioner, provided he satisfies the contributory conditions. The benefit is payable for a maximum number of 91 days in any two consecutive benefit periods. No benefit is payable for the first two days of sickness in case of sickness following, at an interval of not more than 15 days, the spell of sickness for which sickness benefit was last paid. Now the sickness benefit under the Scheme is at par with the standards laid down in the ILO Convention of Minimum Standards of Social Security (1952) for developing countries. The standard daily rate of benefit payable is equivalent to about one half of the assumed average daily wages as given in Schedule II to the Act, but since the benefit will be payable for the days of sickness, including holidays and Sundays, the rate of benefit will actually come to 7/12th of the wages. A person in receipt of benefit is required to remain under medical treatment at a dispensary or other medical institution provided under the Act.

Rates applicable at different ranges of average daily wages with effect from January 1, 1985 are shown in column 2 of Table 2.

An insured person suffering from any specific long term ailments (21 diseases) like tuberculoses, leprosy, mental diseases etc. is eligible for extended sickness benefit at a rate of 25 per cent more that the sickness benefit rate rounded to the next higher multiple of 5 paise, for a period of 124/309 days, if the insured person was in employment for a continuous period of preceding two years. Initially, the extended sickness benefit is now paid for 124 days which may be extended upto 309 days in chronic suitable cases on confirmation by R.D.M.C. Medical Refree/Chief Executive of ESI Scheme, of the State or his nominee. An insured person is paid twice the ordinary sickness benefit rate (practically full daily wage) for 7 days for vasectomy and 14 days for tubectomy operations as an incentive for family planning. This benefit is without bar of two days waiting period, and is in addition to the usual sickness benefit. To be eligible for the sickness benefit during any benefit period, an insured person must have paid for not less than half the number of days of that period.

TABLE 2

Rates of Weekly Contributions

Group of Employees whose average daily wages are	*Corresponding daily standard and benefit rate*
1. Below Rs. 6.00	2.50
2. Rs. 6.00 and above, but below Rs. 8.00	3.50
3. Rs. 8.00 and above but below Rs. 12.00	5.00
4. Rs. 12.00 and above but below Rs. 16.00	7.00
5. Rs. 16.00 and above but below Rs. 24.00	10.00
6. Rs. 24.00 and above but below Rs. 36.00	15.00
7. Rs. 36.00 and above	20.00

Source: P.L. Malik, *Industrial Law*, (14th ed.) p. 618.

(ii) Maternity Benefit

An insured woman is entitled to maternity benefit at double the standard benefit rate. This is practically equal to full wages for a period of 12 weeks of which not more than six week can precede the expected date of confinement. Previously it was consisted of periodical cash payments at the sickness benefit rate or 12 annas a day, whichever is higher.

By the Amendment Act of 1966, an additional maternity benefit is given in case of miscarriage, on production of such proof, for a period of 6 weeks immediately following the date of miscarriage during which she does not work for remuneration with effect from January 28, 1968. In case of sickness arising out of pregnancy, confinement, premature birth or miscarriage, an additional benefit is given for all days on which she does not work, for a period not exceeding one month. The Act further provided that where the insured woman dies during her confinement or during the period of six weeks immediately following her confinement for which she is entitled for maternity benefit, leaving behind in either case the child benefit is payable for whole of that period, but if the child also dies during the said period then, for the days upto and including the day of the death of the child to the person nominated by the woman.

To qualify for the maternity benefit, the conditions of contributions are the same as in the case of sickness benefit excepting that in the former case one of the contributors must have been paid between 36 and 40 weeks before the week of confinement or as the case may be.

(iii) Disablement Benefit

If an insured person is injured in the course of his employment and permanently or temporarily disabled, he will get what is called 'disablement benefit' in the form of cash in instalment. That is to say, he will not receive a lumpsum once for all. The minimum period of disablement which will entitle him to the benefit is 3 days, excluding the day of accident. In the case of permanent disablement, the employee will get the benefit as long as he lives unless a change in the nature of permanent disability calls for review.

In case of temporary disablement, an insured person will be given the cash payment at the 'full rate' during the period of disability, if it last for over 3 days. In case permanent disablement whether total or partial, the person will be entitled to periodical payment for such disablement in accordance with the provisions of the First Schedule to the Act. The daily rate of disablement benefit is 25 per cent more than the standard benefit rate rounded to next higher multiple of 5 paise corresponding to the average daily wages in the contribution period in which the employment injury occurs, this is called the 'full rate.'

The rate of disablement benefit and dependants benefit has been increased from 125 per cent to 140 per cent of the standard benefit rate with effect from January 1, 1981.

In view of the recommendation of the Review Committee, the ESI Corporation had accepted that in cases where the estimated permanent disablement was more than 25 per cent, provisional payment upto 75 per cent of the benefit might be made subject to adjustment when the award of Medical Board became available. The recommendation which was given effect in March 1970 on an experimental basis, has now been adopted permanently.

(iv) Dependants Benefit

If an insured person is hurt in the course of his work and dies as a result, his dependants, i.e., his widow, legitimate sons and legitimate unmarried daughters will get a pension. The widow will get a pension all her life or until re-marriage, an amount equivalent to 3/5th of the full rate. If there are more than one widow, the amount payable is to be divided equally amongst them each. Each legitimate or adopted son will get an amount equivalent to 2/5th of the full rate until he attains the age of 18 years. The same amount of benefit is paid to each legitimate or adopted unmarried daughters until she attains eighteen years of age or until marriage, whichever is earlier. If the sons or daughters are infirm at the time of death, the benefit is paid till infirmity last and daughter continue to be unmarried.

In case the deceased person does not leave any of the above mentioned dependants, then the parents or grandparents are eligible to get the dependants benefit. The dependant benefit may be reviewed subject to the provisions of Section 55-A of the Act.

(v) Medical Benefit

Whenever any insured person or a member of his family needs medical aid, he or she will have it free. Medical benefit is considered to be the king-pin of the ESI scheme which consists of medical attendance and treatment of insured persons and their families in the form of out-patient treatment and attendance in a hospital or by visit to their home or treatment as indoor patient in a hospital clinical. This benefit has been divided into three parts: (a) *Restricted Medical Care*—It consists of out-patient medical care at dispensaries or panel clinics. At these places, facilities of consultation with medical officer, supply of drugs, pre-natal and post-natal rare family planning and immunization services are available. Home visit of a doctor is also available: (b) *Expanded Medical Care*—This service consists of consultation with specialises and supply of medicines and drugs. This also includes the facilities of laboratory tests and X-ray facility; (c) *Full Medical Care*—It provides hospitalization facilities, services of specialists including drugs and diet for in-patients.

A person is entitled to medical benefit during any period for which contributions are payable in respect of him or in which he is qualified to claim sickness benefit or maternity benefit or is in respect of such disablement as does not disentitled him to medical benefit under the regulations.

A person on becoming an insured person for the first time is entitled to medical benefit for a period of three months, provided he remains in service, continuous for 3 months. By a regulation, it has been provided that even when an insured person ceases to contribute, he will continue to get medical benefit for such period as may be provided in the regulations.

A tuberculosis patient is entitled to medical care for about one year following the date on which he otherwise becomes disentitled to it provided he had 2 years continuous service. Artificial limbs, appliances necessary for treatment are now provided as a part of medical benefit. The ceiling expenditure on medical care with effect from April 1, 1980. Though the insured persons under the scheme are being provided with full medical care, yet the restricted medical care is at present available only in Uttar Pradesh at Pipri, where a 50-bed ESI hospital is to be constructed.

In addition to above benefits, funeral benefit upto R. 100/- is also payable to the eldest surviving member of the decreased insured person.

Finance: The scheme is financed by ESI Fund created by the contribution from employers, employees and grants, donations, and aid from Central and State Governments, or any individual or body. The State Governments also share the costs of the scheme by contributing towards medical treatment which is to be determined by an agreement between Corporation and State Governments.

Payments: Speedier cash payments have also now been ensured by reducing the statutory time-limits for payment of various benefits under the ESI Scheme. Regulation 52(1) has been amended in 1972 so that (a) sickness benefit is paid not later than 7 days; (b) funeral benefit is paid not later than 15 days, (c) the first payment of maternity benefit is paid not later than 14 days; (d) first payment of temporary/permanent disablement benefit is paid not later than one month; (e) first payment of dependant benefit is paid not later than 3 months. These limits are maximum and most of the payments are made well within the limits. The amount of cash benefits paid by the Corporation during 1983-84.

In addition to the above, at present, there are altogether 85 fulfledged ESI hospitals as on March 31, 1984. These hospitals taken together provided 17,102 beds for patients. At the end of December 1984, it covered about seven million workers in 513 centres and the total number of beneficiaries including family members was over 27 million.

Administration

The Employees State Insurance Scheme is administered by a Corporate body called the 'Employees' State Insurance Corporation (ESIC) which has members representing employees, employers, Central Government, State Governments, the Medical profession and Parliament. A Standing Committee constituted from the members of the Corporation acts as the Executive Body for the administration of the scheme. There is also a Medical Benefit Council to advise the Corporation regarding matters connected with provision of medical benefit. The Director-General, who is the Chief executive officer of the Corporation, is an ex-officio member of the Corporation and of its Standing Committee. For administrative convenience, the Corporation has also set up Regional Boards, which are functioning in all the States.

Thus, it may be concluded that the provisions of the ESI Act, 1948 is an improvement in this matter on the workmen's Compensation Act, 1923 under which compensation was paid in lump-sum and the party responsible for the payment of compensation was the employer. This insured person can claim the relief by option under any of the said Acts.

It may also be stated that the ESI Act, is a beneficial piece of social legislation in the interest of labour in factories at the first instance and with power to extend to other establishments Provisions of the Act will have to be constructed with that end with a view to promote the scheme and avoid the mischief.

The Employees' Provident Funds and Miscellaneous Provisions Act, 1952

The Employees' Provident Funds and Miscellaneous

Provisions Act provides for the institution of compulsory provident functions for employees in factories or other establishments with the object of making "some provision for safeguarding the future of workers after he retires, for the dependents in case of his early death, and to cultivate among workers the spirit of saving."

On a review of the working of the scheme over the years, it was found that Provident Fund was no doubt an effective old-age and survivorship benefit, but in the event of the premature death of the employees, the accumulations in the Provident Fund might not be adequate to render adequate and long-term protection to his family. This led to the introduction of the Employees' Family Pension scheme with effect from March 1, 1971. The Act was further amended in 1976 with a view to introduce an insurance to cover linked to the deposits in the Fund in the credit of the decreased worker. The Employees' Deposit Linked Insurance Scheme was accordingly framed and introduced with effect from August 1, 1976.

The Act, which initially applied to six major industries—such as Cement, Cigarettes, electrical, mechanical and general engineering products; iron and steel, paper and textile in 1952, is now applicable to 173 industries and classes of establishments employing 20 or more persons. However, any newly started undertaking remains exempted for a period of five years if it employees less than 50 employees and for three years if it employs 50 or more persons. Once the establishment covered under the Act, it remain continue, to be so covered unless the number of persons employed is reduced to less than 85 for a period of persons employed is reduced to less than 85 for a period persons employed is reduced to less than 15 for a period continuous period of one year. The Act does not, however, apply to:

(i) establishments registered under the Cooperative Societies Act, 1912, if the establishment employees less than 50 person and work without the aid of power

(ii) tea plantations in State of Assam; and

(iii) charitable institutions.

The total number of establishments including with exempted and unexempted establishments was 1,51,936 affording shelter to 127.61 lakhs of subscribers as on September, 1984.

Applicability

Earlier, the period of service for eligibility to become a member of the EPF Scheme was one year's continuous service or 240 days of actual work during a period of 12 months or less or on becoming permanent whichever is earliest. In order to liberalise these rules, the scheme was amended (with effect from August 19, 1974) and the period of eligibility for membership was reduced to 6 months continuous service or 120 days of actual work. The Act was further amended with effect from January 31, 1981 by which the eligibility of membership was reduced to three months continuous service or 60 days of actual work during a period of 3 months or less or becoming permanent. The maximum pay limit of Rs. 1000 p.m. for eligibility of membership has also been raised to Rs. 1600 p.m. With effect from December 1, 1976, employees drawing more than Rs. 1600 p.m. are also eligible to become members on certain conditions. This pay limit, however, is not applicable to newspaper establishments, seasonal establishments, in case of an employee who has worked for 2/3rd of the period during which the establishment remains in operation.

Rate of Contribution

The employees statutory contribution to the Fund was originally fixed at 6 per cent of the basic wages, dearness allow-including cash value of food concession and retaining allowance (if any). However, with a view to provide better and more substantial social security benefits to more and more number of workers, the rate of contribution was raised to 8 per cent, which was applicable to 108 industries with effect from Sept. 1, 1983.

The Employees' Family Pension Schemes, 1971

With a view to providing substantial long-term protection to the family of the worker member who dies prematurely while in service, as scheme of Family Pension-cum-Life Insurance came into force with effect from March 1, 1971. The Scheme is applicable compulsorily to all the employees, who become members of the Employees' Provident Fund Scheme on or after March 1, 1971. But it is optioned to those who had become members of the provident fund prior to that date. The total number of Subscribers covered under the family pension scheme as on September 30, 1984 were 82.05 lakhs. The Scheme is financed by diverting $1^1/_6$ per cent of pay of the employees from out of their share of contribution towards provident fund with an equal amount from employers' share. The Central Government also contributes to the family pension fund at $1^1/_6$ per cent of the pay of the member and also bear the expenditure on the administration of the scheme.

All money belonging to Family Pension Fund is kept in deposits in "Public Account" and interest at the rate of 7½ per cent per annum is allowed thereon with effect from April 1, 1981. Prior to this, the rate of interest was 5½ per cent per annum. The benefits provided under the Scheme are given below:

(i) *Family Pension*—If a member of the Scheme dies during reckonable service before attaining the age of 60 years, Family Pension will be paid at the prescribed rates, provided the member had contributed to the Family Pension Fund for not less than one year. The family pension is to be payable:

(a) to the widow or widower up to the date of death or remarriage whichever is earlier;

(b) failing the above, to the eldest surviving minor son until he attains the age of 21 years;

(c) failing this too, to the eldest; surviving unmarried daughter, until she attains the age of 21 years or marries, whichever is earlier. The family pension is payable from the day immediately following the death of member.

(ii) *Life Assurance Benefit*: A lump sum amount of Rs. 2000 will be payable to his her family as life assurance benefit subject to condition that a member has contributed to the family pension fund for a period not less than one year, dies while in reckonable service.

(iii) *Retirement-Cum-Withdrawal Benefit*: The retirement-cum-withdrawal benefit became payable to the members either on attaining the age of 60 years or on cessation of membership from the family pension fund before attaining the age of 60 years for reasons other than death, provided the member has contributed to the fund for not less than one year. The rate specified for retirement-cum-withdrawal benefit varies with number of full years of contributions paid subject to minimum of Rs. 110 (with one year contribution) and a maximum of Rs. 9000 (with 40 years contribution.)

The Scheme has been amended to liberalise the benefits provided under the Act with effect from January 1, 1983 giving additional facilities of (a) Remittance of family pension straight in the bank account of the pensioner every month; (b) Remittance of family pension up to Rs. 250 per month through money order to the pensioner; and (c) One time ad-hoc relief ranges from Rs. 20 to Rs. 35 has also been granted to the family pensioners as on March 31, 1982. In addition, an ad-hock annual increase ranging from Rs. 3 to Rs. 10 shall also be paid to those who are in receipt of pension for one year or more.

The Government has accepted most of the major recommendations pertaining to pensionary benefits of the Fourth Pay Commission. The Government had accepted the rationalised pension structure, the family pension will be subject to a minimum of Rs. 375 and maximum of Rs. 1250 per month, as against Rs. 300 and Rs. 1000, the recommendation to introduce death gratuity for government servants during in harness. The ceiling on gratuity which operated at Rs. 50,000 has been increased to Rs. 1 lakh.

Employees' Deposit-Linked Insurance Scheme, 1976

The Scheme is applicable to all factories establishments to which the E.P.F. and Misc. Provisions Act., 1962 applies, he was brought into force with effect from August 1, 1976. The Scheme provides that in the event of the death of an employee who is a member of the E.P.F. Scheme or of the exempted provident fund, the persons entitled to receive the provident fund accumulations are paid an additional amount equal to the average balance in the provident fund account of the deceased during the proceeding three years, subject to a maximum of Rs. 10,000. The amount payable will be deposited in the Saving Bank Account to be opened in the name of the beneficiary in any Nationalised Bank. The Special feature of the Scheme is that the employee is not required to make any contribution to the insurance fund, but he is required to keep a minimum average balance of Rs. 1000 in the provident fund so as to entitled him to the benefit under this Scheme.

As regards the contribution under the Scheme, the employers and the Central Government are required to pay contribution to the Insurance Fund at the rate of 0.5 per cent and 0.25 per cent respectively of the total emoluments i.e., basic wages and dearness allowance including cash value of any food concession and retaining allowance, if any. In addition to this, the employers and Central Government are to contribute at the rate of 0.10 per cent, and 0.5 per cent respectively of the wage bill towards administrative charges. Total contribution received under the Scheme up to the end of March 1984 was Rs. 201-42 crores.

All these three Schemes are administered by the Central Board of Trustees, a tripartite body consisting of representatives of employers and employees and persons nominated by the

Central and State Governments. The Central Provident Fund Commissioner is the Chief Executive Officer of the Organization and Secretary to the Central Board of Trustees. Apart from the Central Office, there are at present 16 Regional Offices and 29 Sub-Regional Offices functioning in various States for implementation of the Act, and the schemes thereunder.

In pursuance of a recommendation made by the Public Accounts Committee in its 110th report, the Ministry of Labour appointed a high level committee under the chairmanship of Shri G. Ramanujan in April, 1980 to review the working of the E.P.F. Organization with Special reference to the problems of mounting arrear of provident fund contributions. The Committee submitted its report on January 28, 1981, and made some important recommendations including the extention of the coverage of the Scheme to all establishments employing ten or more persons regardless of industry in which they were engaged, and all establishments employing more than 100 workmen may be allowed to manage all the Schemes under the Act through a Board of Trustees etc.

The Maternity Benefit Act 1961

In this direction, the ILO has drawn up long bank a Convention pertaining to women workers known as Maternity Protection. Convention, 1919 (No. 3), with a view to enable working woman to discharge family as well as health care during the period of pregnancy and confinement without loss of wages. In 1921, the Government of India reported to the ILO that it was not possible to adopt the said Convention on the ground that it may cause adverse repercussions on the employment of women and the economic conditions then prevailing in the country. Though the Royal Commission on Labour stressed the need for suitable maternity legislation for women employed permanently in non-seasonal factories, yet the Government of India was slow to act in this direction. However, the State Governments took the lead and the

Government of Bombay passed the first Maternity Benefit Act long back in the year 1929. The period of leave, the quantum of benefit and the qualifying conditions varied slightly from State to State. Besides the state legislations for providing maternity benefit to women employees in factories, there are three Central Acts, viz., the Mines Maternity Benefit Act, 1941; the E.S.I. Act 1948; and the Plantation Labour Act, 1951, which also provide similar benefits. In order to even out the disparities in various Acts, the Central Government enacted a new Act, called the Maternity Benefit Act in 1961. This Act applies to every factory, mine or plantation sectors including Government establishments excluding those establishments which are covered under the E.S.I. Act, 1948. The Act, was amended in 1972 and a new Section 5-A was added as follows:

"Every woman entitled to the payment of maternity benefit under this Act shall, notwithstanding the application of the E.S.I. Act, 1948 to the factory or other establishments in which she is employed, continue be so entitled until she become qualified to claim maternity benefit under Section 50 of that Act."

The act was further amended in 1976 which provides for payment of maternity benefit under the Act to the women employees covered by E.S.I. Act, 1948 and in receipt of wages exceeding entitlement limit of wages (Rs. 1000) specified in that Act.

The Act regulates the employment of women employees in certain establishments for certain periods before and after child birth and provides for the maternity benefits to them at the rate of average daily wage for the period of their actual absence immediately preceding and include the day of their delivery and for six weeks immediately following that day. The maximum period for maternity benefit is 12 weeks, i.e., six weeks up to and including the day of her delivery and six weeks immediately following that date.

In order to qualify for maternity benefit the women employee should have rendered 160 days service during preceding one year.

For nursing mothers the Act provides two nursing break of prescribed duration in addition to rest interval for nursing the child. The Act also entitled to nursing mother from her employers a medical bonus of Rs. 25; if pre-natal and post-natal care is provided by the employer free of charge. In a period of six weeks immediately following the day of her miscarriage. In case of illness arising out of pregnancy, delivery, premature birth of the child or miscarriage, a woman is entitled, in addition to the period of absence allowed to her under section 6 or 9, to leave with wages at the rate of maternity benefit for a period of one month.

In order to safeguard the interest of pregnant women workers, the Act provides that such a woman shall not be dismissed nor be discharged during the period of maternity leave. The Act further provides that no pregnant woman should be required to do any work which is of an arduous nature or which in any way is likely to interfere with her pregnancy etc. during six weeks before the day of her expected delivery.

A Bill seeking amendments to the Maternity Benefit Act, so as to provide for enhanced maternity benefits was introduced in the Rajya Sabha on December 1, 1987 by the Labour Ministry. The amending provisions are based on the recommendations of a Working Group of the Economic Reforms Commission. Reduction in the qualifying period for the grant of maternity benefit to half of the present 160 days of actual work in the proceeding 12 months is one among the several proposals contained in the Bill. When the Bill become effective, women workers will be entitled for maternity benefit, if they put in 80 days of actual work in the proceeding ten months. It sought to extend it to shops and establishments employing ten or more workers. The rate of maternity benefit payable to women employees for each day of absence due to maternity is proposed to be fixed at the average daily wages or the minimum rate of wages under the Minimum Wages Act or Rs. 10 which ever is higher. The existing rate is average daily wage or one rupee a day, whichever is higher.

The rate of medical bonus to women employees in case the employer does not provide pre-natal confinement and post-natal care free of charge is being raised from Rs. 25 to Rs. 250/-. A provision is being made for filling of complaints with the competent Court by the aggrieved woman or an office bearer of the registered Trade Union of which such woman is a member, or a voluntary organization or an Inspector for the purposes of the Act. Presently, complaints can be filed only with the previous sanction of the Inspector.

The Payment of Gratuity Act, 1972

Gratuity is a kind of retirement benefit just like provident fund or pension. It has been conceded as a provision for old age and a reward for good, efficient and faithful service for a considerable period. In the early days, gratuity was considered as a payment gratuitously made by an employer to his employee at his own will and pleasure. In course of time, gratuity came to be paid as a result of bilateral agreements or industrial adjudications as a legal claim.

Before the enactment of the Payment of Gratuity Act. 1972, the first Central legislation on the subject was the Working Journalists (Conditions of Service) and Miscellaneous Provisions Act, 1955. The Kerala and West-Bengal State Governmental, were also enacted legislation for payment of gratuity to workers in 1970 and 1971 respectively. Since the enactment of these two State Acts, some other States have also voiced their intention for similar legislation, it became necessary to have a Central legislation to ensure a uniform pattern of payment of gratuity to the employees throughout the country. The proposal for Central legislation on gratuity was discussed in Labour Minister's Conference and also in Indian Labour Conference held at New-Delhi on August 24-25, 1971 and October, 22, 23, 1971 respectively. The consensus was reached in these two conferences and consequently the Payment of Gratuity Act, 1972 was passed in light of Select Committee recommendations. The Act applies to every factory, mine, oil-field, plantation, port and railway company, shop and other establishments in which 10 or more persons are working or were working on any day of preceding 12 months, and such other establishments in which 10 or more persons are working or were working on any day of preceding 12 months as the Central Government notify in this behalf.

The benefit under the Act is available to a person who is drawing wages not exceeding Rs. 1600 per month (w.e.f. July 1, 1984 instead of Rs. 1000 per month) and has completed 5 years of continuous service immediately before his superannuation, retirement or resignation or death or disablement. The condition of continuous service of 5 years, however, does not apply in the case of death or disablement. If an employee has been in service for 5 years on a monthly salary not exceeding Rs. 1600 he will not loose his right when the wages cross the mark.

The amount of gratuity payable by the employers to an employee is equivalent to the fifteen days wages for every completed year of service or part thereof in excess of six months. The maximum ceiling for payment of gratuity is 20 months wages. In case of piece rated employee daily wages are to be calculated on the average of the total wages received by him during a period of three months immediately preceding termination of his employment and in case of an employees employed in a seasonal establishment, the gratuity is to be paid at the rate of 7 days wages for each season. But the gratuity of an employee whose services have been terminated for any act causing any damage or loss to or destruction of property belonging to the employer, shall be forfeited to the extent of the damage or loss so caused. The gratuity shall be wholly forfeited if his services have been terminated for riotous or disorderly conduct in the course of employment which constitutes an offence involving moral turpitude.

The gratuity under the Act is not liable to attachment in execution of any decree or order of the court. If the amount of gratuity is not paid within the prescribed time, than 9 per cent compound interest will be charged from the date of expiry of prescribed time.

A Bill to amend further the payment of Gratuity Act, 1972, enlarging coverage, fixing a monetary ceiling of Rs. 50,000 and making the penalties more stringent, was introduced in the Rajya Sabha, on March 18, 1987 by the then Minister of Labour for State, Shri P.S. Sangma. Some of the important amendments are: The coverage of the Act is being extended to persons drawing wages upto Rs. 2500 per month and an enabling provision is being made for raising the wage limit for coverage from time to time.

The existing ceiling of 20 months wages for payment of gratuity is being replaced by a monetary ceiling of Rs. 50,000. A provision is also being made for depositing the amount of gratuity payable to a minor with the controlling authority who shall invest the money in a bank or a financial institution for the benefit of the minor. A provision is also being made for compulsory insurance of employers liability to pay gratuity fund under the Act or in the alternative for the setting up of a Gratuity fund under the provisions of the Act in relation to establishment employing 500 or more persons. A provision is also being made for payment of simple interest at a specified rate, if the amount of gratuity is not paid within 30 days from the date it becomes payable. Penalties prescribed under the Act are being made more stringent. Gratuity Trust Fund shall be established. The Indian Labour Conference held in November, 1985 had recommended that a provision for compulsory insurance be incorporated in the Act.

Finally, it may be concluded that social security is a part of labour welfare. Labour welfare secures the workers and his family the fullest life in the comprehensive sense of the term. Social Security covers the various risks and contingencies in the life of individuals in society through appropriate organizations. They are intimately interrelated in policy perspectives, plans, and ends to be achieved. Thus, labour welfare without social security or vice versa are inconceivable. It can be said that the labour welfare is a total concept and social security for labour is an integral part of it. Although, social security for labour is a well established global phenomena and has acquired a separate entity, yet it remains an inherent and counter part of labour welfare.

REFERENCES

Article 16(1) Constitution of India, See also Article 19(i)(g).

ILO, *Approaches to Social Security*, p. 80.

Declaration of Philadelphia (1944) Part III.

Robson W.A., *Social Security*, p. 428.

Sharma A.M. *Aspects of Labour Welfare and Social Security*, (1981) See also pant S.C. *Indian Labour Problems*, p. 275.

Giri V.V., *Labour Problems in Industry* (1962).

Saxena, R.C., *Labour Problems and Social Welfare* (1981).

Ramanujam, G. *Indian Labour Movement* (1986).

Indian Labour Year Book (1983), Government of India.

See Regulation 103-A of the ESI (General) Regulations, 1950.

Annual Report (1984-85), Vol. I, Government of India.

B.M. Lakshmana Murty v. ESI Corporation (1974) 4 SCC 365.

See Section 6 A, E.P.F. and Misc. Provisions Act, 1952.

The Payment of Gratuity Act, 1972, Section 4.

7

Labour Welfare Administration

The labour administration of state government or that of a union territory has the important wing namely 'Enforcement machinery' for factory establishment. The Chief Inspector of Factories heads this enforcements machinery. The primary function of factory inspection services is to ensure enforcement of statutory provisions in respect of safety, health and welfare of employees.

Similarly, Enforcement machinery for mining establishments is a part of the labour administration of the Government of India. The Director General of Mines Safety, who is also the Chief Inspector of Mines under the Mines Act, is responsible for the enforcement of statutory provisions relating to safety, health and welfare measures in mines. According to the Mines Act, 1952 the Chief Inspector of Mines and other Inspectors to whom the Chief Inspector delegates powers, may make examination and enquiry in order to ascertain whether the provisions, rules and bye laws, and orders made thereunder are observed. The Inspector may examine and make enquiry regarding condition of any mine or any part thereof. It is his responsibility to enforce properly the provisions in all matters relating to health, safety and welfare of persons employed in mines. For enforcement of the statutory welfare measures in coal mines, the Central Government has declared some offers of the Coal Mines Welfare Organization to be ex-officio Inspectors of Mines, subordinate to the Chief Inspector of Mines for the purpose of the Mines Act. The Coal Mines Welfare Commissioner enforces statutory welfare measures such as pithead baths, creche, and maternity benefits. The enforcement machinery also assists employee in various ways by advising them on the adoption of proper measures to safeguard against accidents and for this purpose the Directorate General of Mines Safety conducts regular research, the benefits of which goes to the employer.

Enforcement machinery for plantations is a part of the labour administration of a state government. The Labour Commissioner of each state is in overall charge of the administration of the Plantations Labour Act in the respective states. The enforcement of the Act is the responsibility, of the Labour Commissioner or is entrusted to his senior deputy. Generally, in all plantation states the enforcement agency is headed by the Chief Inspector of Plantation. Under Section 4 of the Plantations Labour Act, the stage governments are empowered to appoint by notification duly qualified persons to be Chief Inspectors of Plantations. Similarly the state may notify officers to be Inspector of Plantations. The Act also provides for the appointment of qualified medical practitioner to be certifying surgeons for plantations.

Apparently there is no uniformity in the existing setup of factory inspectorates in the states. In most of them, the Chief Inspector of Factories is a independent full-time functionary under the administrative control of the Labour Commissioner. In few states, he is a separate head of department, responsible to the Labour Secretary. In some others, the Labour Commissioner himself is designated as the Chief Inspector of Factories.

Factory Inspection

During the plans, labour administration has been accorded due importance in the execution of welfare measures. The first plan while laying down the frame work of labour policy, referred specifically to the administrative aspects of enforcement and implementation and called for effective implementation of the existing legislation "to improve working conditions and promote the general well-being of the worker." It also made specific recommendations for this purpose. While reviewing the extent of implementation, the second plan pointed out inadequate implementation of legal provisions and enforcement of awards and agreements and recommended that the penalities should be sufficiently deterrent. Referring to working conditions, safety and welfare, the third plan stressed the need for more effective implementation of the statutory provisions. It also stressed upon the strengthening of the inspectorates to the extent necessary.

Planning Commission's panel on Labour Policy considered the area of labour administration. It observed that there was a need for a comprehensive examination of the whole question of labour administration in the country because the problems of labour administration have not been reviewed in a detailed manner in spite of the marked changes which have occurred in the size and the composition of the labour force and legislative measures undertaking to protect the labour interest."

On the administrative aspects of enforcement and implementation the fourth plan observed that: "Improvement in working conditions depends in large part on the effectiveness with which the existing labour legislation is enforced. In this respect, there appears to be considerable room for improvement. In particular, it is felt that existing provisions for penalties in case of default are not adequate and minimum penalties should be laid down at least for the graver offences. At present the labour inspectorates in states are not adequately staffed and equipped." There has thus been an increasing emphasis throughout the plans on the effective implementation and enforcement of the labour laws which have been enacted for the betterment of the workers.

The legislation relating to factories has been progressively expanded and improved upon over a period of years by conditions and occupational diseases. The administration of the Factories Act was from the beginning entrusted to the then local governments (now called state governments) and thy were given the option to appoint special factory inspectors or entrust the work of inspection to district magistrates. The first Factories Act enacted in 1881, as also the subsequent Act of 1891, did not provide for any factory inspection to enforce their provisions. The district magistrates and civil surgeons were ex-officio inspectors under those Acts. The Factory Labour Commission (1906) severely criticized the system of inspection by district magistrates and civil surgeons and felt that most of the then existing abuses in the implementation of statutes were the result of inadequate an inefficient inspection. The Commission recommended the strengthening of the inspection staff to cope with the needs of inspection and leaded for more full time inspectors. As a result of this recommendation, the Factories Act, 1911 made a special provision for the appointment of factory inspectors. The subsequent enactments made further improvements in this direction. The Factories Act, 1922 made the penalties for breaches more deterrent.

The Royal Commission on Labour which was set up in 1929 also reviewed the general administration of the Factories Act in detail With a view to improving the enforcement of the Factories Act it made specific recommendations for strengthening of the inspectorates and for the appointment of medical inspectors. As a result of its recommendations the factories Act, 1922 was repealed and a new Act of 1934 was placed on the statute book, improving still further the provisions for strengthening the inspectorates.

The Labour Investigation Committee appointed in 1944, also reviewed the functioning of the enforcement machinery. It felt that inspection was inadequate and enforcement not up to the mark. It observed thus: "it is a regrettable fact that the enforcement of labour laws has not been up to the mark and although much has been done by way of putting the workers' rights on the statute book, on the whole the worker has not been able to obtain a fair deal.' With a view to improving the enforcement, the Committee recommended strengthening of the machinery of inspection. More frequent inspections and more stringent enforcement of the existing provisions could, in its opinion, go a long way in improving the conditions of work, reducing the number of accidents, and maintaining the efficiency of workers.

Obviously the need for introducing measures for the effective administration of the Factories Act was recognized by all the investigating bodies set up from time to time. The problem was, however, given a serious attention only when the Government of India in 1946 requested for the services of Sir Wilfrid Garrett to advise on the administration of the Factories Act and the improvement of working conditions in factories. He also acted as Chief Advisor of Factories in India for some time in 1946-47. He undertook the task of examining Indian Factories Act and of suggesting ways and means by which improvements could be brought about. He made many valuable suggestions for improving the quality and effectiveness of the factory inspection services. Most of these suggestions were incorporated in the Factories Act, 1948.

The Committee on Labour Welfare made the following recommendations for improving the inspection services:

1. The Committee recommended that the norm of one inspector for every 150 factories as suggested by Labour Ministers' Conference in 1960 is quite reasonable and should be implemented by each State without any further delay. The state governments should make adequate and speedy arrangements to ensure that at least two inspections of a factory are carried out every year.
2. It recommended for suitable amendment of the Factories Act by the central government so as to make it binding on

the state governments to utilise the money collected by ways of registration fees solely for the purposes of the enforcement of the provisions of the Factories Act.

3. The Committee felt that wherever suitable arrangements to collect the statistics do not exist at present, early steps be taken to establish a suitable machinery for compilation and publication of statistics as an integral part of factory inspectorates.
4. It agreed with the recommendations of the 16th session of the Labour Ministers' Conference (1960) that the existing factory inspectorates should be bifurcated into technical and non-technical wings. Further, wherever necessary the strength of non-technical inspectors may be suitably strengthened.
5. It suggested for suitable re-orientation courses for giving refresher training to factory inspectors of the State Governments.
6. One of the main recommendations of the Committee was to appoint a safety officer in all factories employing 500 or more workers. To ensure effective control, the appointment of safety officers may be regulated by the state governments.
7. Other recommendations of the Committee relate to: (a) Modifications in the penal clauses of the Factories Act; (b) Transport facilities to inspectorate staff (c) Organization of annual meetings of chief inspectors of factories; (d) Tripartite committees for enforcement of factories Act provisions at plant level; (e) Setting up of specialist and research units; and (i) constitution of an all India inspectorate service.

The following are the recommendations of the National Commission on Labour (1969) for strengthening the factory inspectorate:

1. Appointment of factory inspectors with non-technical qualifications to look after routine matters and non-technical provisions of the Act.
2. Use of licensing and registration fees by the state governments for expanding the inspectorate and making it more efficient.

3. Effective enforcement: of the Act by increasing the frequency of the factory inspections. Ordinarily, a factory has to be visited twice annually; factories where managements are known to be slack in implementation have to be inspected more often.
4. Development of frequent and informal contacts by the inspectorate with management and unions, so that the inspectorate will be in a position to play the effective role of an adviser, a role expected of it in these changing times.
5. Qualitative and qualitative improvement of the inspectorate by appointing specialists in different disciplines.

The following are various other suggestions of improving the inspection services:

1. Normally the factories are to be visited twice in a year for checking the extent of compliance. Besides, factories with sub-standard working conditions and factories having high accidents have to be visited more often to ensure effective compliance with the provision of the Factories Act.
2. One of the main obstacles in effective enforcement of the welfare provisions of the Factories Act has been the numerical inadequacy of thc inspection staff in almost all the states. For adequates and vigorous inspections, the strength of factory inspectorate in the states should increase correspondingly with the rise in the number of factories.
4. Not only the number of inspections but their quality should improve. The inspections should not be of a routine nature; it should; be through in all respects and should have the aim of correcting promptly the deficiencies noted. In this regard there should be close co-operation between inspection service, the employers and workers. Moreover, the frequency of inspections should be evenly spread over between small-sized and large-sized units and inspection reports should clearly depict the real position of the factory regarding implementation of various measures relating to health, safety, welfare, etc.
4. It is essential that the Inspectorates are equipped with qualified and trained personnel to ensure that statutory provisions are enforced properly. Moreover, the

Inspectorates should have specialists in the disciplines of Industrial Hygiene, Industrial Medicine, etc. to tackle the various problems in the areas of safety and health.

Factory Inspectorate of the Govt. of Maharashtra

The factory inspectorate of the state mainly enforces the Factories Act along with other Acts like Payment of Wages Act, Cotton Ginning an Pressing Act, Employment of Children Act, and Maternity Benefit Act. The Chief Inspector of Factories is the head of the inspectorate and is under the administrative control of the Commissioner of Labour. There is also one Joint Chief Inspector of Factories. There are ten Deputy Chief Inspectors of Factories, four for Bombay Region and one each for Nagpur, Pune, Thane, Nasik, Kolhapur and Aurangabad and 110 Inspectors of Factories as on 1.1.1985. There is an Industrial Hygiene Section in the Inspectorate which looks into the health hazards faced by the Industrial workers employed in various factories.

The Chief Inspector of Factories is responsible for the enforcement of Factories Act in the whole of the Maharashtra State. There are 20 sub-offices in the mofussil. The Inspector in normally required to do the following duties broadly classified as field work and office work.

Field Work: (i) Inspection of factories (ii) Enquiry into complaints (iii) Enquiry into accidents (iv) Survey work of factories not registered under the Act (v) Follow up action regarding inspection remarks (vi) Check up whether factory is constructed as per plans (vii) Check illegal overtime working, holiday working, night employment of female employees (viii) Court attendance (ix) Enquiry into complaints regarding payment of wages, deductions, etc. (x) Talks to be delivered to the workers, supervisors, etc.

Office Work: (i) Security of plans (ii) Scrutiny of accident reports and classification, (iii) proposal for legal action, warning etc., (iv) To attend to the workers and their representatives, (v) Preparation of reports of complaints, accidents, etc.

The Inspector helps the worker in settling his grievances regarding payment of dues, etc. The inspectorate also extends help to the Maharashtra Welfare Board to collect unpaid accumulations. Safety posters are distributed to the factories free of cost. Training class are conducted for training the representatives of the factories in regard to filling up of various returns under the laws enforced by the Inspectorate.

The factory inspectorate receives complaints under the Factories Act, Payment of Wages Act, Maternity Benefit Act, Workmen's Compensation Act, etc. Most of the complaints are in respect of non-payment of wages, overtime wages, accidents, compensation etc. The inspectorate takes legal action against defaulting factories and cases are decided by the courts of Law. However, the inspectorate prefers the enforcement of the Act through perusasion rather than through penalties.

REFERENCES

1. *Report of Labour Investigation Committee* (main report), p. 9.
2. *Fourth Five Year Plan: A Draft Outline*, p. 395.

8

Welfare Legislation and Health

In the beginning attempts at Labour welfares Legalistation in India were aimed at regulating employment, particularly of children and women, and safety rather than at improving conditions of work, health, and welfare. The concept of labour welfare was then, quite understandably, confined to the provision of employment generally. This character of legislation continued for decades before a shift in the emphasis became discernible. Measures such as canteens, creches, rest-rooms, drinking water, first aid appliances, dispensaries, etc., which are now taken for granted, took a long time to appear on the industrial horizon of India.

Growth of Welfare Legislation

Though the bulk of the labour legislation has been enacted after Independence, yet its origin can be traced to 1837 when, following the abolition of slavery in 1833, the British colonies started importing Indian labour under various types of contracts. The first enactment to be made was the Apprentices Act in 1850. The object of this Act was to enable children, specially orphans and poor children brought up by public charity, to learn trades, crafts, and employment by apprenticing them to craftsmen, by which, when they were grown, they might earn their livelihood. In 1853, the Fatal Accidents Act was passed to "provide compensation to families for loss occasioned by death of a person caused by actionable wrong". The Merchant Shipping Act, passed in 1859 sought to regulate the employment of seamen and made provisions for their health, accommodation, and protection from imposition. A perusal of these enactments suggests that they were framed to meet special contingencies and were not indicative of any sustained or continuous legislative policy. The next enactment came in 1881 after a gap of over twenty years. The history of labour welfare legislation thereafter shows a steady movement and its progress can best be followed in a schematic manner.

Factories

The first cotton textile mill in India was set up in 1851 in Bombay by a local merchant, Cawasjee Nanbhai Davar. the industry grew rapidly thereafter and in 1872-73 there were 18 cotton mills employing about 10,000 workers.[1] The conditions of work, especially those of women and children employed in these mills, were inhuman. Public attention was drawn to the subject for the first time, by Major Moore who published his report on "Administration of Bombay Cotton Department". The author dwelt at length with long working hours, condition of women labour, and young age of children employed in the factories. Instructed by the Secretary of State for India, the Government of Bombay appointed a commission in 1875 to determine whether legislation was necessary. The commission recommended against legislation.

However, the developments in England were to bring factory legislation into India. Britain was experiencing a movement for reforms in labour legislation and the Lancashire textile magnates were affected by it. They were further alarmed by the growing Indian textile industry where labour costs were very low. About this time, Miss Carpenter of Bristol, founder of the National Indian Association, visited India, made inquiries into the factory conditions, and published her report. Assisted by the report of Miss Carpenter, the Lancashire employers seized the opportunity to divert criticism from conditions at home to those in India. They waited upon the Secretary of State for India to plead their inability to compete with foreign industry where labour was cheap. The

Secretary of State wrote to the Government of India urging legislation in respect of factory work and confessed that pressure was being brought to bear on him. Consequently, the local government started moving in the matter, which was resented by Indian industrialists who saw the hand of "ignorant British philanthropists and gasping English manufacturers" behind the move. However, facts could not be ignored for long and the first Indian Factories Act was passed in 1881. The Act defined a "child" as a person below 12 years of age, and prohibited employment of children below 7. "Child" workers were to work for nine hours a day with a rest interval of one hour and were to be given four holidays a month. This Act, however, failed to provide any protection to women, and even to children it gave only insufficient protection. It, thus, failed to satisfy the interested parties.

The First International Labour Conference (that met at Berlin in 1890) recommended, among other things, the regulation of women and child labour. Pressed by the British employers that the recommendations of the Berlin conference be applied to India, the government set up a Factory Commission on whose recommendations the Indian Factories (Amendment) Act was passed in 1891. In the amending Act, the age of the "child" was raised to 14 years; the employment of children below 9 years of age was prohibited, and the working hours of children were brought down to 7 per day. Weekly holiday and rest intervals for all workers per also introduced.

In 1905, the Association for Labour Legislation, a forerunner of the ILO, held a conference at Berne and made a number of recommendation pertaining to working hours and working conditions of factory labour. Armed with these recommendations, interested parties in Britain revived their agitation for further factory legislation in India. A delegation waited upon the Secretary of State for India in 1906 to demand restrictions on hours of work for men workers in India. A

Textile Committee in 1906 and a Factory Commission in 1907 were set up, on whose recommendations the Factories Act, 1911, was passed.

Employment in certain dangerous occupations and during night was prohibited for both women and children. Children were required to produce medical certificates of age and fitness.

The World War-I and the formation of the ILO in 1919 materially changed the situation, making it necessary to amend the existing Factories Act. An amending Act was, therefore, passed in 1922 in which the working hours for both men and women were fixed at 60 a week and not more than 11 a day. One hour rest for every six hours of work, a weekly day of rest, at least one holiday during a consecutive period of 10 days, and an overtime rate of 1¼ times the ordinary rate of payment were introduced. The age of the child was raised to 15 years. Employment of children below 12 years of age was prohibited and child workers were required to produce certificates of fitness and age.

The Royal Commission on Labour in its report in 1931 pointed to a number of shortcomings in the existing statute and suggested its revision. Accordingly, the Factories Act, 1934, was brought into existence. The new Act was a landmark in the history of the growth of welfare legislation. It retained the provisions regarding weekly holidays, prohibition of night work for women and children, age of "child", etc., and introduced for the first time shelters, restrooms, and creches. The concept of "adolescent" (between the ages of 15 and 17 years) as a protected person was also brought in. The administration and inspection were also improved.

Its is obvious from the outline of the provisions of the Factories Act, 1934, that with the passing of this Act, legislation reform movement gained considerable ground. The Act was mended, off and on, during and after the Second World

War. It was, however, repealed by the Factories Act, 1948. The need to bring into existence and enforce a more comprehensive legislation has been brought out in the Statement of Objects and Reasons of the 1948 Act. It says:

> Experience of working of the Act [1934] has revealed a number of defects and weaknesses that hamper effective administration. Provisions for the safety, health and welfare of workers are generally found to be inadequate and unsatisfactory and even such protection as it provided does not extend to the large mass of workers employed in work-places not covered by the Act. In view of the large and growing industrial activity in the country, a radical overhauling of factories law is essentially called for ... The proposed legislation [Act of 1948] differs materially from the existing law [Act of 1934] in several respects. It is essential that important basic provisions relating to health, safety, working conditions, working hours, holidays, lighting, ventilation, etc., should be extended to all work-places. ... The minimum age of employment of children has been raised and their working hours reduced. The present Act [1934] is very general in character and leaves too much to the rule-making powers of Provincial governments ... leaves complex and important points to the discretion of inspectors placing heavy responsibilities on them. The detailed provisions in the proposed legislation [1948] will go a long way in lightening their burden.

The Factories Bill was passed on 28 August 1948, received the assent of the Governor-General on 23 September 1948, and came into force on 1 April 1949. A few amendments have been made in the Act since then.

Mines

Although excavation of coal started in India late in the eighteenth century, mining of other minerals was introduced in the middle of the nineteenth century. Modern mining is of recent origin. The paid-up capital of the joint-stock companies engaged in mining and registered in India was Rs. 19.2 million in 1890 and the coal production amounted to 1.7 million tons in the same years. Absence of foreign competition, nature of mines which were mostly near the surface, and general unawareness of labour conditions in the mines were responsible for the apathetic attitude of the government towards this important and growing sector of the Indian industry. It was only in 1895 that a Mining Committee was appointed to go into the matter. As a result of the recommendations of the Mining Committee, a bill was drafted in 1899 which was passed into the Mines Act, 1901, and enforced on March 22 of the same year. This Act defined "child" to be a person who was under the age of 12, and granted powers to the chief inspector to prohibited the employment of women and children in mines where conditions, in his opinion, were dangerous to their health and safety.

In pursuance of section 5 of the Act, the Governments of Bihar, Bengal, Orissa, C.P., and Madras framed some rules. Under these rules, the powers of inspectors were specified; instructions were laid down for the control and guidance of persons acting in the management of, or employed in, the mines; and bigger mining companies were requested to frame bye-laws to prevent accidents and to provide for the safety, convenience, and discipline of persons employed therein. These bye-laws were subject to the approval of local governments, after which they had the statutory status.

Although a major step forward in the legislative history of India and a pioneering statute in mines, the Act had many defects. Basically, it lacked in provisions for the regulation of conditions of employment. It also made inadequate provisions for the regulation of the conditions of employment of women and children.

The mining industry grew steadily. In the early twenties, there were about 1,800 registered mines employing over 200,000 workers. Inspectors appointed under the Act of 1901 were reporting increasing difficulties due to the inadequacies of the Act. Moreover, the Government of India Act, 1919, made the administration of mining laws a Central subject. Further, the ratification by the Government of India in 1921 of the Hours Convention of the ILO committed it to the principle of 60-hour working week. A new Act was, therefore, passed in 1923 and enforced on 1 July 1924. Under this Act, the age of the "child" was raised from 12 to 13 and employment of children below ground was prohibited. Weekly hours of work were limited to 54 below ground and 60 above ground. Working days were limited to six a week.

However, the Act contained no provisions for limiting daily hours of work of men and for restricting employment of women below ground. A number of amendments were made thereafter. The amendment of 1928 concerned itself with the spread-over of daily hours of work and introduction of shift system. I was made illegal to employ any person in a mine for more than twelve hours in any period of consecutive twenty-four hours. All mines working longer than 12 hours a day were to introduce shift system and shifts were not to overlap. It was made obligatory for all mines to maintain registers fo workers and the hours of work.

By another amendment in 1929, the employment of women below ground was prohibited in all mines except in coal mines in Bengal, Bihar, Orissa, C.P., and salt mines in the Punjab. The exempted mines were to introduce a system of gradual reduction of their women work force working below ground, leading to a total elimination of the practice in 1939.

By an amending Act in 1935, weekly hours of work and daily spread-over were reduced. For surface workers, 54 hours a week and 10 hours a day with a daily spread-over of not more than 12 hours, and for workers below ground, 54 hours a week and 9 hours a day with a daily spread-over of 9 hours, were introduced. The surface workers were to have one hour's rest for every six hours of work. The age of the "child" was raised from 13 to 15. The concept of "young person" was introduced, who could take up work after the usual physical fitness certificate. In 1936, the Act was again amended to make further provisions for the safe working conditions of workers. In 1937, the Act was further amended to provide for the establishment of rescue stations and rescue station boards and to levy an excise duty of six pies per ton of coal or coke produced and despatched from mines and its utilization. During the Second World War, restrictions on the employment of women below ground were lifted, but were reimposed after the war.

Provisions for the health and welfare of mining workers were thought of for the first time by the Bihar Labour Enquiry Committee in 1938. During the war and post-Independence period there has been a plethora of statutory measures for the welfare, health, and safety of mining workers.

Rules such as the Coal Mines Rescue Rules and Coal Mines (Pithead) Bath Rules were framed. The Mica Mines Labour Welfare Fund Act and the Coal Mines Labour Welfare Fund Act were passed in 1946 and 1947 respectively. In 1948, the Coal Mines Provident Fund and Bonus Schemes Act was passed. The plethora of mining legislation with its ad hoc nature and often conficting administrative set-ups created considerable confusion and the need for a comprehensive legislation incorporating all the basic provisions on working hours, working conditions, health, safety, and welfare was increasingly being felt. Consequently, the Mines Act, 1952, was brought into existence, which still remains in force.

Plantations

Plantations is the oldest among Indian industries. Assam tea gardens are among the earliest plantations in India. "The paucity of population in Assam and the location of tea gardens in isolated districts made it necessary to import labour from outside and a class of recruiters, therefore, grew up for the supply of labour to tea gardens. This unregulated recruitment of labour gave rise to many abuses." As a result, the plantations legislation was first concerned with the regulation of recruitment and transportation of labourers from outside districts to tea gardens. Legislation to regulate employment and working conditions of the plantation labour came much later.

The first Act to come was the Transport of Native Labourers Act, 1863, enforced by the Government of Bengal (Assam, Cachar, and Sylhet were parts of Bengal at that time). The Act sought to regulate the passage and transport of the native labourers from and through the notified districts of Bengal. It required recruiters to be licensed, emigrants to be registered, and sanitation facilities to be provided on the way to labour districts. The period of contract was restricted to five years. By an amendment to the Act in 1865, the period of contract was reduced to three years and protectors were appointed to supervise the working of the Act. By another amendment in 1870, the Government of Bengal made provisions for the regulation of the manner of engagging and contracting with native labourers. In 1873, by another amendment, the government was authorised to declare certain districts as "unhealthy" for the residence of labourers if the mortality rate during the year or its average during the preceding three years exceeded seven per cent.

By now, the tea gardens had expanded and recruitment was being done from area outside Bengal where the local government had no jurisdiction. An enquiry commission was set up in 1881 on whose recommendations the Government of India passed the Inland Emigration Act in 1882. The passing of this Act set the clock back. The Act removed "unnecessary restrictions on recruitment and provided protection to planters against desertion, absence and idleness of workers". Its immediate effect was that planters indulged in some of the grossest abuses and the mortality rate went very high. The Government of Bengal was obliged to set up another commission in 1895 and on its recommendation, the Assam Labour and Emigration Act was passed in 1901. This Act repealed all the existing legislation. It extended to the whole of India and gave powers to the local governments to prohibited all or any person from recruiting or eagaging any person or class of persons to emigrate from any part of India to any tea district. It provided for the nature of contract, wages, increments, and right of repatriation to labourers. The recruiting agencies were to be licensed. They were obliged to transport workers through specified routes only. The Act was amended in 1908 and 1915. The matter was examined by the Royal Commission on Labour (1929-1931) which in its report criticised the Act and recommended freer movement of, and greater security to, labourers besides better administration of the law. Accordingly, the Government of India passed the Tea Districts Emigrant Labour Act in 1932 and enforced it on 1 October 1933.

Till 1950, Cochin was the only State in India to have adopted legislative measures for the direct control of labour conditions in plantations. In this State, rules were framed and put into force on 1 May 1937. Complete absence of regulation of conditions of work on plantations in all other Provinces was commented upon by the Labour Investigation Committee (1946). Since the conditions of life and employment on plantations differed from those in other industries, the committee suggested enactment of a separate Plantations Labour Code for the whole of India. In 1947, a tripartite Industrial Committee for Plantations was set up by the Government of India to consider the problems of plantation industry. At its first meeting, the committee recommended that an inquiry should be made into the cost and standard of living of workers in the plantation industry so that reasonable wages could be fixed. It also decided that a medical expert should be deputed to study the existing standards of medical care in plantations. The investigations were undertaken and the committee considered these reports in March 1948. It agreed that the standards of medical care should be prescribed by law and that employment of children below the age of 12 in plantations should be prohibited. Meanwhile, the government drafted a Plantations Labour Bill which was discussed by this committee in September 1949 and November 1950. On the basis of these discussions the government re-framed the Bill which was passed into the Plantations Labour Act by Parliament on 15 October 1951. It was enforced on 2 November 1951.

Transport

Railways

The railways form the most important part of Indian transport. The first railway train that made its appearance in India ran a distance of 20.5 miles from Bombay to Thana on 18 April 1853. Its expansion has never looked back since that date. In 1958, the railways employed over 1.1 million workers. The conditions of railway employees had been determined by the Board of Directors located in Britain and its Resident Agents in India. The Railway Board was constituted in 1905 to take charge of the state-owned railways. The question of regulating employment of railway labour excepting those working in workshops covered under the Factories Act was not taken up till the ILO passed the Hours Conventions in 1919 and the Weekly Rest Convention in 1921. These conventions were ratified by the Government of India, and in 1926 an advisory committee was appointed by the Indian Railways Conference to devise methods to give effect to these conventions. This chapter deals with the regulation of employment of railway servants. The workers covered by this Act were classified into two categories, namely, "continuous" and "essentially intermittent". Hours of work for essentially intermittent workers were specified at 84 a week and for continuous workers at 60 a week. Provisions were made for a weekly day of rest, overtime rate, and administration of the Act. The Labour Investigation Committee (1944) in the course of its investigation was presented with a number of complaints on a variety of issues. The All India

Railwaymen's Federation demanded the appointment of an adjudicator in respect of certain demands. The government appointed Justice Rajadhyaksha as the adjudicator who gave his award in May 1947. The Railway Servants (Hours of Employment) Rules were framed in 1951 to meet the provisions of the award. All the provisions were, however, incorporated in the Indian Railways (Amendment) Act, 1956.

Shipping, Ports and Docks

"The origin of legislation for mercantile marine workers can be traced as far back as the middle of the nineteenth century. Since then, a series of Acts have come into operation. Most of these Acts were amended and consolidated by the Indian Merchant Shipping Act, 1923." Part II of the Act regulates the conditions of employment of Indian seamen. Since its enactment, the Act has been amended several times. Among the important amending Acts are the ones passed in 1949 and 1951. The amending Act of 1949 was passed to regulate the supply of maritime labour by providing for the setting up of seamen's employment offices, while the amending Act of 1951 was passed to provide for the medical examination of seamen and to authorise the Central government to notify the authorities by whom such an examination might be conducted.

The new Merchant Shipping Act was passed in 1958. Besides other things, this Act relates to the establishment of a National Shipping Board, formation of the Shipping Development Fund, registration of Indian ships, and other details of a highly technical nature.

Though a series of legislations relating to docks and ports has been passed since 1889, it was only in 1908 that a consolidating Act, the Indian Ports and Docks Act, was brought into existence. The Act was amended in 1922 to prohibit the employment of children under the age of 12. The Indian Dock Labourers Act was legislated in 1934. It afforded safety and protection to workers engaged in loading and unloading operations in the docks. This Act was passed to implement the recommendations of the Royal Commission on Labour and the ILO Convention (No. 28) concerning protection against accidents of workers employed in these occupations.

Shops and Commercial Establishments

"The Government of India first examined the question of granting protection to workers employed in shops and commercial establishments in connection with ratification of the ILO's Hours of Work (Commercial and Offices) Convention of 1930. It was, however, decided not to ratify the convention. The lead in the matter was given by the Government of Bombay which brought an Act into force on this subject in November 1940." The Act was revised in 1949. Other States followed suit and now similar Acts for regulating the conditions of employment of persons employed in shops and commercial houses are operating in all the States.

Besides the above State Acts, there is a Central legislation known as the Weekly Holidays Act, 1942. This Act is permissive in character and applies to only those States which may notify its application in their territory. It has been made applicable in seven States so far.

FACTORS STIMULATING GROWTH OF WELFARE LEGISLATION

A careful study of the historical development of labour welfare legislation reveals a number of factors which accelerated its growth and stimulated its progress. A few important ones could be mentioned at this stage.

A dominant factor, particularly during the early period, was the vested interest of the British manufacturers. India was one of the major suppliers of raw material to the British industries and a principal market for their finished products. The development of indigenous industries was a threat to the British industrialists. Availability of low-cost raw material and cheap labour at home gave a competitive advantage to Indian industries and they could outsell British products, at least in Indian markets. Alarmed by the fast growing textile industry in India, the Lancashire and Manchester employers repeatedly waited upon the authorities to press their demand for more rigorous legislation in India. This would at least increase labour costs. Every time a delegation met the Secretary of State for India, a commission or a committee was set up and new measures adopted to regulate Indian industries.

The social reform movement and the growth of strong trade unions in Britain also influenced the speedy ushering in of labour legislation in India. On the other hand, the growth of the movement for reforms in existing labour standards in Britain inconvenienced British employers and forced them to press for similar measures in India and, on the other, it brought to bear pressure on the British government to grant and ensure similar human standards for Indian labour. The government was, therefore, obliged to move in the matter. The dispatch from Colonial Secretary, Lord Passifield (Sydney Webb), to all colonial governors makes an interesting reading.[8] It said that "the growth of trade unions was a desirable and legitimate feature of industrial and social development. The government should be sympathetic to any existing unions, and in those territories where there were no unions provisions should be made for their establishment. The unions should be given legal protection to enable them to grow and develop into strong organizations."

Similarly, as the British trade unions grew in power and strength, they started demanding more human rights and better working conditions for labour in British overseas territories. The British Trades Union Congress intervened more than once in Indian labour affairs. A strong public opinion in Britain against the arrest of B.P. Wadia for organizing a strike of Binny Mills workers in Madras was largely due to the interest taken in the matter by the British Trades Union Congress. Its leaders visited India to make a first-hand study of labour conditions prevailing in the country. It will strengthen the point further if a resolution adopted by the British Trades Union Congress is mentioned here. It reads: "Believing that the British colonial and mandated territories require a free trade union movement with the same rights and privileges as British trade unions, so as to ensure that the working conditions are safeguarded and higher standards of living secured, requests the General Council to give all possible assistance to trade unions in these territories."[9]

The two world wars made considerable impact on labour legislation movement. New needs created by war conditions and lack of transport facilities for shipment of raw material and finished goods to and from the United Kingdom forced the government to encourage the growth of local industries. Heavy industrialization resulted in heavy increase in the industrial work force who were soon organized or at least became conscious of their rights and started agitating for better conditions of work. Huge profits were made by employers of which little was passed on to workers. This added to the latter's feeling of being aggrieved. The government was obliged to take notice of the same and quite a few provisions, particularly those regarding the payment of dearness allowance and bonus, health, welfare, and safety, owe their origin to the war periods. The development of labour standards in India owes a good deal to the work of the ILO. Early factory legislation was a direct result of deliberations of their first International Labour Conference held at Berlin in 1890 and the conference of the Association for Labour Legislation held at Berne in 1905. The ILO was formed in 1919 and India was one of its founding members. The ILO through its conventions and recommendations set up numerous labour standards that its member-countries were morally bound to implement. Some conventions were implemented by the Government of India on its own while others had to be implemented because of the criticism made year after year by non-government members at the annual conferences of the ILO.

The movement for political freedom and the development of trade unions in India exercised a strong influence on legislative reforms in the country. Trade unions were organized by political parties and they functioned as the labour wing of the freedom movement. Industrial cities became strongholds not only of trade unions but also of political movement. With the rise of M.K. Gandhi on the national horizon of India, the programmes of both the movements were transformed from liberal deliberations to aggressive action. This increased labour demands as well as union strength to win them.

The dawn of freedom and political democracy in India gave a new angle to the movement of labour legislation. The industrial labour had to be granted and ensured of rights due to them in a welfare state. The country launched a massive programme of economic development industrialization. Industrial peace, which is a prerequisite to any development, is mainly dependent on an efficient, contented, and conscious work force. Labour occupies a crucial position in the new social order. Further, industrial labour is always more vocal and assertive about its rights and forms the single largest block of voters which no political party can afford to neglect or overlook. Thus, we find that in the course of fifteen years following Independence, Indian labour legislation has been so enacted that it could be favourably compared with that of the most industrialised countries.

It has often been said that there has been a plethora of labour legislation unwarranted by the economic and social conditions prevailing in the country at present. While conceding the point that the government has enacted voluminous legislation after Independence, it has to be stated that it is not unwarranted by the prevailing conditions. All this legislation has not been thought of overnight, but is the result of gradual growth over a period of one century. Experimentation has been the spirit of legislation. Labour legislative measures of the nineteenth and the early twentieth centuries were humble in nature. The country was new to industrialization and lacked in administrative experience as well as in basic statistics. As it progressed, it faced new problems. New solutions and suitable administrative machinery were devised and incorporated by amendments in the existing statutes till a saturation point was reached and a new consolidating Act was brought in.

The pace of labour legislation in ensuring minimum standards of safety, health, and welfare for workers was very slow during the British period. The British government must accept responsibility for it, but it has to be granted that the British administration could not be expected to do something which it did not know. Social reconstruction in Britain started only after 1911, particularly after the First World War. British administration in India during that period could not be judged by the now current social and labour standards.

By enacting numerous labour statutes, the Government of the Republic of India appears to have made use of the experience of the former rulers and only hastened the process of creating new labour standards worthy of a government committed to social justice. Further, a rapidly developing community has to look ahead and decide upon the social and economic conditions that it likes to have at the end of a given period of time. Its statutory measures should not only fit into the existing conditions but should also direct them towards desired objectives. The present body of labour legislation reflects the spirit of planned progress of a democratic socialist society.

BASIC HEALTH PROVISIONS

Factories

The Factories Act, 1948, lays down that dust and refuse shall be removed daily; floor shall be washed at least once a week; and walls, partitions, and ceilings of work-places shall be painted at least once in 14 months (for water colour) and once in five years where oil paint is used. Temperature shall be kept at a level comfortable to workers, and the appropriate government may prescribe standards of temperature and ventilation. In work rooms, a workers should be provided with space at the rate of 350 cubic feet in old factories (factories that were in existence on the day when this Act came into force) and 500 cubic feet in new factories. Similarly, the appropriate governments have been authorised to make rules requiring specified factories to make arrangements for providing space for storing and drying wet clothes. Drinking water should be made available at work-places. Provisions of the Act and rules framed thereunder by State governments regulate sources of water supply, its quantity, and cooling arrangements. Water supplied from sources other than municipal hydrants has to be approved by a competent authority. It should be available during all working hours, be clearly marked "drinking water" in regional languages, and be stored at the rate of one gallon per worker per day. Factories employing 250 or more workers should supply "cool water" during the period from March 1 to November 30.

Conservancy arrangements are required to be made by employers in all factories. There should be separate arrangements for men and women workers. Privacy should be secured and water supplied inside the cubicles. Scales for providing seats have been laid down in the rules. There should be one seat for 25 male workers up to 100 and one seat for every additional 50 workers. For women, there should be one seat for every 25 persons. Urinals should be provided for male workers at the rate of one urinal for every 50 men up to 500, and one for every additional 100. Spittoons should be provided and conveniently located. The rules lay down that a worker found dirtying a place by not using the proper place can be fined up to five rupees. The employers are also required to provide washing facilities of an approved type, separately for men and women, at a scale as laid down by the government.

The Act requires that at least one first aid box having prescribed contents be kept in all factories. In addition to this, there should be at least one first aid box per 150 workers ordinarily employed at a time. Trained men to dispense first aid should be available during working hours. A first aid register should always be kept along with the box and all dispensations should be entered in it. Further, every factory employing 500 or more workers should maintain an ambulance room, staffed by a doctor, a compounder, and a nurse and equipped with at least the minimum prescribed articles. Such factories should also make arrangements to have an ambulance van available at call. Sitting arrangements should be made for all workers obliged to work in a standing position, in order that they take advantage of any opportunities for rest which may occur in the courts of their work.

Mines

The Mines Act, 1952, lays down provisions for drinking water which are similar to those in the Factories Act, with the exception that the scale of water to be supplied is at the rate of half a gallon per day per worker employed. Conservancy arrangements are to be made on the lines of factories and at the scale of one seat for every 50 workers on the surface and one seat for every 100 workers working below ground.

As regards first aid, the Mines Act, 1952, requires that first aid boxes should be made available at suitable places on the surface and first aid stations should be set up below ground. There should be at least one trained person for every 100 workers working above ground and one for every 50 persons working below ground. Every supervisor or an officer while going below ground should carry first aid equipment on his person. Provisions similar to factories are required to be made in respect of ambulance room and ambulance vans.

The Coal Mines (Pithead) Bath Rules were framed in 1946. Under these rules, the manager of every coal-mine is required to construct a pithead bath as per specifications approved by the competent authority. The bathrooms should be constructed separately for males and females, and attendants should be on duty during all working hours. Adequate water supply, lighting, and drainage arrangements should be made in the bathrooms.

Shipping

The Indian Merchant Shipping Act, 1923, requires that every seaman aboard a ship must be allotted accommodation as specified in the Act. Water of good quality and fit for use of crew, free medical treatment, and free medicines should be available to the master, seamen, or apprentices while aboard a ship. The Act provides for relief to distressed seamen and their maintenance until such time as the local authority is able to provide them with a passage home.

Central Public Works Department

The C.P.W.D. has made rules for sanitary arrangements and protection of the health of workers employed by contractors. According to these rules, first aid appliances should be made available at readily accessible places on the work site. Where hospital facilities are not available within an easy distance of the works, first aid posts should be established and staffed by trained compounders. Where large work-places are remote from regular hospitals, indoor wards should be added to the first aid posts and one bed for every 250 employees be made available. Arrangements for speedy availability of ambulance van should also be made. Sufficient supply of drinking water must be provided at easily accessible places in all work-places. The water stores should be away from latrines, drains, or other sources of pollution. All wells must be entirely closed and provided with dust and leakage proof trap-doors. Adequate bathing and washing facilities should be provided separately for men and women.

BASIC WELFARE PROVISIONS

Factories

The Factories Act, 1948, lays down that the appropriate government may make rules requiring that in specified factories where more than 250 workers are ordinarily employed, a canteen (or canteens) shall be provided and maintained by the occupies for use of workers. The standards in respect of construction, accommodation, furniture, and other equipment, the foodstuffs to be served and charges thereof shall also be subject to the rules so framed. The occupies of a factory should make arrangements for the constitution of a canteen committee to supervise the working and accounts of the canteen. The committee shall consist of employers' nominees and workers' representatives. The representatives of workers will be elected directly department-wise. The ultimate responsibility of maintaining the canteen according to prescribed standards is that of the occupies although the canteen may actually be run either through his own servants or through an agent or a contractor or a cooperative society. There has been no unanimity among the adjudicators on the point whether a canteen constitutes a part of the factory and whether the employees of the canteen are "workers" under the Factories Act, 1948, or the Industrial Disputes Act, 1947.

Again, if more than 150 workers are employed in a factory, adequate and suitable shelters or rest rooms and a lunch room with provision for drinking water where workers can eat meals brought by them shall be provided and maintained by the occupies. But if the canteen has a hall, no additional shelters, rest rooms, etc., may be necessary. If a lunch room is provided, workers are expected to use it and are prohibited from taking their meals in work rooms.

In every factory where more than 50 women workers are ordinarily deemployed, there shall be provided and maintained a suitable room (or rooms) for use of their young age children. Such room shall provide adequate accommodation, be well lighted and ventilated, maintained in clean and sanitary conditions, and will be under the charge of a woman trained in the care of infants and children. Rules have been made by the appropriate governments laying down the standards of this service, free supply of milk and other nutritious diet as well as daily wash and change of clothes.

In every factory where 500 or more workers are ordinarily employed, the occupies shall employ in the factory such number of welfare officers as may be prescribed. The appropriate governments have been authorised to frame rules for the appointment, qualifications, and service conditions of labour welfare officers. Details of these rules have been discussed elsewhere in this book.

Mines

The Mines Act, 1952, makes provisions regarding the appointment of welfare officers, which are similar to those in the Factories Act, 1948. An additional provision has been made in the case of canteens under which a group of employers can submit for approval plans of a common canteen. Provisions made in the Plantations Labour Act, 1951, are more elaborate and extensive. This has been warranted by the special nature of problems faced by plantation workers. The Act requires that every worker working on a plantation shall be provided with housing accommodation for himself and his family. In addition, a worker will be given a piece of land where he can grow things of his choice. Every plantation employing 150 or more workers shall have a canteen of standards similar to those in factories. The provisions for creche are at par with the Factories Act, 1948. If more than 300 workers are employed on a plantation, the employer shall apoint one or more welfare officers as prescribed in the rules.

Plantations

In addition to the above, the Plantations Labour Act, 1951, makes provisions for recreational, educational, and medical facilities for workers. Recreational facilities of prescribed standard have to be provided on all plantations. Where the number of employees' children between the ages of 6 and 12 exceeds 25, the employer is obliged to set up a school. The Act lays down that the employer shall make arrangements for the medical care of woerkers and their families. The standard of medical care has been specified by the government. Provisions have also been made for the supply of "water proof" dress to all workers.

C.P.W.D.

The C.P.W.D. Rules make provisions for a creche and a canteen to be established and maintained by contractors, of standards similar to those laid down in the Factories Act, 1948.

Protection to Children and Women

Children

One of the major concerns of the state is to protect and safeguard children and women against exploitation and victimization. We found in an earlier section of this chapter that it was not until 1881 that concrete steps were taken to regulate working hours of children. The Factories Act, 1881, defined "child" as a person below 12 years of age, and prohibited the employment of children below 7. Child workers were to work 9 hours a day. Through repeated amendments, the conditions of work were made more favourable to children. The Factories Act, 1934, introduced the concept of an adolescent (between 15 and 17 years) as a protected person and required that children should work for not more than 5 hours a day with a maximum spread-over of 7½ hours. The position has been made still better under the Factories Act, 1948. The Act defined "child" as a person who had not completed 14 years of age, and prohibited the employment of children below the age of 14 in factories. Young persons (between 15 and 18 years) could be employed in factories subject to certain conditions. The occupies of a factory, before employing a young person, must be in possession of a certificate that the person concerned is more than 14 years of age and a certificate of medical fitness issued by a surgeon. The young person must be issued a token marked "P" (protected person) which he must carry on his person during working hours. He shall not be allowed or required to work for more than 5 hours a day or in more than one relay. He also earns leave with wages at the rate of one day for fifteen days of work. Again, a young person cannot be employed during night or in cleaning, oiling and repairing jobs, or in hazardous occupations.

Provisions for young persons made in the Mines Act, 1952, are similar to those made in the Factories Act, 1948. In addition, the Mines act prohibits the employment of young persons below ground and requires that they be given safe work under the supervision of an adult worker.

In 1938, the Government of India enacted the Employment of Children Act prohibiting employment of children in certain occupations. The Act laid down that no child who has not completed his fifteenth year of age shall be employed or permitted to work in any occupations connected with the transport of passengers, goods, or mail on the railways and in the ports. It also prohibited the employment of children below the age of 14 at night and in workshops where any of the following processes is being carried on: bidi making, cement works, cutting and smelting of mica, shellac works, tanning, carpet weaving, printing, dyeing and weaving of cloth, manufacture of matches and fire works, soap making, and cleaning of wool.

Another Act that protects children against exploitation is the Children (Pledging of Labour) Act, 1933. It declares any agreement to pledge the labour of children whereby the parent or guardian of a child in return for any payment or benefit to be received, undertakes to cause or allow the services of a child to be utilised in any employment to be void. However, an agreement made without detriment to the child and not made in consideration of any benefit other than reasonable wages to be paid for child's services and terminable at a week's notice, will note be deemed illegal. The Tea Districts Emigrant Labour Act, 1932, lays down that no child shall be employed and immigrated to tea districts unless accompanied by his parents or guardians. The Mines Act, 1952, holds the guardian responsible if a young person is found engaged in double employment on any one day.

Women

Most of the Acts make special provisions for women workers. The Factories Act, 1948, provides for separate toilet, washing, and resting facilities for them. It prohibits their employment during night or in hazardous occupations. it makes special safety provisions by disallowing their employment in cleaning, oiling or repairing, moving machines or to lift heavy weights. If she has a young child whom she has left in the factory creche, she has to be given time off at stated frequencies to go and suckle her baby. The Mines Act, 1952, makes all of the above provisions besides prohibiting women's employment below ground. The Merchant Shipping Act, 1958, prohibits recruitment of women except as nurses to take employment on board sea-going ships.

MISCELLANEOUS WELFARE LEGISLATION

In addition to the above mentioned enactments, there are various other measures adopted to improve the social conditions of industrial labour. Legislative measures to liquidate debts of industrial workers have been taken in many States. Development of industrial cooperatives has been given special attention in the Third Five Year Plan, as discussed in a subsequent chapter. The government has undertaken special studies to assess the incidence of gambling and drinking in mining areas. It has set up labour welfare centres in most of the principal industrial cities.

AN ASSESSMENT

Educative Value

The details of basic provisions of health and welfare as given above indicate that these provisions are relatively more regulative and comprehensively instructional. Provisions have been made not only for cleanliness, washing facilities, toilets, etc., but the rules have also prescribed the manner and frequency of dusting and washing of floors, painting of walls, number of water taps, scale of lavatory seats, type of latches to be fixed to doors, and water taps in the cubicle. In Western countries, these things are taken for granted, and hopefully it will be so in India also. But at the time of making these provisions, conditions in work-places were such that it was thought better to lay down the details. The face that improvement has been registered in the manner of providing and usage of these services shows that they have a great educative value.

Democratic Participation

Though responsibility to comply with legal provisions rests with employers, yet workers have been statutorily associated with the administration of many welfare measures. The canteen is to be looked after by a canteen committee, half the members of which are elected workers' representatives. The works committee is competent to discuss all or any of the welfare measure and to advise on their improvement. All welfare funds are administered by boards on which workers are adequately represented. The labour welfare officer whose specific responsibility is to run welfare services has been enjoined upon to work closely with welfare programmes not only brings in a sense of reality to the programmes but it makes the services efficient and the staff more vigilant. It develops a feeling for the undertaking in the minds of workers and gives them experience in democratic functioning which should be of significant value to workers in the discharge of their duties as citizens.

Need for Amendment

Recent investigations conducted by independent sources show a great deal of discrepancy in the manner in which employers comply with legal requirements as well as the extent of their utilization by woerkers. It can generally be said that in big and medium-sized establishments, most of the welfare services have been well provided. Canteen, creche, drinking water, washing and toilet facilities, shelters and rest rooms, lockers, first aid boxes, etc., in work-places are not merely items of legal requirement but are the usual facilities expected in urban industrial environment. Today, an employed in an urban centre will have to provide most of these facilities at the required minimum standard even if there was no legal enactment. The problem is presented by small employers everywhere and in most of the establishments located in outlying rural areas. A survey of fifty creches in Dhanbad and Asansol coalfields showed almost no no utilization of them. Women woerkers who were contacted by the investigators stated that they preferred to leave their children at home rather than in the creche because the creche staff used the same feeding bottles for all children and this polluted their caste. Another workers visited a number of new plants set up in rural areas where work force was recruited from the neighbouring villages. It was found that workers did not utilise the canteen. Most of them were surplus agricultural workers who travelled to the work-place every day. They brought their own food and were not in the habit of spending anything on themselves. Dirty and fly-infested tea stalls and eating places as well as pan shops are a common sight outside most of the factories and mills. They are well patronised by workers. Is it that the workers feel more relaxed and free in these places? Or, is it that they pay less here as compared to the canteen inside? Small size factories are notorious for not providing any facilities and have a way of getting away with it, too. It is in respect of the small establishments that administrative authorities should be most vigilant.

Proper legislation on welfare and health was framed in 1947-48. Things have substantially changed since then. Some services that were introduced at that time are now well accepted, at least by a major part of the industry. A need exists to revise and amend the welfare and health measures in factories, mines, and elsewhere. Workers' health is very precious and canteens could be used effectively to promote it. it should be made a legal requirement for employers to provide a subsidised balanced meal to all workers and for woerkers to take at least one meal at the canteen. Such a practice is being followed in many of the continental countries and in Japan. Similarly, the problems in creche utilization should be looked into. A creche costs at least eight thousand rupees as non-recurring expense and steps should be taken to make the money spent on it more fruitful. The problem of drinking water in mines continuing to be acute. The pithead bathrooms in the mines need improvement. In many cases, usefulness of the pithead baths is nullified by the practice of issuing coal to workers. On coming out of the pit, a worker takes bath after which he carries home coal on his back. This makes him dirty all over again. There is a need to integrate legal provisions with current local practices.

Problems of Young Persons

The legal protection provided to young persons is no doubt adequate, but it does not meet the total needs of the citizens of tomorrow. Though they have been provided with shorter hours of work, selective employment, and more leave, yet their educational and vocational needs have been overlooked. It will be appropriate to make statutory provisions for their education and training after five hours of work. In many countries, the employers are required to give two off-days a week to children for attending schools or vocational training centres. The pledging of children's labour is still widespread in unregulated industries in the south. The inspection and administration needs to be strengthened in this respect. The concept of "parental guilt" for double employment and other types of exploitation of children should be introduced in factories also. The procedure of certification for fitness of young persons should be amended. At present, the certifying surgeon certifies general physical health of a child. The certificate should be issued in relation to the specific job that a child has to take up. It should be certified whether the child could take up a specific work without impairing his health.

Summing Up

Finally, it should be stated that law is essentially an educative process and its objectives can be met only when all parties, particularly the employers, give their willing cooperation. The state sets pace and gives direction to the social process through legislative measures. It should keep a careful watch on its development, should undertake periodic evaluation, and should introduce suitable amendments as and when necessary. The entire body of welfare legislation has grown old and needs revision.

REFERENCES

1. *Gazette of India, 1947*, Part V, pp. 580-585.
2. *Statistics of British India, 1922*, Vol. 1, p. 19.
3. *Imperial Gazette of India 1908*, Vol. 3, p. 197.
4. Indian Mines Act (VIII), 1901; Report of the Chief Inspector of Mines in India 1901, p. 43.
5. *Indian Labour Year Book, 1950-51*, p. 68.

9

Legal Provisions

Though, enough legislations are there in books, ensuring safety at work place and social security to employees. The Employers in India are statutorily required to comply with the provisions of various welfare amenities under different labour legislations. The statutory welfare facilities provided under the Factories Act, 1948, Plantations Labour Act, 1951, Mines Act, 1952, Motor Transport Workers Act, 1961, and Contract Labour (Regulation & Abolition) Act, 1970, have been discussed in this chapter.

Shelters, Rest Rooms and Lunch Rooms

Every factory employing more than 150 workers must provide, adequate and suitable shelters or rest rooms and a lunch room, with provision for drinking water, where workers can eat meals brought by them. But in case a canteen is maintained in accordance with the provisions of Section 46, it will be regarded as part of this requirement. If a lunch room exists no worker will be allowed to eat food in the work-room. These are to be sufficiently lighted and ventilated and to be maintained in a cool and clean condition. The state government may prescribe the standards in respect of construction, accommodation, furniture and other equipment for shelters, rest rooms and lunch rooms. It may, by notification in the official Gazette, exempt any factory or class or description of factories from the requirements of Section 47.

According to Section 9 of the Motor Transport Workers Act, the employer is required to provide rest rooms or any other suitable alternative accommodation at places where motor transport workers employed in a motor transport undertaking are required to halt at night. They are to be maintained in a clean and comfortable condition and are to be provided with proper lighting and ventilatory arrangements.

Section 17 of the Contract Labour (Regulation and Abolition) Act also made it obligatory on the part of the contractor to provide for rest rooms of such other alternative accommodation where contract labour is required to halt at night, in connection with the work of an establishment. Separate rooms are to be provided for women employees under the Central and Maharashtra Rules. The rest room or other suitable alternative accommodation is to be located at a convenient distance from the establishment with adequate supply of wholesome drinking water. If it is not provided by the contractor within the prescribed period the principal employer will have to provide the same.

The Mines Rules have laid down that in every mine where more than 50 persons are ordinarily employed, adequate and suitable shelters at or near loading wharves, open cast workings, work-shops, etc., are to be provided for taking food and rest. Any canteen maintained under these rules may be regarded as part of the requirements of this rule.

Facilities for Storing and Drying Clothing

It is only the Factories Act which has incorporated such a provision. Under Section 43 of the Act, a state government may make rules for the provision of suitable places for keeping clothing not worn during working hours and for the drying of wet clothing. As per the Maharashtra Factories Rules, 1963, such facilities shall, include the provisions of separate rooms, pegs, lockers or other arrangement approved by the Chief Inspector in all classes of factories such as engineering workshops, iron and steel works, oil mills, chemical factories, motor garages, tanneries, etc.

Facilities for Sitting

Every Factory has to provide necessary sitting arrangements, particularly for workers who are obliged to work in a standing position. It enables them to take advantage of any opportunity for rest which may occur in the course of their work. The Chief Inspector of Factories may direct the occupier of any factory to provide suitable seating arrangements as far as practicable.

In Maharashtra, sitting facilities have been provided in a number of factories, *viz.*, electrical goods manufacturing, pharmaceutical, garment factories, radio assembling factories, biscuit manufacturing, telephone industries, etc.

Washing Facilities

It was the Royal Commission on Labour which noted that the provision of suitable washing facilities for all employees though desirable was deficient in many factories. The worker who lives in crowded areas has inadequate facilities for washing and bathing, etc., at home. Provision of such families would add to his comfort, health and efficiency. The Commission recommended that for workers engaged in dirty processes, suitable washing place and water should be made available compulsorily.

Section 42 of the Factories Act lays down that every factory has to provide adequate and suitable washing facilities separately for the use of male and female workers. In this regard the state government may prescribe standards of adequate and suitable facilities for washing.

Section 18 (c) of the Contract Labour (Regulation and Abolition) Act, provides that every contractor employing contract labour in connection with the work of an establishment has to provide and maintain washing facilities. As per the Contract Labour (Regulation and Abolition) Central Rules 1971 and the Maharashtra Contract Labour (Regulation and Abolition) Rules, 1971, the contractor has to provide and maintain adequate and suitable washing facilities. Moreover, separate and adequate screening facilities are to be provided for the use of male and female workers at convenient points. They are also to be kept clean and in hygienic condition.

First-Aid Appliances

The Royal Commission on Labour recommended that, in the case of all factories where mechanical power is used, a first-aid box of prescribed standard, which need not involve any great outlay, should be provided and maintained in different departments according to the number of workers employed, on the basis to be laid down by local governments. Steps should be taken to ensure that there are persons on the staffs of the different departments in every large factory capable of utilising the appliances in the proper manner in the case of need.

Every factory must provide and maintain first-aid boxes or cup-boards equipped with the prescribed contents. The number of such boxes or cupboards must not be less than one for every 150 workers. Each first-aid box or cupboard is to be kept in the charge of a separate responsible person who holds a certificate in first-aid treatment recognized by the state government. These should be readily accessible during all working hours. In case there are more than 500 workers, an ambulance room of the prescribed size and containing the prescribed equipment is to be provided under the charge of qualified medical and nursing staff.

Section 21 of the Mines Act provides for first-aid boxes and medical appliances on the same lines as that of the Factories Act. In addition, it provides for conveyance to hospital or dispensaries of persons who, while employed in the mines, suffer bodily injury or become ill. The Mines Rules, 1955 (Rules 40 to 45) have imposed and obligation on the owner of the mine to provide first-aid rooms, first-aid station, first-aid personnel, etc.

Section 12 of the Motor Transport Workers Act has laid down a statutory obligation on the employer to provide first-aid boxes equipped with the prescribed contents in every transport vehicle, under the charge of the driver or the conductor.

Under Section 19 of the Contract Labour (Regulation and Abolition) Act, the contractor is required to provide and maintain a first-aid box equipped with the prescribed contents at every place where contract labour is employed so as to be readily accessible during all working hours. In accordance with the Central and Maharashtra Rules, the contractor is required to provide first-aid boxes at the rate of not less than one for every 150 contract labourers or part thereof ordinarily employer. The first-aid box is to be marked distinctively with a red cross on a white background. Noting except the prescribed contents are to be kept in the first-aid box. A separate responsible person trained in first-aid treatment and who will always be readily available during the working hours of the establishment will be incharge of the first-aid box.

Canteen

The Royal Commission on Labour and the Labour Investigation Committee have laid considerable emphasis on the provision of canteen at the work-place. The observation of the Labour Investigation Committee is as follows: "The works canteen is increasingly recognized all over the world as an essential part of the industrial establishment, providing undeniable benefits from the point of view of health, efficiency and well-being." The I.L.O. recommendation No. 102 adopted in 1956 in its 39th session gave further impetus to the establishment and improvement in the existing canteens in factory establishments in the various countries of the world. In most of the developed countries, canteens have already become an established feature of industrial life. In many countries, canteens have been set up under stature and in some others through the efforts of workers and collective negotiation between the management and the workers. In most of the developing countries, Legislation empowers the competent authorities to ensure the setting up of canteens in all undertaking employing more than a stipulated number of workers.

Different statutory requirements for provision of canteens for the use of the workers are as follows:

According to Section 46 of the Factories Act, a state government may make rules for provision of canteen by the occupier in any specified factory wherein more than 250 workers are ordinarily employed. Rules 79 to 85 of the Maharashtra Factories Rules, 1963 deal with canteens. The Inspectorate notifies all factories employing 250 workers or more to provide canteens and it is left to any individual unit, to justify and seek relaxation, if any, from the government. As per the Rules the canteen building is to be constructed in accordance with the plans approved by the Chief Inspector of Factories and must accommodate at least a dining hall, kitchen, store room, pantry and washing place separately for men and women. The dining hall of the canteen must have accommodation for at least 35 per cent of the workers at a time. However, the state government may alter and percentage of workers to be accommodated. A portion of the dining hall and service counter must be partitioned off and reserved for women workers. Sufficient chairs, tables, stools, benches, utensils, crockery, cutlery and other necessary equipments must be provided for efficient running of the canteen. Where the canteen is managed by a Co-operative Society registered or deemed to be registered under the Maharashtra Co-operative Society's Act, 1960, the occupier has to provide the initial equipment for the same. The price list of foodstuff, beverages, and any other item served in the canteen must be conspicuously displayed. All books of accounts, registers and any other document used in connection with the running of the canteen must be produced on demand to an Inspector. The accounts partaining to the canteen are to be audited, once in every 12 months, by registered accountants and auditors, and the balance-sheet prepared by the said auditors is to be submitted to the Canteen Managing Committee. The Canteen Managing Committee, which consists of equal representatives of employers and the employees, is to be consulted from time to time regarding quality and quantity of foodstuffs to be served in the canteen, the arrangement of menus, times of meals in the canteen and on any other matter pertaining to its administration. The employer is not required to constitute such a committee in case the canteen is being run by the Co-operative Society. The Chief Inspector may, by an order in writing, direct the Manager to provide in the canteen any item of foodstuff s if he is satisfied that such item is in general demand. Food, drink and other items served in the canteen are to be sold on no profit basis.

Under Section 394 of the Bombay Municipal Corporation Act, 1888, a municipal license for the eating house is necessary. Industrial canteens are licenstable as catering establishments and the conditions of license applicable to the canteen are the same as applicable to a eating house. Since a canteen is a catering establishment, a license is necessary under the aforesaid section even if it is not conducted with profit motive or no members of public are entertained. Under Section 394 of the Bombay Municipal Corporation (Amendment) Act, 1962 a form of application for license is prescribed for various commodities and trades in Schedule M of the Act.

Provision of canteen in all plantation employing 150 or more workers is a statutory obligation under Section 11 of the Plantations Labour Act. In pursuance of these provisions, most of the state governments have framed rules requiring such plantations to provide and maintain canteen or canteens.

Section 16 of the Contract Labour (Regulation and Abolition) Act provides for the constitution of one or more canteens in every establishment covered under the Act. In establishment where contract labour numbering 100 or more is employed by a contractor, one or more canteens must be provided by him for the use of such workers. If the contractor falls to provide the canteen within the time limit laid down, the same is to be provided by the principal employer within 60 days of the expiry of the time allowed to the contractor. This is common in both the central and state rules.

In accordance with the Mines Rules, 1955, in every mine wherein more than 250 persons are ordinarily employed and where the Chief Inspector or the Inspector so requires, a canteen must be provided within the precincs of the mine, for the use of all persons employed. The rules also prescribe certain requirements relating to standards of canteens, furniture, utensils and other equipment, cleanliness, etc.

Under Section 8 of the Motor Transport Workers Act, the state government may make rules for provision of one or more canteens by the employer in every place wherein 100 or more motor transport workers are employed in a motor transport undertaking.

The canteens could be broadly divided into three types: In the first type, we may include canteens organized and administered directly by the employer. In such canteens, the staff are appointed by the employer and paid from the factory fund. They enjoy all other benefits as are admissible to other factory employees. The second types of canteens are those run by the contractors who are in charge of appointment and supervision of the canteen staff. The necessary pavement to the staff is also made by them. Obviously the intention of the contractor will be to make point. The employers normally entrust the canteen to the contractors to get rid of some of the problems and also to free themselves from certain statutory liabilities. In the third category are included canteens run on co-operative basis. Here the employers with or without the assistance of the employer take upon themselves the responsibility of administrating a canteen. However, the union co-operation is vital for successful running of canteens on co-operative lines.

The Committee on Labour Welfare recommended the following measures for improvement in the canteen services:

(i) The canteens should preferably be run by workers on cooperative basis and employers and the state governments should give necessary encouragement for this purpose. The managements/employers should provide canteen facility even in establishments employing less than the prescribed limit of workers, if a request is made by them on this behalf and the workers agree to run the canteen on cooperative basis.

(ii) Both managements and the workers' organizations should take active interest in the running of the canteens. Tripartite bodies should be constituted to ensure that the canteens are run properly and are popular with the workers.

(iii) It is necessary that the spirit behind the provision of canteens be borne in mind by the employers. They should take due interest in providing eatables of requisite standards and nutritive value to the workers employed in their establishments and should not view the provision of canteens as a routine statutory and should not view the provision of canteens.

(iv) Credit facilities should be provided to the employees making use of the canteen services. For this purpose, it is also necessary that the Payment of Wages Act, 1936 should be suitably amended so as to include deductions for credit to workers in respect of purchases made from the canteen.

(v) To mitigate the hardships of workers in small factories including those in industrial estates, the competent authority should be authorized to permit joint service by small employers situated in the same area/industrial estates and, if necessary, amendments to the existing provisions of the Act should be made for setting up of joint canteens.

(vi) The canteen should be situated in a clean and hygienic place, and its kitchen, counter as well as the eating place

> should be maintained in clean and healthy conditions, free from flies, dust and dirt. The welfare personnel of the establishment, the union leaders and the more literate and enlightened workers should ensure that the workers who take advantage of this service appreciate the value and importance of a clean and hygienic canteen service.

The National Commission on Labour observed that: (a) even after years of development, canteens and rest shelters have not received adequate attention from management; (b) the present employment limit for requiring the employer to set up a canteen compulsorily should be brought down to 200 in units where there is an established demand for a canteen from a majority of workers; (c) it should be automatically obligatory for the employer to provide a canteen whenever the employment exceeds the prescribed limit. The need for notifying the establishment should be done away with; (d) establishment which operate over a wide area should consider the running on a mobile canteen; (e) canteens should provide at least one balanced meal a day; and (f) workers should precierably run the canteens themselves on a co-operative basis. In any case they should be associated with canteen management. Wherever canteens are run on co-operative basis, employers should give subsidies in the shape of free accommodation, fuel and light, utensils and furniture.

Creche

The need for setting up creches in industrial establishments was stressed by the Royal Commission on Labour in its report way back in 1931. It recommended that the provision of creches should be made a statutory obligation in all factories employing not less that 250 women. At the same time is suggested that discretionary powers may vest with the provincial governments to provide creche facilities even in the units employing lesser number of women workers, where, in their opinion, the circumstances warranted establishment of such creches. The then Government of India, after examining the position prevailing in India and practices obtaining in other countries, decided to make provision of creches in such factories that employed more than 50 women workers, a staturoty obligation on the employers under the Factories Act, 1934. The provincial governments were authorized to make rules under the Act.

The creche facilities in different countries are provided either under law or by public authorities or by local bodies as a part of the community facilities Section 48 of the Factories Act provides for the setting up of creches in every factory wherein more than 30 women workers are ordinarily employed for the use of children under the age of 6 years of such women. The rooms must provide adequate accommodation, and they should be adequately lighted and ventilated and under the charge of women trained in the case of children and infants.

Rule 87 of the Maharashtra Factories Rules, 1963 provides that the creche is to be conveniently accessible to the mothers of the children. As far as practicable it is not to be situated in close proximity to any part of the factory where obnoxious fumes, dust or odours are given out or in which excessively noisy processes are carried on. The building in which the creche is situated has to be soundly constructed and it is to be adequately furnished and equipped. The mother of a child left to the care of the creche is to be allowed in the course of her daily work two intervals of at least fifteen minutes each to feed the child. For children above two years of age, an adequate supply of wholesome refreshment should be provided in addition. For each creche, a woman incharge with prescribed qualifications and an adequate number of female attendants should be appointed. The creche staff is to be provided with suitable clean clothes for use while on duty. The state government may by notification in the Official Gazette, exempt any factory in which the number of married women or widows employed does nor exceed 20 from the provisions of Section 43 and of the Rules made thereunder subject to the condition that the number of married women and widows employed in such factory is reported every six months to the Chief Inspector.

Section 12 of the Plantation Labour Act provides for a creche in every plantation wherein 50 or more women workers are employed or were employed on any day of the preceding twelve months.

The Mines Creche Rules, 1959 provide for the maintenance of creches in mines where women workers are employed and also for the amenities to the provided in creches. Owner, agent or manager of every mine wherein 50 women are employed or were employed on any day of the preceding 12 months, are required to construct a creche as specified and planned by the competent authority under the Rules. In case any mine owner is not capable of providing a creche of the prescribed standard, the competent authority may approve of the erection of a temporary creche to be replaced by a permanent one within a stipulated time. The competent authority may also authorize erection of a joint single creche on certain conditions. The creches are to be adequately lighted, properly ventilated and maintained in a clean and sanitary condition. In each creche, amenities like medicines for first-aid, cradles or beds, bed sheets, feeding bottles, utensils and toys for children should be provided. Arrangements for cool and wholesome drinking water, supply of milk, soap, towels, etc., for children attending the creche must be made. A trained and qualified woman must be appointed as a full-time creche-in-charge for ensuring the clealiness of the creche. The Coal Mines Welfare Commissioner and the Chief Inspector of Mines respectively are the competent authorities to administer and enforce the Rules in respect of coal mines and mines other than coal.

Creche facilities are extended to the contract workers by the Contract Labour (Regulation and Abolition) Central Rules, 1971. It provides that in every establishment where 20 or more women are ordinarily employed as contract labour, there must be provided two rooms of reasonable dimension for the use of their children under the age of six year. One of such rooms is to be used as a play room for the children and the other as bed room. The contractor has to provide adequate number of toys and games in the play room and sufficient number of cots and beddings in the sleeping room.

The Committee on Labour Welfare made certain suggestions for improvement of creche facilities. They are listed below:

(a) The creches set up for the first time in new industrial establishments should be well-furnished and properly supervised by trained personnel. It is also equally important that the standard prescribed in respect of creches should be strictly maintained even if the number of children decreases.

(b) The smaller industrial establishments, situated in a continuous compact area and employing 10 or more women workers should arrange for common creche facilities on joint basis.

(c) The provision of nurseries/kindergarten classes in creches is essential for that up-bringing and growth of children and they should form an integral part of the creche facilities.

(d) With a view to meeting the appropriate needs of the children of the employed women workers, the municipalities, local bodies and state governments should set up community creches near the residential areas, labour colonies or central places in big cities and towns so that the working mothers are able to utilise this amenity to the maximum possible extent.

The National Commission on Labour recommended that (a) the standard of creches in a majority of factories and mines needs to be improved; (b) the state should provide creches as part of its labour welfare activity in the case of smaller units. It should be possible in such cases, for the states to recover a part of the expenditure on running a creche from the employers concerned; (c) the children of women workers employed through the contractors should also be covered by this facility.

The factories having creches have come down from 75 in 1971 to 41 in 1982 in the State of Maharashtra. The number of children taking advantage of the creche facilities have also indicated a sharp fall from 1860 in 1971 to 546 in 1982. The reason may be that the units where creches existed nominally only, with hardly any children, have been able to persuade the female workers to discontinue bringing their children to factories on some consideration. In some cases there are written agreements while in some others, it may be only an understanding. The transport difficulties also discourage female workers from carrying young children to the places of work. The reduction in the number of creches appears to be rather conspicuous in the textile industry.

Welfare Officer

The industrial undertakings were in firm grip of "jobbers" (in the textile industry) or "mukadams" (in the engineering industry) or "sirdars" (in plantations). They recruited and disciplined workers, took care of output requirements and often kept at bay the unions in plants. They engaged in large scale victimisation of labour. The Royal Commission on Labour in 1831 recommended the abolition of the jobber system and the appointment of labour Officer. The Commission said: "We advocate for all factories the exclusion of the jobber from the engagement and dismissal of labour. This can best be achieved by the employment of a labour officer, and this is the course we recommend wherever the scale of factory permits it. he should be subordinate to no one except the General Manager of the factory, and should be carefully selected. Integrity, personality, energy, the gift go understanding individuals and linguistic facility are the main qualities required. No employee should be engaged except by the labour officer personally, in consultation with departmental heads, and none should be dismissed without his consent, except by the manager himself, after hearing what the labour officer has to say. It should be the business of the labour officer to ensure that no employee is discharged without adequate cause; if he is of the right type, the workers will rapidly learn to place confidence in him and to regard him as their friend. There are many other duties which such an officer can fulfill, particularly, in respect to welfare." Thus, the post of labour officer was instituted initially (a) to eliminate the evils and malpractices of the jobber system; (b) to develop and improve labour adminsitration in mills; and (c) to serve as a liaison with the State Labour Commissioner. The cotton textile mills in Bombay and the jute industry in Calcutta pioneered the appointment of labour officers in the 1930s. The then labour officers were expected to discharge the placing function including maintenance of law and order in an organization. However, the policing function gradually changed to welfare activities and the labour officers introduced certain welfare services like the setting up of food-grain co-operatives, the organization of sports, etc. In due course, the labour officer became a Labour Welfare Officer.

The Labour Investigations Committee also gave importance to the institution of labour officers. Its recommendations had considerable impact on the thinking of the government before independence.

The Factories Act of 1948 provides for the statutory appointment of a welfare officer in a factory. Section 49 (1) and (2) of the Factories Act, lays down that: (1) In every factory wherein five hundred or more workers are ordinarily employed the occupier shall employ in the factory such number of welfare officers as may be prescribed; (2) The State Government may prescribe that duties, qualifications and conditions of service of officers employed under sub-section (1).

The lead given by the Factories Act was subsequently

followed by the statutes enacted for plantation and mining industries. According to Section 18 (1) and (2) of the Plantation Labour Act, 1951: (1) In every plantation wherein 300 or more workers are ordinarily employed the employer shall employ such number of welfare officers as may be prescribed; (2) The state government may prescribe the duties, qualifications and conditions of services of officers employed under sub-section (1) In the Mines Act, 1952, this provision has been made under Section 58 (q). Rule 72 of the Mines Rules, 1955 provides that every mine wherein 500 or more persons are ordinarily employed, the owner, agent or manager has to appoint a suitably qualified person as Welfare Officer. The Rules further lay down the qualifications, duties and conditions of service of the Welfare Officers.

The state governments are required to frame the necessary Rules laying down qualifications, duties, conditions of employment, etc., of the Welfare Officers under the respective Acts. The central government has also framed the Model Rules under the above three Central Acts of provide necessary guidelines for this purpose. All the three Model Rules have laid down the following qualifications for the post of Welfare Officer.

(i) A degree of a University recognized by the state government in this behalf; (ii) Degree or Diploma in Social Science (or Social Work or Labour Welfare in the case of mines), recognized by the state government in this behalf. In addition to this, the Mines Rules lay down the following: "Preferably practical experience of handling labour problems in any industrial undertaking for at least three years." (iii) Adequate knowledge of the language spoken by the majority of the workers in the area where the factories, mines and plantations are situated.

The Model Rules framed under the Factories Act have laid down a chart of duties for the Welfare Officer. These duties are: (1) Supervision of safety, health and welfare programmes like housing, recreation, sanitation services as provided under law or otherwise; (2) Counseling workers in personal and family problems and in adjusting to work environment; (3) Advising management in formulating labour welfare policies and training programmes; (4) Maintaining liaison with workers, management and with other outside agencies like Factory Inspectorate, Central Labour Institute and other social welfare agencies; (3) Suggesting measures for promotion of harmonious industrial relations and general well-being of the workers by adopting various measures in the plant for the redressal of grievances and for increasing the productive efficiency of the workers.

The functions of a Welfare Officer could broadly be classified under three areas of manpower management: (a) labour welfare (welfare function), (b) labour adminsitration (personnel function), and (c) labour relations (conciliation function). His labour welfare function includes advise and assistance in implementing legislative and non legislative provisions relating to health, safety and welfare, hours of work, leave, formation of welfare committees. His labour adminsitration responsibilities may cover organizational discipline, safety and medical adminsitration, liaison, wage and salary administration, education of workers. His labour relations activity may consist of settlement of grievance, adminsitration of standing orders, steps to increase productive efficiency, peaceful settlement of disputes, promotion of harmonious labour-management relations. It is mainly, a staff function with the role of a staff advisor or specialist. He is expected to act as a advisor, counsellor, mediator and liaison man between management and labour.

In exercise of the powers conferred by sub-section (2) of Section 49 and Sections 50 and 112 of the Factories Act, 1948 (LXIII of 1948), the Government of Maharashtra made the following rules, namely:

Duties of Welfare Officers

The duties of the Welfare Officer, Additional Welfare Officer and Assistant Welfare Officer shall be: (i) to establish contacts and hold consulations with a view to maintaining harmonious relations between the factory management and workers; (ii) to bring to the notice of the factory management the grievances of workers, individual as well as collective, with a view to securing their expeditious redressal; (iii) to stay and understand the point of view of labour in order to help the factory management to shape and formulate labour policies and to interpret these policies to the workers in a language they can understand; (iv) to watch industrial relations with a view to using his influence to prevent a dispute arising between the factory management and workers and in the event of a dispute having arisen to help to bring about a settlement by persuasive efforts; (v) to advise workers against going on illegal strikes and the management against declaring illegal lockouts and to help in preventing anti-social activities; (vi) to maintain an impartial attitude during legal strikes or lockouts and help to bring about a peaceful settlement; (vii) to advise and assist the factory management in the fulfilment of obligations, statutory or otherwise, concerning the application of provisions of the Factories Act, 1943, and the rules made thereunder and to establish liaison with the Factory Inspector and the Medical Service oncerning medical examinations of employees, health records, supervision of hazardous jobs, sick visiting and convalescene, accident prevention and supervision of safety committee, systematic plant inspection, safety education, investigation of accidents, maternity benefits and workmen's compersation; (viii) to promote relations between factory management and workers which will ensure productive efficiency as well as amelioration in the working conditions and to help workers to adjust and adapt themselves to their working environments; (ix) to encourage the formation of Works and Joint Production Committees, Co-operative Societies, Safety First and Welfare

Committees, and to supervise their work; (x) to advise and assist factory management in provision of amenities, such as canteens, shelters for rest, creches, adequate latrine facilities, drinking water, sickness and benevolent payments, pension and superannuation funds, and gratuity payments; (xi) to help the factory management in regulating the grant of leave with wages and explain to the workers the provisions relating to leave with wages and other leave privileges and to guide the workers in matters of submission of application for grant of leave for regulating authorised absence; (xii) to advise and assist factory management in providing welfare facilities such as housing facilities, foodstuff, social and recreational facilities, sanitation, education of children and advice on individual personal problems; (xiii) to advise the factory management on questions relating to training of new starters, apprentices, workers on transfer and promotion, instructors and supervisors, supervision and control of notice board and information bulletins for further education of workers and to encourage their attendance at technical institutes; (xiv) to suggest measures to raise the standard of living of workers and in general promote their well-bring; (xv) to bring to the notice of workers their rights and liabilities under the Standing Orders of the factory and order rules which grant rights to, and define the duties of workers or which are directed to the discipline, safety and protection of workers and the factory.

Non-performance of Other Duties

If the Chief Inspector of Factories, Bombay, is of opinion that a Welfare Officer, Additional Welfare Officer or an Assistant Welfare Officer is being required or permitted by the occupier of the Factory to do work which is inconsistent with or detrimental to the performance of his duties prescribed by rule 7, the Chief Inspector of Factories may, by an order in writing direct that such Welfare Officer, as the case may be, shall not be required or permitted to do such work.

The role and status of Welfare Officers have been a matter of controversy. The Committee on Labour Welfare sought the views of various parties, namely state governments, public sector undertakings, private employers' organizations, workers' organizations and eminent persons in the field of labour relations on the role and status of Welfare Officers. Some of the opinions expressed in this regard are given below:

(1) It has been suggested that Welfare Officers should be appointed by the government and employers should deposit their pay and allowances with the government. Their functions should be supervised by the state labour department to whom they should be made answerable.

(2) A Welfare Officer should not be allowed to represent employers in disputes. Personnel and welfare functions should be clearly defined and assigned to different officers. He should not be allowed to handle personnel matters as a representative of the management unless the establishment is too small.

(3) One view in that a Welfare Officer should be statutorily protected so that be may give his independent view without any fear. Without such protection, he may become a tool in the hands of management which may go against the interest of the workers. On the other hand, a different view has been expressed by some that statutory protection is not necessary or desirable for a Welfare Officer to function effectively. Statutory protection may encourage a tendency to adopt the role of as outside authority.

(4) Compulsory appointment of Welfare Officers by law should be done away with because the institution of Labour Welfare Officer does not serve the workers at all. It is used by the employers against the workers and the designation only creates and maintains an illusion.

(5) Relevant sections of the Acts should be amended to enable a Labour Welfare Officer to discharge all such functions as are assigned to him by the management, other than the prohibited functions. The prohibited functions might be the following: (a) to appear in law-courts on behalf of the

management or to prepare briefs or the purpose and (b) to take disciplinary action against the workers.

(6) The "neutrally" concept of the function of Labour Welfare Officer, howsoever well-intended is poorly conceived, ill-defined and generally meaningless. The Labour Welfare Officer is recruited and paid by the management. The latter laos evaluate his performance, determine increments and promotion. Under these circumstances, he cannot be the "Third Force", between labour and management having independent status and decision-making power of his own.

(7) There is a significant feeling among the professional training institutes that the Welfare Officer plays the role of a social worker in the industry. It is assumed that the role of Welfare Officer is a strange admixture of social work orientation and business orientation.

Having gone into all the relevant factors and views expressed, the Committee on Labour Welfare recommended that the managements should designate one of the existing officers of their personnel departments as Welfare Officers to fulfil the purpose of the law. The managements should ensure that only such officers of the personnel department are designated to look after the welfare activities as are properly qualified to hold these posts and have attitude for welfare work.

To conclude, in the words of the National Commission on Labour "the care of workers in all matters affecting their well-being, both at the place of work and outside, puts a special responsibility on the welfare officer who has to be a maintenance engineer on the human side. However, in many cases, the welfare officers also handle grievances and complaints of workers relating to terms and conditions of service and domestic and other matters which he is the domain of personnel management. There is, thus, virtually no demarcation between personnel management functions and welfare functions. The welfare officers, at present, do not have job satisfaction, since the subject of welfare is not generally accorded adequate importance. It is treated more as a statutory requirement to be tolerated."[1]

Act-wise Outline of Welfare Facilities

A brief outline of various welfare facilities provided under different labour enactments is given below:

The Factories Act, 1948

The welfare amenities provided under the Act are given below:

(a) Washing facilities (S. 42)

(b) Facilities for storing and dry clothing (S. 43)

(c) Sitting facilities for occasional rest for workers who are obliged to work standing (S. 44)

(d) First-aid boxes or cupboards—one for every 150 workers and ambulance facilities if there are more than 500 workers (S. 45)

(e) Canteens if employing more than 250 workers (S. 46)

(f) Shelters, rest rooms and lunch rooms, if employing over 150 workers (S. 47)

(g) Creche, if employing more than 30 women (S. 48)

(h) Welfare Officer, if employing 500 or more workers (S. 49)

The Mines Act, 1952 and the Mines Rules

The main obligations of the mine owners regarding health and welfare of their workers are as follows:

(a) maintenance of creches where 50 women workers are employed;

(b) provision of shelters for taking food and rest if 150 or more persons are employed;

(c) provision of a canteen in mines employing 250 or more workers;

(d) maintenance of first-aid boxes and first-aid rooms in mines employing more than 150 workers (Section 21)

(e) provision in coal mines of (i) pit head baths equipped with shower baths; (ii) sanitary latrines and (iii) lockers, separately for men and women workers.

(f) appointment of a Welfare Officer in mines employing more than 500 or more persons to look after the matters relating to the welfare of the workers.

The Plantation Labour Act, 1951

The following welfare measures are to be provided to the plantation workers:

(a) Canteens in plantation employing 150 or more workers (S. 11).

(b) Creches in plantations employing 50 or more women workers (S. 12).

(c) Recreational facilities for the workers and their children (S. 13).

(d) Educational facilities in the estate for the children of workers, where there are 25 workers' children between the age of 6 and 12 (S. 14).

(e) Housing facilities for every worker and his family residing in the plantation. The standard and specification of the accommodation, procedure for allotment and rent chargeable from workers, etc., are to be prescribed in the Rules by the state governments. (S. 15 and 16)

(f) The state government may make rules requiring every plantation employer to provide the workers with such number and type of umbrellas, blankets, raincoats or other like amenities for the protection of workers from rain or cold as may be prescribed (S. 17).

(g) Appointment of a Welfare Officer in plantations employing 300 or more workers (S. 18).

The exact standards of these facilities have been prescribed under the Rules framed by the state governments.

The Motor Transport Workers Act, 1961

The Motor Transport Undertakings are required to provide certain welfare and health measures as given below:

(a) Canteens of prescribed standard, if employing 100 or more workers (S. 8).
(b) Clean, ventilated, well-lighted and comfortable rest rooms at every place wherein motor transport workers are required to halt at night (S. 9).
(c) Uniforms, raincoats to drivers, conductors and line checking staff for protection against rain and cold. A prescribed amount of washing allowance is to be given to the above-mentioned categories of staff (S. 10).
(d) Medical facilities are to be provided to the motor transport workers at the operating centres and at halting stations as may be prescribed by the state governments (S. 11).
(e) First-aid facilities equipped with the prescribed contents are to be provided in every transport vehicle, (S. 12).

The Contrast Labour (Regulation and Abolition) Act, 1970

The following welfare and health measures are to be provided to the contract workers by the contractor:

(i) A canteen in every establishment employing 100 or more workers (S. 16).
(ii) Rest rooms or other suitable alternative accommodation where the contract labour is required to halt at night in connection with the work of an establishment, (S. 17).
(iii) Provision for a sufficient supply of wholesome drinking water, sufficient number of latrines and urinals of prescribed types and washing facilities (S. 18).
(iv) Provision for first-aid box equipped with the prescribed contents (S. 19).

The Act imposes liability on the principal employer to provide the above amenities to the contract labour employed in his establishment, if the contractor fails to do so.

The Merchant Shipping Act, 1958

Provision in the Act relating to health and welfare cover:

(i) Crew accommodation;
(ii) Supply of sufficient drinking water;

(iii) Supply of necessities like beddings, towels, mess utensils;
(iv) Supply of medicines, medical stores, and provision of surgical and medical advice, etc.;
(v) Maintenance of proper weights and measures on boards; and grant of relief to distressed seamen aboard a ship;
(vi) Every foreign-going ship carrying more than the prescribed number of persons, including the crew, is required to have on board as part of her complement a qualified medical officer;
(vii) Appointment of a Seamen's Welfare Officer at such ports in or outside India as the government may consider necessary;
(viii) Establishment of hostels, clubs and canteens, libraries etc.;
(ix) Provision of medical treatment and hospitals; and
(x) Provision of educational facilities etc.

The governments have been authorized to frame rules, *interalia,* for the levy of fees payable by owners of ships at prescribed rates for the purpose of providing amenities to seamen and for taking other measures for their welfare.

Dock Workers (Safety, Health and Welfare) Scheme, 1961

A comprehensive Dock Workers (Safety, health and Welfare) Scheme, 1961, has been framed for all major ports and is administered by the Chief Advisor, Factories (Factory Advice Service and Labour Institutes). It is framed under the Dock Workers (Regulation of Employment) Act, 1948.

Amenities provided in the port premises include provision of:

(i) urinals and latrines;
(ii) drinking water;
(iii) washing facilities;
(iv) bathing facilities;
(v) canteens;
(vi) rest shelters;
(vii) call stands, and;
(viii) first-aid arrangements.

Other welfare measures provided are: (a) housing; (b) schools; (c) educational facilities; (d) grant of scholarships; (e) libraries; (f) sports and recreation; (g) fair price shops; and (h) cooperative societies, etc.

Cost of amenities, welfare and health measures and recreation facilities for registered workers shall be met from a separate fund called Dock Workers' Welfare Fund which shall be maintained by the Board. Contributions to this Fund shall be made by all registered employers at such rate as may be determined by the Board. The Board shall frame rules for contributions for the maintenance and operation of the Fund. Different rates of welfare levy at different ports have been fixed.

Inter-State Migrant Workmen Act, 1979

Section 16 of the Act stipulates that every contractor employing inter-state migrant workmen in connection with the work of an establishment to which this Act applies will have to provide the following facilities:

(a) The ensure regular payment of wages to such workmen (at least minimum wages have to be paid as fixed under the Minimum Wages Act, 1948);

(b) To ensure equal pay for equal work irrespective of sex;

(c) To ensure suitable conditions of work to such workmen having regard to the fact that they are required to work in a state different from their own state;

(d) To provide and maintain suitable residential accommodation to such workers working during the period of their employment;

(e) To provide the prescribed medical facilities to the workmen, free of charge;

(f) To provide such protective clothing to the workmen as may be prescribed; and

(g) In case of fatal accident or serious bodily injury to any such workman, to report to the specified authorities of both the states and also the next of kin of the workman.

10

Codes of Conduct

In principle, private-sector initiatives reflect commitments made voluntarily—in response to market incentives rather than regulatory compulsion. The "mismatch of regulatory scope and actual economic structures", arising from the growth of contractual and joint-venture arrangements across borders, has contributed to public demands for ways of ensuring accountability for the social and environmental impacts of enterprise operations. As a result of public pressure, enterprises feel vulnerable to exposure of potentially abusive labour practices on the part of their foreign business partners in the commodity or service chain. Private-sector initiatives thus seek to establish commitments across the chain, which commonly aim to reinforce or, in some cases, improve on existing legal requirements. This, however, raises the question of whether such initiatives are genuinely "voluntary." Indeed, private-sector initiatives are supposed to be voluntary only because they are not directly enforced by law, but some — particularly representatives of developing country enterprises or governments—contend that market pressure effectively renders them compulsory on terms which can be unfair.

However, the growing number of private-sector initiatives concerned with labour practices raises a host of other issues as well. For example, how do such initiatives relate to other efforts to achieve social justice through better working conditions and fuller employment, particularly those made through public policy or regulation? And what sort of effects, if any, do they have on the social dimension of international trade, and on economic development in particular? Is it fair to be sceptical of their value, or should they be welcomed as a step in the right direction? Even if transnational private initiatives can present a sustainable "high road" for business conduct amidst the complexities of global transactions over time, claims by enterprises and other actors concerning social improvements achieved through private initiatives are not easily categorised, evaluated or compared. Some controversy may thus be inevitable. These initiatives operate across diverse economic, political and legal contexts, without standard reference points or generally accepted methods of development, implementation or assessment. A number of implications therefore arise from limitations inherent in the way such initiatives are developed implemented and ultimately assessed.

Private-sector initiatives spring from the desire to add value to the enterprise, generally by fostering relationships with customers (including consumers), intermediary buyers and other business partners. The need to preserve or legitimise a reputable public image, including the reputation of brand names, has prompted such initiatives at all stages from production to retail sectors active in outsourcing consumer goods internationally, especially in those with labour-intensive operations. Producers of capital goods and intermediary products, who do not independently respond to consumer demands, may in turn be pressed by intermediary buyers to satisfy the demands of consumers. Besides, evidence that good corporate behaviour may enhance financial performance has tended to reinforce the moral incentives for firms to act as "good citizens."

Preventive action has contributed to the growth of private-sector initiatives as well. By displaying efforts to improve workplace conditions, enterprises can pre-empt consumer boycotts as well as formal accusations of unacceptable or illegal business practices. Such efforts may also obviate the need for government regulation by demonstrating that industry best practice satisfies the public interest. Indeed, in some cases, governments may encourage enterprise initiatives as a substitute for social regulation of trade or business. Some countries may also view such initiatives as a way of improving labour practices or public image for trade and investment purposes. None the less, debate continues over whether other considerations, such as protectionist instincts, may contribute to some government efforts to encourage voluntary initiatives. A wide range of actors contribute to the development, implementation and assessment of private-sector initiatives. Initiatives led by enterprises or enterprise associations appear to be the most rapidly proliferating; these vary widely in membership, activities and priorities. Local and international workers' organizations view enterprise social initiatives as a tool to enhance or supplement—rather than replace—collective bargaining processes. Non-governmental organizations and coalitions employ combative as well as collaborative approaches, including negative publicity campaigns, boycotts and court actions against enterprises. Debate persists on the efficacy of such methods. Some argue that boycott hurt the workers they are intended to help, while others believe that, at times, negative publicity operates to complement collaborative efforts. Professional accounting firms and new consulting firms are increasingly offering services in social accounting and monitoring, though few have expertise in labour relations or inspection.

PRIVATE-SECTOR INITIATIVES

At the heart of any private-sector initiative is a decision to communicate a message about the social behaviour of enterprise. The message may target various recipients, including investors, employees, managers, consumers, business partners, local community members, governmental entitles. NGOs and media watchers. The means chosen to communicate that message—and its ultimate impact on enterprise social behaviour—vary considerably depending upon operational circumstances, although they do share functional and normative similarities.

The following typology of initiatives is structured around codes of conduct, social labelling programmes and investor initiatives. But given the difficulty of drawing the precise boundaries of each of these three categories of initiatives at this stage in their development, some overlapping is unavoidable. Any attempt to categorise them is therefore bound to be imperfect. Besides, initiatives aimed at enhancing enterprise social responsibility may include other forms of action as well.

Codes of Conduct

Codes of conduct are written statements of principle or policy intended to serve as the expression of a commitment to particular enterprise conduct. As such, information about the code must be communicated externally to become known to consumers, suppliers and others, whether through company advertising, published annual reports, audit letters or third-party certification which itself is communicated to the outside world.

Although many codes fall within the realm of general business ethics with no implementation methods, this article is concerned only with those that enterprises adopt with the intention of applying them internationally, particularly as "sourcing guidelines" to specify requirements for the workplace conduct of their business partners. In such cases, the code of an international buyer or retailer, for example, is applied to other enterprises in supply (or "value") chains which are not necessarily directly owned, operated or controlled by the enterprise having adopted the code. Such codes may be adopted unilaterally by enterprises, negotiated between management, workers and/or NGOs, or influenced in some way by shareholders.

Enterprises apply *operational codes* directly to themselves and their business partners to articulate commitments to specific conduct, or subscribe to such codes through systems sponsored by third parties (typically enterprise associations or conditions of enterprises, trade unions and/or NGOs). Most of the codes which have propelled the topic into the spotlight are operational codes in large retailing and manufacturing operations engaged in international trade. or developed by industry associations of export suppliers or import retailers, especially for use by their small and medium-sized enterprise members. This latter category of operational codes, sometimes called *subscription codes,* may involve a system for self-reporting by subscribers, or certification by the third-party sponsors themselves. *Model codes,* by contrast, are generic statements intended to serve as a basis for enterprises to develop their own codes. Model codes are generally issued by industry associations, trade unions, NGOs and/or governments. Although these codes do not operate directly within enterprise or through enterprise subscriptions, their provisions may be reflected, in full or in part, in the codes adopted by enterprises.

Social Labelling Programmes

Social labelling programmes operate as verification systems for enterprise social performance by using a highly visible means of communication: a physical label about the social conditions surrounding the production of a product or rendering of a service. Labels show symbols such as legos, trade marks and, in some cases, text, which seek to differentiate the product or enterprise. If the label has no text, its meaning must usually be acquired from some other source, *e.g.* advertising or the media. Like codes of conduct, labels are considered to be voluntary responses to market demands. Aimed at consumers and/or potential business partners, social labels may be affixed to products or their packaging, displayed at the retail site, or assigned to enterprises (usually producers or manufacturers).

Stand-alone social labelling programmes sponsoring *independent labels* often involve a high degree of NGO participation and indeed leadership, reflecting the fact that civil-society processes, including campaigns and public demands, create the perceived market for social labels. Yet independent labels have been developed and administered not only by NGOs, but also by workers' organizations (union labels), industry and trade unions or other enterprise associations, or hybrid partnerships of one or more of those actors. Social labelling programmes run by NGOs or hybrid partnerships tend to be dominated by organizations in developed countries, particularly in their initial phases. However, some of those led by enterprise associations or public/private partnerships have involved coalitions in developing countries, such as Abrinq in Brazil and Kaleen in India. In some cases, small and medium-sized enterprises, or enterprises in industries enjoying little brand loyalty, have shared the costs and higher visibility of an independent social label, usually administered by an enterprise association or hybrid partnership on the basis of a commonly accepted code of conduct. In such situations, the label may be affixed to the product, as with RUGMARK, or may consist of a trade name used by certified companies, as with Responsible Care, a chemical industry initiative. Some programmes which start as multi-stakeholder subscription codes may eventually adopt a certification label as, for example, the Clean Clothes Campaign.

Single enterprises engaged in production, export or retail sales, and enterprise/government partnerships, may also develop social labels to affix to products, using slogans and symbols distinct from brand names, and applying the system to outsourced operations with external suppliers. Some labelling programmes, both stand-alone and enterprise-generated, operate with specific codes of conduct to guide enterprise efforts to obtain licence or use of a label. Operating costs may be subsidised by importers who pay levies on labelled products, or by producers or distributors. Some of these costs are usually passed on to the consumer or, in programmes run by individual enterprises, sometimes absorbed in some internal way.

Investor Initiatives

Private-sector initiatives seeking to leverage financial capital—as well as market share—contribute to enterprise responsiveness to the concerns of prospective investors and present shareholders in the context of the "socially responsible investment" (SRI) movement that has grown recently in certain developed countries. Although there is no single accepted definition of SRI, the term generally indicates investment-related decisions that seek social change while maintaining economic returns. Two SRI approaches seek to influence enterprises in development or implementation of codes, labels and other private initiatives, though their social objectives vary considerably and appear to be based on highly subjective judgements. The first is *investment fund screening,* i.e. the inclusion in investment portfolios (investment)—or exclusion therefrom (divestment)—of publicly traded corporate securities based on the social performance of companies. The second consists of *shareholder initiatives* that involve the exercise of rights based on established share ownership as a means of influencing company behaviour. These two approaches differ in timing and orientation. In principle, fund screening occurs prior to the purchase of company stocks, though subsequent verification may lead to withdrawal of money from a company deemed socially irresponsible. In contrast, shareholder initiatives occur after purchase and seek to influence corporate policy decisions by maintaining a relationship rather than through a "boycott" approach.

Both screening by investment fund managers and shareholder initiatives appear to be gaining ground, at least in industrialised countries. Overall, formal shareholder activism has recently increased in the United States, Japan—

albeit with an overwhelming proportion of environmental concerns—and Germany, distantly followed by other European countries and Canada. The geographic distribution of these initiatives reflects various cultural, legal and economic factors, including civil-society involvement in share ownership, level of development of publicly held corporations, and legal restrictions on grounds for shareholder activism.

Shareholders are influenced to take action by many of the same forces that put pressure on enterprises to act, including media coverage, boycotts, support by public authorities for private initiatives, and reports of research organizations, universities and NGOs. Coalitions among different types of institutional investors have emerged as the main driving force behind many successful share holder actions. The most important sponsors of labour-related resolutions are indeed institutional investors, including insurance companies, pension funds, church funds, union funds, local authority funds and also fund managers who manage investments for other people. Public employees' pension funds and church investors are particularly active, but the evidence is inconclusive as to their specific action on labour issues. As a group, trade unions and union pension funds only occasionally sponsor labour-related shareholder proposals, although they do support such resolutions when they are submitted by other sponsors.

LINKAGES & AGENTS

Commodity Chains

Private-sector initiatives—particularly operational and model codes and social labelling programmes—appear to operate primarily in relation to sectoral concerns or commodity linkages. Indeed, the structure and operation of commodity chains play a defining role in the development and implementation of transnational private-sector initiatives, especially in the case of codes of conduct (see van Liemt, 1998). Codes of conduct with labour-related provisions are known to exist in nearly all catalogued sectors of activity, though the extent of participation by sector varies widely. Some codes develop by virtue of common ownership or equity relationships between enterprises in the chain (*e.g.* tea plantations and packaging). Others are applied as conditions to contractual arrangements, which may represent long-term relationships or fragmented, highly opportunistic outsourcing arrangements. The closer and more long-lasting the relationship between retailer and supplier, the easier the application of the code appears to be. The longer the production chain and the more complex the levels of contractors. subcontractors and buying agents, the more daunting the code's application becomes. Manufacturers with wholly owned facilities abroad or ongoing relationships with contractors have built-in arrangements for code implementation, while retailers removed from their suppliers must use bargaining power to ensure compliance with code standards. Retailers who directly contract out manufacture of private-label merchandise can directly influence their contractors. A global "solidarity negotiation" between international trade secretariats and MNEs, in some cases across commodity chains and sectors, has emerged with code systems and other initiatives that involve varying degrees of participation by local unions. The effectiveness of the chain-wide model, however, depends in part on the degree of cohesiveness of the commodity chain involved.

Role of Trade Unions and NGOs

In a trend that appears to be increasing, codes of conduct are being negotiated and implemented jointly between workers' organizations and enterprises or enterprise associations, especially in regional initiatives in Europe. This feature may be attributed in part to the effect of pre-existing regulations which nurtured a culture of consultation between labour and management, hence a predisposition to extend discussions to new issues and ultimately arrive at code agreements (see, for example, European Union 1994). Such codes apply increasingly to operations owned or managed by European enterprises, or operations in Europe owned or managed by United States and other foreign MNEs. Most of them incorporate international labour standards in a more consistent pattern than do other types of codes reviewed. One innovative approach has been to commit the enterprise, within the "code agreement," to incorporating that agreement into its existing local-level collective agreements. This approach has developed primarily in the context of a leading regional agreement in the textile sector between the European sectoral industry association, EURATEX, and its worker counterparts, ETUF-TCL, and reflects national variations in law and practice relating to collective bargaining relationships. Transposition of collective agreements to the national level brings with it the framework of existing implementation systems and relationships, and a method for achieving uniformity of standards among enterprise operations in various countries and circumstances.

Hybrid systems involving enterprise, workers' organizations and NGOs concerned with labour practices are often initiated by NGOs and operate as code systems and/or social labelling programmes primarily through the subscription method. Sensitive to public and media attention, hybrid code partners tend to concentrate on labour practices in particular sectors, *e.g.*, textiles, clothing and footwear; forestry; or food and agriculture. In contrast to the traditional balance of bargaining power between workers and employers, the participation of NGOs has lent a more piecemeal character to negotiations over hybrid codes. The priorities of civic groups are marked by negotiation processes with few rules of procedure and little transparency. In several high-profile efforts, workers' organizations have been noticeably outweighed by their enterprise and NGO counterparts. Recently, however, workers' organizations have become increasingly important contributors to such initiatives. For example, social labelling programmes aimed at non-labour issues, such as fair-trade labelling programmes and the Forest Stewardship Council, have recently added labour issues to their agendas as workers' organizations become more involved in the programmes; and the Flower Label Programme incorporated labour issues from the start due to early trade union involvement. Governments and inter-governmental organizations (IGOs) tend to play supportive roles in such systems.

PRIVATE-SECTOR INITIATIVES: LABOUR CONTENT

Recent efforts at assessing the labour dimensions of private-sector initiatives have yet to identify either the extent to which enterprises around the world are engaged in promoting labour-related standards or the extent to which such initiatives result in actual improvements in their social conduct. Most available surveys of codes of conduct are specific to particular enterprises in developed economies, to only a few labour issues, or both. Case-study approaches by sector or issue have been undertaken, with some notable contributions (see also UNCTAD, 1994; Burns et al. 1997). Studies on the labour dimensions of social labelling are similarly limited in number, scope and methodology—partly because of the relatively few years of experience with social labels, and the limited number of programmes in operation. Information on investor initiatives in likewise sporadic and non-comprehensive.

From a public-policy perspective, self-regulation of the type reflected in enterprise codes of conduct and private-sector labelling programmes offer certain advantages. In principle, such initiatives can promote corporate behaviour in line with the spirit of the law and thus complement public regulatory efforts. This is particularly evident where the scope of codes or labelling programmes is extended to suppliers in countries and situations where the will or capacity to enforce labour laws or policies is lacking. Some private initiatives move beyond mere compliance requirements and serve as catalysts to advance law or policy beyond the current thresholds that shape commercial behaviour. But despite these advantages, private-sector initiatives are fraught with special challenges arising from their private character and development outside traditional regulatory frameworks. A first step in understanding these challenges involves assessing whether such initiatives consistently complement public policy goals and regulatory efforts and, if not, how they could do so.

The Selectivity of Codes and Labelling Programmes

Based on the ILO's preliminary review of approximately 215 codes and 12 social labelling programmes, significant discrepancies in content and operation have been found both from one code or label to another and between private-sector initiatives and public regulatory frameworks. The review focused on labour practices reflecting internationally recognized fundamental principles and rights—i.e. freedom of association, the right to collective bargaining, elimination of all forms of forced or compulsory labour, the effective abolition of child labour and the elimination of discrimination in employment and occupation—and on wage levels and occupational health and safety. A high degree of selectivity was discovered as to which of these labour issues was taken up in the codes and labelling programmes reviewed.

Appearing in about 75 per cent of the codes reviewed, occupational health and safety was the most frequently addressed issue. Discrimination in hiring or terms and conditions of employment was variously addressed in approximately two-thirds of the codes reviewed. Elimination of child labour-orrefusing to use child labour or to work with companies that did employ children — appeared in 45 per cent of the codes reviewed. The issue of wage levels followed, appearing in about 40 per cent of the codes reviewed. Prevention of forced labour—or refusing to contract with companies that used forced labour—was found in only 25 per cent of the codes reviewed. Strikingly, the principles of freedom of association and collective bargaining, which are fundamental to trade union development and functioning, were addressed, in varying ways, in only 15 per cent of the codes reviewed.

The selectivity reflected in the labour issues covered by codes of conduct can be attributed to various factors. Firstly, the content of codes often appears to be largely decided in non-transparent and non-participatory processes, which may be conducted within executive boardrooms or through ad hoc negotiations between parties with varying degrees of access to information and bargaining power. Secondly, concern for particular labour problems also varies from one sector of commercial activity to another because of the specific nature of the industry or service concerned and, perhaps, its degree of exposure to negative publicity. For example, codes in the TCLF sector tend to concentrate on elimination of child labour and forced labour. Similarly, special attention to occupational health and safety was apparent in the codes of enterprises in the chemical, transport, TCLF, mining, commerce, postal and toy-manufacturing sectors. And thirdly, the selection of labour issues is also conditioned by the degree to which a particular labour practice is — in principle at least—considered acceptable by enterprise itself. This may help to explain the wide gap between the high proportion of codes (representing most sectors of activity) which address employment discrimination, and the relative few which address freedom of association and collective bargaining.

The 12 labelling programmes reviewed displayed similar selectivity in the labour issues they addressed. As with codes of conduct, some social label focus on a single labour issue (*e.g.* child labour), while others address multiple labour issues, or a broader range of issues that includes not only labour practices but also matter such as far trade or forest conservation. The issue most frequently targeted among the programmes reviewed was child labour (11 out of 12 programmes). Half of the programmes addressed wage levels, and one-third took up one or more of the following issues: freedom of association, collective bargaining and occupational safety and health. Other labour-related concerns were less frequently addressed, including forced labour and non-discrimination. A number of factors contribute to the selectivity of social labelling. Labelling programmes naturally reflect the concerns of the consumers, media and civil society campaigns from which they arise. They primarily cover export markets involving retail trade, with market "niche" products, affluent consumers and eye-catching circumstances. In addition, products vary in amenability to social labelling depending on the price sensitivity of the sector, the role of brand recognition and consumers' concern for social issues.

Definitions & Reference Sources

Codes & Labels

With a high degree of selectivity in the choice of labour issues, the review of codes and labels uncovered wide variation in the way in which the targeted labour practice was defined. Most codes and labelling programmes tend to reflect their drafters' own definitions of what the desired improvements in labour practices should be. Among the codes reviewed, such "self-definition" was the most widely used means of setting "standards" concerning wage levels, health and safety, and certain fundamental labour rights. Other code provisions referred to one or more of the following sources: national law, industry practice, and international labour standards.

National law is the most frequently cited of those three reference sources for code "standards." General provisions guaranteeing respect for national law appear frequently in the commerce sector, and industry associations regularly choose to refer to national law. A few codes mentioned national law as a minimum standard only. References to industry standards, by contrast, appear to play a lesser role in code provisions than do references to either national law or international standards. The nature of code initiatives as tools for enterprise leadership might explain this.

To sum up no more than one-third of the codes and labels reviewed referred to international standards, whether general human rights standards or labour-specific standards. References to international standards occur proportionately more often in joint enterprise/workers codes and in hybrid codes than they do in codes developed by industry associations, employers' organizations or enterprises alone. Many of the codes developed by enterprises widely considered to be pioneers in social responsibility make no reference to international standards or other ILO instruments.

Many self-definitions differ from, and even contradict, international labour principles. For example, although some of the codes that address freedom of association affirm that principle and the right to collective bargaining, others only allude generally to respect between labour and management. Other codes favour the elimination of trade union activities, while some propose a combination of approaches. Even on labour issues which enterprise initiatives have addressed for some time, such as employment discrimination, there appears to be very little convergence of content or approach as between codes. Many of those reviewed dealt with non-discrimination in general allusions to respect and dignity of workers, although some did directly refer to eliminating discrimination. Others specifically rejected certain grounds of discrimination, but few reiterated all the internationally recognized grounds of discrimination, Some of the codes promoted not only freedom from discrimination by also equal opportunity for advancement. Mention of equal pay for work of equal value appeared in only a handful of codes.

Despite its overwhelming international recognition, the prohibition of forced labour is treated through self-definition in roughly 80 per cent of the codes that address this issue. Most definitions are limited to prohibiting forced labour in the production of goods; services are added only exceptionally. Many also mention prison labour to qualify or extend the concept of forced labour, and some focus on physical or mental abuse as well. Similarly, the issue of child labour, which has received much media and international attention in the past decade, is addressed primarily through self-definitions, many of which lack specificity as to what a "child" is. References to national laws are common on this issue, although some enterprises might supplement such a reference with a minimum-age standard of their own, which applies only if the national standard is lower. Others defer to national law in the event of conflict between their self-defined minimum age and the age set by international standard. Still others make their own minimum-age standard applicable where no national law addresses the question of child labour. Very few refer directly to the ILO's Minimum Age Convention, 1973 (No. 138), although those that determine their own minimum-age standard typically specify 14 or 15 years which, in certain respects, resembles the general minimum-age standards set in the Convention for work that does not jeopardise the health, safety or morals of young persons. Similarly disparate definitions are given in code provisions addressing wage levels, and occupational health and safety.

Investor Initiatives

Although shareholder resolutions address a wide range of issues, the number that directly address international labour issues in relatively small. And by comparison with codes and social labeling programmes, the labour criteria used in screening by managers of investment funds appear to be less specific, with no apparent standardization among screens.

Moreover, financial analysts tend to judge "socially responsible" funds primarily in terms of comparability of financial performance with funds which make no distinction between general and potentially "cleaner" investment options, including those with notable anti-discrimination and social protection programmes (see, for example, Glassman, 1999). About one quarter of the "socially screened" mutual funds in the United States use labour-related criteria such as "no sweatshop labour," advancement of women and people of colour in the workplace and issues of concern to unions.

IMPLEMENTATION & IMPACT OF PRIVATE-SECTOR INITIATIVES

Without a generally accepted methodological framework that result in the reporting of comparable data, it is difficult to arrive at any objective assessment of efforts to implement codes or labelling systems, and impossible to measure progress even within a single enterprise, let alone within or across industry sectors. Most efforts to establish principles and procedures for the implementation of labour-related codes emphasise the need for participation by all interested parties, comparability of reported data, periodic evaluation and revision of methods, transparency (including disclosure of reports), and the need for external auditing to verify and validate such processes and are used. However, private-sector initiatives generally remain lacking in standardised principles and procedures for defining criteria and conducting assessments.

Monitoring & Assessment

Actual implementation of any commitment involves, in the first instance, the application of management systems within the enterprise, but [v]ery few ... codes emphasise or discuss in detail internal oversight and personal integrity" (Lefebvre and Singh, 1992, p. 807, whose study of Canadian codes exhibits this tendency in almost 70 per cent of cases).

Common management systems to implement private-sector initiatives include the establishment of a clear and detailed enterprise policy, allocating managerial resources for effective dissemination of the policy (including translation) and staff training, and developing and implementing tools for monitoring, reporting, and taking corrective action.

Enterprise-based tools for monitoring and reporting on performance range from self-certification of code compliance by managers, suppliers or affiliates, to active monitoring, evaluation and reporting processes conducted by enterprise personnel or consultants, or externally by third parties or professional inspectors. Enterprises generally favour internal reporting because of concern abut leaks of confidential information. According to one study, the more vertically integrated the enterprise is, the more likely monitoring is to be conducted through an in-country or regional presence that facilitates frequent inspections (United States Department of Labour, 1996). Less monitoring occurs with less integrated relationships in the chain or in the company's own operations.

Self-policing methods for monitoring the implementation of private-sector initiatives have both advantages and drawbacks. Not infrequently, a code launched with much publicity in an industrialised country is unknown, unavailable or untranslated at producing facilities; and even where it is made available, workers may have no way of reading the code or reporting non-compliance without risking disciplinary treatment or dismissal (van Liemt, 1998). Reports from practice suggest that code implementation systems often lack sufficient human resources, adequate participation by workers, and transparency in application. Such reports have increased both consumer scepticism about private-sector claims and public pressure for credible and independent methods of reporting on enterprise performance.

In contrast to self-policing methods, third-party reporting offers various models for balancing control by the enterprise concerned with the perceived need for credibility derived from independent assessment. Growing numbers of enterprises are choosing to call upon professional inspection or auditing firms which may be providing other inspection or auditing services to them already. In general, however, such firms are thought to be less experienced in the detection of workplace violations and less independent due to pre-existing contractual relationships with enterprise management. NGO assessors have also been hired, but without notable success. Small and medium-sized enterprises, especially those in developing countries, have chosen to develop industry association programmes for monitoring and reporting; these programmes provide some degree of independent assessment at lower cost and, presumably, with higher visibility than could be achieved by a single enterprise. Increasingly joint implementation structures between trade unions and enterprises are being recognized as a means of operating independently of management control and enlisting worker participation. Under other arrangements, NGOs work together with international workers' organizations and enterprise to pursue accreditation systems with certification fees.

Assessment methods for social labelling systems generally mirror hybrid code certification arrangements. Most of these systems use NGO or professional auditors, with various forms of self-monitoring found in one-third of the programmes reviewed. Arrangements for worker input were found in very few of the programmes reviewed, and typically took the form of an opportunity to provide information to monitors (Abrinq), to comment on certifiers' reports (FSC), or to be represented as observers (FLO tea registry).

The problem of cost associated with independent inspection arises under codes and labelling systems. This problem is particularly acute for producers subject to varying requirements of different buyers and retailers. In many cases, the added costs of code systems are reflected in a retail mark-up, but if the cost is significant it can damage the competitive position of enterprises. Some have responded with sectoral initiatives, such as those taken under ILO technical assistance programmes to eliminate child labour, while others have opted for the uncertain shelter of social labelling programmes. However, the costs of running of social labelling programme have not yet been proven to operate on a self-sustaining basis, nor has the investment yet proven its worth in terms of added market share.

Effects of Implementation

The effects of private-sector initiatives on their purported aim of improving labour practices are not easily measured, nor are their potential collateral effects on enterprise growth (especially in developing countries), employment, and comparative advantage in international trade and investment. Indeed, whether they stem from codes, labelling programmes or other initiatives, socially responsible sourcing conditions can have critical implications for developing country enterprises in a value chain, especially for small and medium-sized enterprises. In many cases, such conditions require enterprises to find cost-effective ways of making the technical and managerial changes needed in order to maintain, or obtain, access to foreign markets or the large international buyers or investors who impose social requirements (on these difficulties of compliance, see WTO, 1997a: Kumar, Gessese and Konishi, 1998). Private-sector initiatives have been at the root of the summary termination of supply contracts where plants have been exposed for non-compliance with code standards imposed from the outside.

Social labelling programmes also produce direct and indirect effects, both helpful and adverse. They may improve working conditions, raise funds for educational and rehabilitation programmes for former child workers, and improve compliance with labour laws. However, they may also bring adverse effects, including financial difficulty among participating enterprises and consequent loss of jobs. Higher prices of labelled products may result in lower penetration of the market, and child workers may be driven into less formal sectors where their exploitation is more difficult to eliminate.

Debate on how to determine the effects of social labelling focuses on the use of such factors as market share of the label, consumer recognition, percentage take-up of participating companies, number of beneficiaries involved and magnitude of change involved in beneficiaries' income and consumer spending. In the context of ecolabelling, economic theory (unsupported by empirical data) has been used to suggest that negative effects could arise when successful labelling schemes drive down the price of unlabelled goods, thereby increasing demand for those goods (Mattoo and Singh, 1994). A counter argument is that the increased sale of labelled goods would result in increased economies of scale and consequently lower prices, which could in turn be expected to result in diminished sales, reduced economies of scale and higher prices for unlabelled products (Appleon. (1998), and that awareness-raising itself may result in increased demand for labelled goods.

As with codes and labels, the impact of shareholder proposals is difficult to measure, given the number of intervening factors. Even a modest vote in favour of a resolution can assist proponents in discussions with management since it demonstrates a measure of shareholder support for the spirit of the resolution. But measurable progress may take several years, since proponents often put a resolution to the vote several times. The impact is perhaps most visible when the effort results in an agreed plan of action with management leading to withdrawal of the resolution. This is what happens to about one-third of the resolutions submitted in the United States. The action taken often mirrors that requested in the proposed resolutions, whereby shareholders ask management to take score voluntary initiative to address labour practices within the enterprise's operations or outsourcing partners. In various cases, shareholders have asked the enterprise to develop a code of conduct, adopt a third party (subscription) code, amend its articles of incorporation to include international labour standards as binding provisions, increase activity under a code of conduct, or monitor and report on contractors' compliance with the enterprise's code of conduct. Shareholders have even accepted an active role in the monitoring process. In other efforts, shareholders have requested enterprises to restate formal company policy in response to various labour concerns, or prepare a report on the enterprise's labour practices abroad or its supplier standards. As a means of circumventing a rule excluding shareholder proposals concerning the "ordinary business" of the company, shareholders in the United States have proposed linking executive compensation to social performance of the company. In any event, it is clear that enterprises targeted by shareholders face unpredictable parameters in designing and implementing initiatives to satisfy their demands, and in reporting to, and negotiating with them. In turn, shareholders have few reliable ways of assessing enterprise progress on issues of concern.

As to social screening by investment funds, the criteria used by fund managers—*e.g.* "no sweatshop labour" or the advancement of women — may serve as a basis for excluding or including a particular company's shares. But differences between the criteria used by various investment funds tend to weaken their ability to send a clear message to enterprises; indeed, in some cases, the act of divestment could amount to nothing more than a silent withdrawal of money. As some advocates of these initiatives acknowledge, screened funds may have to operate in combination with other instruments to have an effect. In most cases, screened funds do not own enough shares in single companies to influence their decision-making by damaging share prices, but they may make a difference when combined with campaigns and other social strategies.

Social Policy Implications

Overall, private-sector initiatives share certain potential benefits and draw-backs. On the positive side, they stimulate social concern among enterprises and consumers through market mechanisms. To the extent that they complement, supplement or catalyse government policy goals, they offer alternative means of leveraging public efforts. However, these benefits apply selectively as to the labour practices and sectors concerned. Moreover, the initiatives tend to lack transparency, and reliable and comparable verification methods. To the extent that they differ in content from public objectives of social justice, they may even undercut national efforts to improve labour practices, increase employment, liberalise trade and, ultimately, distribute gains equitably. In addition, they may ultimately discriminate against producers in developing countries who face undue costs or other constraints in the process of assessment/certification of conformity. The balance of such risks against the benefits of private-sector initiatives is a matter of concern to policy makers and enterprise stakeholders alike.

Though it is difficult to predict the future of private-sector initiatives, as to both their sustainability and their direction, the fact remains that the market alone has so far failed to produce generally accepted principles for their content or implementation. The degree to which coordination of public and private action, and even regulation, is needed to enhance the benefits and minimise the risks inherent in the operation of such initiatives has been the subject of vigorous debate.

Concern for greater coordination of public and private action marks the approaches of the Governments of the European Union countries and the United States. At the World Economic Forum in January 1999, the Secretary-General of the United Nations noted the relevance to private initiatives of the universal aims reflected in ILO principles and methods of work. He urged multinational investors, employers and producers to "uphold human rights and decent labour and environmental standards directly, by your own conduct of your own business" by promoting universal values in their dealings (Annan, 1999, p. 3). A promotional approach has been adopted thus far in discussions within the ILO itself. The Organization has embarked on a research agenda focusing on the effects of private-sector initiatives on working conditions and job creation. It has also been mandated to provide assistance upon request relating to enterprise needs in this area to serve the Organization's own objectives.

The World Bank is exploring a global code of social policy, and the United Nations Commission on Sustainable Development is engaged in consultations with enterprises. NGOs, trade unions and governments on a universal set of principles to guide industry in promoting sustainable development (see Chote, 1999; United Nations Commission on Sustainable Development, 1999). The OECD, for its part, is considering a revision to its Guidelines on International Investment which would, among other things, reflect certain core labour standards.

Other approaches have focused more squarely on regulatory means. The European Parliament has recommended, in a resolution to the European Commission, that a model code of conduct incorporating labour and other standards be adopted for European business operating in developing countries (European Union, 1999). But further direct public regulation of private-sector actors—particularly if it is legally binding, such as that proposed by the European Parliament—would appear an inadvisable means of seeking to standardise the content of private-sector initiatives concerned with labour practices. A global system promoting the realization of minimum standards in national law and policy might provide a more appropriate and effective framework by encouraging national authorities to ensure that private action is in line with public policy. Indeed, with strengthened public systems for pursuing universally accepted standards—which would essentially amount to a uniform global "bottom line"—private-sector initiatives would likely reflect at least a coherence based on those minimum standards in most cases.

As regards implementation, however, complementarity between public goals and private-sector initiatives could be achieved more effectively and equitably by promoting a framework for such initiatives that encourages comprehensive, transparent and reliable corporate social policy. Such a framework could aim to uphold a set of widely-recognized basic principles analogous to the "generally-accepted accounting principles" (GAAP) which served to charter the profession of financial accounting. Possible approaches include the use of a multilateral private framework, national-level public regulation, or multilateral public regulation. Yet the most promising solution to date, as out-lined below, involves a combination of those three approaches, supported by concrete technical assistance, provided to the enterprises concerned on the basis of equal access and impartiality.

Approaches using a *privatised multilateral framework* would involve agreements to follow guidelines on a voluntary basis, or a voluntary mechanism for setting benchmarks and assessing enterprise performance. Taken alone, such frameworks present advantages as well as risks, including lack of transparency and narrow participation in the development and implementation of initiatives. The workings of a privatised framework can be illustrated by the experience of the International Organization for Standardization (ISO) generally and, in particular, by its current development of standards for ecolabelling criteria, symbols and verification processes. This effort, promoted by Agenda 21 of the United Nations Conference on Environment and Development, seeks to establish guidelines for standardising criteria, label development and verification systems. Proponents argue that such standards could help prevent confusion among consumers arising from the conflicting criteria and unclear meaning of various labels, minimise the risk of loss of credibility over unverifiable claims, and diminish potential liability if enterprises fail to meet national legal minimum standards.

Other approaches to promoting coherence among initiatives are primarily public in nature. Resort to some sort of *reciprocity or equivalence exchanged at the national level* presents some advantages but also risks imbalance of application globally and distortion of trade. A review of the relevant clauses of bilateral investment treaties (BITs) and treaties of friendship, commerce and navigation (FCN) reflect the patchwork results of such approaches, when taken in isolation.

Another public model—*guidelines on enterprise social policies, developed at the intergovernmental level*—provides a multilateral framework for the realization of voluntary commitments through reporting and application to particular cases. Examples of this model include the ILO Tripartite Declaration of Principles concerning Multinational Enterprises and Social Policy ("Tripartite Declaration"), and the OECD Guidelines on Multinational Enterprises. The follow-up of these systems, however, has demonstrated the difficulty of maintaining, and monitoring, concrete commitments to certain social behaviour under systems that are not legally binding.

In one hybrid model, which adapts voluntary private-sector guidelines to a legally-binding conventional system of *multilateral public regulation.* States assume certain obligations respecting private-sector standardising activities while the voluntary and non-state character of the underlying private-sector initiatives is acknowledged. For example, the Technical Barriers to Trade (TBT) Agreement of the World Trade Organization and its annexed Code of Good Practice govern the development and assessment of technical regulation and standards with a view to preventing unjustifiable non-tariff barriers. Article 2.5 of the TBT Agreement provides that, whenever a mandatory domestic technical regulation is prepared adopted or applied for a legitimate objective (including protection of human health or safety, and the environment) and in accordance with relevant international standards, it is rebuttably presumed not to create an unnecessary obstacle to international trade. Similarly, the TBT Agreement encourages Members to harmonise conformity assessment procedures through the use of international guides and participate in the preparation of those guides by international standardising bodies with a view to reducing unnecessary obstacles to trade that might result from national differences in conformity assessment procedures (Preamble and Articles 5.4 and 5.5). Standardising bodies themselves, including governmental and non-governmental domestic bodies, may register their acceptance of the Code of Good Practice which, in turn, requires that they use international standards in the development of their (national) standards. The Code of Good Practice also encourages transparency and cooperation among standardising bodies at the local, central (*e.g.* national or federal) and regional levels through such requirements as notification of standardising activities, provision of information upon request, and consultations in an objective effort to solve any complaints.

The Code seeks, in the long run, equivalence, mutual recognition and harmonization of public and/or private standards on "as wide a basis as possible" by reference to international standards. It is not clear whether international labour standards are directly relevant to the interpretation of the TBT Agreement and its annexes, but in the context of labour-related private initiatives, a type of framework analogous to that presented by the TBT Agreement and Code of Good Practice is worthy of consideration. This general model offers commercial non-state actors—whose voluntary conduct is guided by governmental commitments to encourage internationally based standards—an opportunity to enter directly into a relationship of commitment and accountability to both public and private actors.

Specifically, it provides a practical means of encouraging coherence in the content of voluntary standards and in procedures for conformity assessment, and of preventing confusion from arising over conflicting sets of voluntary standards and/or distortion in various methods of assessment and certification of conformity with such standards. Some substantive and procedural coherence in the field of labour-related private-sector initiatives could be encouraged by combining a set of recommended principles—like those set out in the ILO's Tripartite Declaration or in the OECD Guidelines, or their more recent outsourcing equivalents — with a sign-on system like a voluntary Code of Good Practice annexed to a commitment binding on governments. To be effective and non-protectionist, the framework would necessarily require support through concrete and targeted programmes of technical assistance and guidance to enterprises, especially in developing countries, seeking to address the challenges inherent in developing and applying private-sector initiatives. Such programmes, financed by private and, as available, public sources, could seek to build capacity and complementarity of approach between private- and public-sector activities. The results of a capacity-building approach, together with a framework for harmonization of procedures, might well bring the uncertain promise of private-sector initiative to fulfilment by preserving the broader pursuit of social justice in the international trade liberalization.

REFERENCES

Annan, Kofi, 1999, *Secretary-General proposes global compact on human rights, Labour, environment, in address to World Economic Forum in Davos.* Address of United Nations Secretary General Kofi Annan to the World Economic Forum in Davos, Switzerland, on 31 January 1999, Press Release SG/SM/6881/Rev. 1. New York, NY, United Nations, 1 Feb.

Blanpain. Roger, Forthcoming, "A general introduction," in Roger Blanpain (ed.): *Multinational enterprises and the social challenges of the 21st century.* Dordrecht, Kluwer.

Barns, Maggie; Forstater, Mayer; Mong, Adrienne; Osgood, Diane; Zadek, Simon, 1997, *Open Trading: Options for effective monitoring of corporate codes of conduct.* London, New Economics Foundations Catholic Institute for International Relations. Mar [for an executive summary see <http//www.oneworld.calvertgroup.com/investor/ind-sri-resolutions.html> (visited 2 June 1999).

Caroll, Archie B. 1996, *Business and society: Ethics and stakeholder management.* Third edition Cincinnati. OH, South-Western College Publishing.

Chote, Robert 1999, "World Bank sets out plans for global code for social policy," in *Financial Times* (London), 22 April, p. 4.

Dickson, Marsha A. 1996, *Socially responsibel consumer behaviour in the appeal marketing system: Preliminary findings from a survey.* Columbus, OH, Ohio, State University (Department of Consumer and Textile Sciences). 18 July.

Diller, Janelle M. Forthcoming. "Social conduct in transactional enterprise operations: The role of the International labour Organization," in Roger Blanpain (ed.): *Multinational enterprises and the social challenges of the 21st century.* Dordrecht, Kluwer.

Ferguson, Clare, 1998. *A receive of UK company codes of conduct.* Report commissioned by the Social development Division, Department for International Development. London, DFID. Aug.

Glassman, James, K. 1999, "Do-good funds that are also doing better," in *International Herald Tribune* (Zurich). 6-7 February, p. 16.

Haas, Daniel, 1998, *Mit Sozialklauseln gegen Kinderarbeit? Das Beispiel der indischen Teppichproduction.* Berliner Studien zur internationalen Politik. No. 4. Minster, Lit.

IRRC (Investor Responsibility Research Center). 1996a *Shareholder action advances worldwide: Investors placed a broader range of topics on more non-US ballots in the 1996 global proxy voting season.* Press release, 29 July. Washington, DC.

Kellerson, Hillary, 1998. "The ILO Declaration of 1998 on fundamental principles and rights: A challenge for the future," in *International Labour Review* (Geneva), Vol. 137, No. 2, pp. 233-228.

Kumar, Ritu; Gessese, Nebiyeleul; Konishi, Yasuo, 1998. *Responding to global standards: A framework for assessing social and environmental performance of industries—Case study of the textile industry in India, Indonesia and Zimbabwe.* Vienna. United Natices Industrial Development Organization (UNDIO), May.

Lefebvre, Maurica; Singh, Jang B. 1992. "The content and focus of Canadian corporate codes of ethics," in *Journal of Business Ethics* (Dordrecht). Vol. 11, No. 10 (Oct.), pp. 799-808.

Mayhew, Nick, 1998, "Trouble with the triple bottom line," in *Financial Times* (London), 10 August, p. 8.

Murray, Jill, 1998. "Corporate codes of conduct and labour standards," in Robert Kyloh (ed.): *Mastering the challenge of globalization: Towards a trade union agenda.* ILO Bureau for workers'; Activities, Working Paper produced under Project INT.97/MO1/ITA ("Information technology, workers' participation and social dialogue"). Geneva, ILO, pp. 45-104.

Sajhau, Jean-Paul, 1997. *Business ethics in the textile, clothing and footwear (FTC) industries: Codes of Conduct.* Sectoral Activities Programme (Industrial Activities Branch) Working Paper, SAP 260/WP.110. Geneva, ILO.

Stuckelberger, Christoph; Eger, Michel, 1996, "A social clause with a TNC: The Migros-Del Monte case," in *Swiss Coalition News* (Bern), No. 7, March, pp. 6-7.

UNCTAD, 1994 *World investment report: Transnational corporations, employment and the workplace.* New York, NY, United Nations.

United Nations Commission on Sustainable Development. 1999. *Voluntary initiatives and agreements.* Economic and Social Council, Commission on Sustainable Development, Seventh session, 19-30 April, Report of the Secretary-General. E/CN 17/1999/12. New York, NY. United Nations, 5 Apr.

United States Department of Labour 1997, *By the sweat and toil of children—Volume 4: Consumer lebels and child labour.* Washington. D.C., Bureau of International Labour Affairs.

Varley, Pamela: Mathiasen, Carolya; Vorthers, Meg (eds.) 1998. *The sweatshop quandary: Corporate responsibility on the global frontier.* Washington, DC, IRRC.

11

Position of Welfare Officer

Labour Welfare Officer's position in Indian industry is one of the most controversial of subjects in the areas of welfare, of industrial relations and of personnel management. The office of the Welfare Officer has a history of its own. It is a fact appertaining to industrial development all over the world that the enterpreneur in early days was his own director, labour officer, accountant and cashier, etc., managing by himself, and perhaps by the help of a few assistants, all the works of management. As industry developed into complex system of large scale production reaching world markets, the early owner, or manager could not alone attend to the growing and multiplying functions of industry. Moreover, legislative regulations, and also advances in social sciences emphasised the need to appoint specialist to deal with all the complex and delicate human problems arising from day to day in industries. Sociology, Psychology, Law and allied subjects gradually moderated the excesses of purely engineering bias and outlook in planning for production. Even purely economic emphasis has been greatly controlled by Psychology and Sociology in industry. Thus industrialists in the West gradually recognized social engineering as an important factor. They appointed Personnel Officers who could bring to bear on human problems in industry a sociological and psychological approach. Some industries—in the U.S.A., notably,—employ their own Sociologists, while some have their own Psychologists in addition to Economists. Yet others have on their staff, Counsellors and even Social Workers.

Emergence

The emergence of the Labour and Welfare Officer in the industry has a curious story in India. In the 1850s when modern factory system was introduced into India, the management had to face keen foreign competition. Moreover, the factory system of production mechanised on a large scale, was entirely new to employers as well as to labour. Lack of technological know-how combined with indifference to human element, naturally resulted in low wages, poor working and living conditions, in accidents, and universal discontent amongst labour. Labour slowly emerged as a unionised pressure group. The then alien government (British) due to pressure from England, as well as on its own account, and also on account of protests from unions, passed some legislation compelling managements to pay more attention to the human element in industry. Slowly and steadily more and more legislation in various fields of work life were passed, enlarging the responsibilities of the employers towards their workers, and making working conditions for workers safer and more convenient.

Inspectorates were appointed to periodically supervise if what was required of the management with regard to safe and convenient conditions of work and other such matters, was properly observed and attended to. Still, employers largely tried to shirk responsibilities. Labour, on the other hand, became more and more united and conscious of its rights. This awakening was assisted by the wave of nationalism surging through the country, particularly after the War of 1914. Discontent was becoming universal. The Inspectorate was inadequate. And legislation, too, was found to be no cure for the ills of labour. In 1929 the Royal Commission on Labour was appointed. This Commission was headed by Lord J.H. Whitley. The Commission investigated intensively and extensively and made several very relevant, constructive and far-reaching recommendations in the fields of working and living conditions and labour-management relations,—

amongst many others. Of these many recommendations of the Royal Commission on Labour the one touching the usefulness and the need to extend welfare amenities in important. This does not mean that there were no Welfare Officers in Indian industries before the recommendations of the Royal Commission on Labour. Along with technological knowledge, knowledge about human technology also grew in India, but at a much slower peace than in the West. It is acknowledged that even in the West, material technology has always far out-stripped human technology. It is a problem in cultural history that human engineering is lagging behind material engineering. According to the readings of social scientists such as Ogburn and Elton Mayo, tensions and inadequacies in productive processes are generally due to this lag.

Industrial organization in India, too, became a complex system affecting and involving community life. Industry touched society in its various phases of life i.e., economic, political, legal, cultural, hygienic, etc. Also as in the West, the development, forcing, or helping such management, to revise their ideas, broaden their outlook and humanise their policies in regard to labour matters. This does not mean that such was the universal trend; but some progressive employers at least were influenced by these factors. Also legislation imposed obligations on managements. Workers became increasingly unionised and hence, required to be dealt with collectively. All these forces necessitated the appointment of an officer who knew some law, some social sciences and some public relations. Thus progressive industrial organizations appointed Labour Officers. Wherever welfare works of a statutory and non-statutory nature were introduced the Labour Officer generally functioned also as a Welfare Officer. The early Labour Officer could be designated as a prototype, or a sort of replica of the Personnel Officer in Western industries. The Labour Officer was mainly concerned with general recruitment, discipline maintenance, grievance settlement, industrial relations, and welfare services. He had an office of his own, and was provided with a small staff to assist him. In companies where any considerable welfare work was done, the work was entrusted to Welfare Superintendents. Thus, even before the Royal Commission on Labour made recommendations for the appointment of Labour Welfare Officers, the functions of the Welfare Officer were, to some extent, combined with the functions of the Labour Officer, who was really a Personnel Officer.

However, the report of the Royal Commission is an epoch making document. It heralded a new approach. The report synthesised and channelled the multifarious social, ethical, economic and industrial trends which were taking shape in the country. In the light of the Commission's recommendations many statutory provisions were introduced in the later Factories Acts, and in Acts pertaining to industrial relations.

Impact of Social Work

We said that the development of social sciences suggested and facilitated the appointment of Labour and Welfare Officers. No discipline has so much contributed to enhance the prestige and value of the Labour and Welfare Officer as the discipline of Social Work. The concept and practice of social work ask forming the equipment of a profession was new to India. In nineteen thirties the Dorab Tata Trust started a post-graduate school for the training of social workers. Dr. J.M. Kumarappa, the second Director of the School saw the need to introduce and practise techniques of social work consistently and steadily in our industries. He observed that the workers were poor. They worked in masses under difficult working conditions. The workers also lived crowded in dismal slums under sub-human conditions. So Dr. Kumarappa felt the need to train Labour and Welfare Officers along modern lines so that these could function effectively in industrial organizations as well as in labour communities. The school itself was organized to train social workers to function in general as well as in particular fields, such as family welfare, child care, delinquents, disabled groups, etc. labour and labour welfare together was one of the fields.

In this Institute (now known as the Tata Institute of Social Sciences) a carefully planned training programme for Labour and Welfare Officers was gradually developed. As graduates got trained they had to be placed in suitable positions of employment. Along side with the training programme, Dr. Kumarappa embarked on a consistent, constant and convincing drive for employing only trained persons as Welfare officers: This was done both at government level as well as at the level of private industrial organizations. In fairness to Dr. Kumarappa we have to record that the zeal he showed in this regard was due both to his desire to promote the interest of his own students equally with the interests of the poor working classes. Further, he felt that properly trained personnel in industries would promote better industrial relations. If any untrained people were already working as Labour and Welfare officers, it was proposed to provide a short term advanced training for them. Running through all these developments was the idea of introducing social work and social sciences in industries. The efforts of Dr. Kumarappa succeeded to some extent when the Factories Act of 1948 statutorily required factories employing 500 or more workers to appoint Labour Welfare Officers. Section 49 of the Factories Act, 1948 says: "In every factory wherein 500 or more workers are ordinarily employed, the occupier shall employ in the factory such number of welfare officers as may be prescribed." This section further states, "the State government may prescribe the duties, qualifications and conditions of service of officers employed under Sub Section one."

Factories Act, and Welfare

Now, the Factories Act of 1948 is a culmination of a series of earlier Acts in the field, and it is rightly described as a Welfare Act. The Act makes extensive provisions for welfare in various areas in the workplace. Thus the whole of chapter three of the Act in ten sections covers items relating to health, such as cleanliness, disposal of wastes and effluents; ventilation and temperature, dust and fume, artificial humidification, over crowding, lighting drinking water, latrines, urinals, spittoons. Likewise chapter four is devoted to provisions regarding safety, such as fencing of machinery, safe working of machines, precautions in case of fire, etc., — all included in 21 sections. Such special welfare sections provide for washing facilities, facilities for storing and drying of clothing, as well as for sitting, first-aid appliances, canteens, shelters, rest rooms and lunch rooms, creches, appointment of Welfare Officers, —all these making up 8 sections. Powers are given to State Governments to make supplementary rules in regard to the welfare provisions. Thus one may see that the Factories Act covers quite a comprehensive field. Other provisions of the Act deal with working hours of adults, rules and prohibitions regarding employment of young persons, leave with wages to workers, special provisions regarding notice in cases of accidents, etc., and penalties and procedures in case of violations; and supplemental sections relating to returns to be submitted to the authorities. Obligations of workers, etc., in observing health and safety precautions are also important section of the Act.

Welfare Work in Community

While the Factories Act embraces a wide field of labour welfare within the workplace, it is interesting to note that it is silent (and naturally so) regarding welfare of workers in the community. Through no legislative provisions have been made for the welfare of the workers in their community environment, a few managements did provide housing, schooling, medical assistance, recreational and transport facilities for their workers and for their families too. Of curse the extent and quality of these welfare services differed according to the standard, resources and service—mindedness of the employers. It should also be mentioned that in the mines and plantations, the very nature of the work in isolated and remote areas made housing of the worker necessary and inevitable.

Again, in public enterprises such as the Indian Telephone Industries in Bangalore, Hindustan Machine Tools, Bangalore, Bhilai Steel Plant and the Steel Plant at Rourkela, the government has built complete communities around or in the neighbourhood of the factories.

Mention should also be made of welfare work in the community taken up by some State governments and municipalities. Big corporation like Bombay built some tenements for their own workers as well as for factory workers. This was done with a view to lessen the hardships in regard to housing of the low income groups which workers generally are. Along with tenements-construction, provision was also made for facilities such as schools, play grounds, dispensaries, libraries, etc. Most State governments also provided for the organization of welfare centres in labour areas. These welfare centres, whether they were organized by State Governments or municipal bodies, functioned as neighbourhood houses, i.e., centralised agencies from which radiated all types of social services.

Training

The point we are aiming at is that while the concept and techniques of Social Work entered workplaces and industries, they also spread into the community life of the workers. While qualified persons were appointed to initiate and organize welfare work in factories, similarly qualified personnel were appointed in the community centres. This intensified the need for a greater number of social workers. To meet the increasing demand for trained personnel for welfare work in factories as well as in communities, schools of social work were instituted in Delhi, in Madras, Baroda, Bangalore, Udaipur, Waltair, Varanasi and in other places. Some institutes like the Indian Institute of Social Welfare and Business Management, Calcutta and the Bombay Labour Institute, Bombay, were started exclusively for the training of Labour or Personnel and Welfare Officers. The others gave generic courses in welfare, also including a training programme for Personnel and Welfare Officer. Again, some of these were independent institutes, while some were sections or departments of universities. In addition to this, Institutes of Business Management were also started with foreign collaboration. Specialised training institutes for management studies also came into existence, notably in Ahmedabad, Bangalore, Calcutta and in Bombay. Enlightened management groups perceived the need to keep their personnel equipped with modern knowledge in the field; and consequently they initiated their own programmes through their staff colleges or by becoming members of a regional or central staff college. Also, several industrial consultants entered the field. They offered periodical, personnel training programmes. Professional associations too organized periodical conferences and seminars at which papers were road, and problems were discussed, and experiences exchanged.

The developments mentioned above have been described only to impress upon the reader the impact of social sciences, particularly of Social Work on the art and science of management, on business administration and particularly on labour welfare. This impact is still being felt and extended. But it is historically true that the regard for the human element and the need to introduce human engineering in our industries received an impetus with the starting of schools of Social Work. It is also possible, and perhaps true, that the Factories Act provision making the appointment of Welfare Officers obligatory on industries has also given a fillip to the training programme offered by several institutes in this regard. However, Social Work or social science training for Labour Welfare Officers (and for Industrial Relations and Personnel Officers too) has come to stay. And largely management have also accepted the need for such training for such personnel.

It is not strictly relevant to enter into a description of the discipline or training offered by the various institutes or schools; but for our purpose it is sufficient to state that generally training programmes include courses in Social Economics, Sociology, Techniques of Social Work, Social Research, Labour Legislation, Industrial Relations and Personnel Management. It is assumed that a graduate going through the discipline of this training will acquire the intellectual knowledge, emotional balance, and human, yet scientific approach required for comprehending and handling the manifold, complex and delicate problems which arise in factories and industrial undertakings.

It is under this assumption that the government has made rules for the employment of qualified Labour Welfare Officers. What are these qualifications? The rules made under the Factories Act require that the Labour Welfare Officer to be eligible for the job should be a graduate in any of the social sciences. We should here state that while the Factories Act makes statutory provision for the appointment of Labour Welfare Officers, it has left it to the discretion of State governments to frame their own rules as regards qualifications and procedures for employment of the Labour Welfare Officers. Though there is no strict uniformity in the qualification required for the Labour Welfare Officer, the rules generally agree that the Officer should possess a degree in social sciences. Now, social sciences are assumed to include Psychology, Economics, Political Science, Sociology, Anthropology, History and also Social Work. Law could also be treated as a social science.

"Is one who is a graduate or a double graduate in any one or two or all of these disciplines and qualified candidate? A specific answer to this is not available from any competent authority. But we think such a person is not a fully qualified candidate.

Some State governments such as the Maharashtra Government also add in the rules that an applicant for a Labour Welfare Officer's post should also have studied as one of his subjects Industrial Relations and Personnel Management. Some other State add that a degree or diploma in Social Work is a preferential qualification—assuming that the candidate will have taken labour Welfare and Industrial Relations in his social work studies.

While this is the general picture regarding the qualification for the Labour Welfare Officer, there are examples of companies who specifically require a candidate to have an additional law degree. Some others give preference to applicants with an additional degree or diploma either in Business Management or in Management Studies. Yet other peculiar, but by no means rare instance is of managements preferring applicants with foreign degree or diplomas!

As a matter of great importance we must draw the attention of the reader to the fact that we are discussing the position of the Labour Welfare Officer as distinguished from the Labour Officer or the Personnel Officers. The Labour Welfare Officer is statutorily required to be appointed. The others are not. But the Labour and Personnel Officers are also generally required by employers to possess more or less qualification similar to those possessed by the Labour Welfare Officer. The confusion between the two distinct posts of Labour or Personnel and Labour Welfare Officer has arisen due to the fact that the posts of Labour or Personnel and of the Labour Welfare Officer are sometimes found combined. Thus we have Labour and Welfare Officers; Personnel and Welfare Officers; Industrial Relation and Welfare Officers, etc. The combining of these two jobs in one person, and the combining of the functions of these two officials have led to much conflict, confusion and criticism,—seriously affecting the position of the Labour Welfare Officer. We shall presently see how this has happened. But we must observe that the functions and post of the Labour or Personnel Officer are historically prior to those of the Labour Welfare Officer, who is required to be appointed in every factory wherein 500 or more workers are ordinarily employed, See 49 Factories Act, 1948.

The Act also provides for the appointment of more Welfare Officers where more number of workers are employed. It should be mentioned here that according to a Cawnpore case the Labour Welfare Officer does not cease to have locus-standi, if in the course of his services, the number of workers in the factory falls below 500 (Ref. Premnarain Srivastava *vs.* The Cawnpore Chemical Works Pvt. Ltd—1974 LIC).

Duties of Welfare Officer

We have outlined above the qualifications required of a Labour Welfare Officer. Let us now discuss what the duties are of such Welfare Officer in industry. We may take as our model the rules framed in this regard by the Maharashtra Government.

The duties of the Welfare Officer shall be:

1. to establish contact and hold consultations with a view to maintaining harmonious relations between the factory management and the workers;
2. to bring to the notice of the management the grievances of workers, individual as well as collective, with a view to securing their expeditious redress;
3. to study and understand the point of view of labour in order to help the factory management to shape and formulate labour policies and interpret these policies to the workers in a language they can understand;
4. to watch industrial relations with a view to using his influence to prevent industrial disputes arising between

the factory management and workers: and in the event of a dispute having arisen, to help to bring about a settlement by persuasive efforts;

5. to advise workers against going on illegal strikes and the management against declaring illegal lock-outs, and to help in preventing antisocial activities;
6. to maintain an impartial attitude during legal strikes, lock outs, and help to bring about a peaceful settlement;
7. to advise and assist the factory management in the fulfilment of obligations, statutory or otherwise, concerning the application of provisions of Factories Act 1948, and the rules made thereunder, and to establish liaison with the Factory Inspector and the medical service concerning medical examinations of employees, health records, supervision of hazardous jobs, sick-visiting and convalescence, accident prevention and supervision of safety committee, systematic plant inspection, safety education, investigation of accidents, maternity benefits and workmen's compensation;
8. to promote relations between factory management and workers which will ensure productive efficiency as well as amelioration in the working conditions, and to help workers to adjust and adapt themselves to their working environments;
9. to encourage the formation of works and joint production committees, co-operative societies and safety first and welfare committees and supervise their work;
10. to advise and assist factory management in the provision of amenities, such as canteens, shelters for rest creches, adequate latrine facilities, drinking water, sickness and benevolent scheme-payments, pension and super-annuation funds, and gratuity payments;
11. to help the factory management in regulating the grant of leave with wages and explain to the workers the provisions relating to leave with wages and other leave privileges and to guide the workers in the matter of submission of application for grant of lave for regulating authorised absence;
12. to advise and assist factory management in providing welfare

facilities such as housing facilities, food stuffs, social and recreational facilities, sanitation, education of children, and advise on individual personal problems;

13. to advise the factory management on questions relating to training of new starters, apprentices, workers on transfer and promotion, instructors and supervisors, supervision and control of notice board and information bulletins to further education of workers and to encourage their attendance at technical institutes;
14. to suggest measures which will serve to rise the standard of living of workers, and in general promote their well-being.
15. to bring to notice of workers their rights and liabilities under the standing orders of the factory and other rules which grant rights to, and define the duties of workers, or which are directed to the discipline, safety and protection of workers and the factory.

Protected Welfare Officer

The duties of the Labour Welfare Officer listed by the Maharashtra State Government could be taken as typical. These duties are along the lines indicated by the central government. The Welfare Officer is required to be given appropriate status corresponding to the status of other departmental heads serving under the chief head of the factory. His conditions of service, it is stated, should be the same as of other members of the staff of corresponding status in the factory. The Labour Welfare Officer cannot be readily dismissed or discharged by the employer. But when a dismissal or discharge becomes necessary, the employer is required to explain to the Commissioner of Labour of the grounds of the proposed action; and the Commissioner, after making such enquiry as he deems fit, will advise the employer on the proposed action.

Here we may mention the case of a Personnel Officer who claimed that he was also a Welfare Officer and sought protection under the Factories Act rules against termination.

P. was recruited as a Personnel Officer in a steel factory in 1947. He continued in service till 1950 as Personnel Officer, when he was assigned to the company's mines in Bihar; and later in 1953 to the company's mines in Orissa. P's services were terminated in 1954 for unsatisfactory work, but without any enquiry. P., moved the Labour Commissioner against the termination. P's application was rejected; but P., filed an application to the High Court. The High Court dismissed the application whereon P., appealed to the Supreme Court. The Supreme Court's ruling in this case was as follows:

There was no specific order of the company appointing or recognizing P., as a Welfare Officer, though the Labour Commissioner had exempted P., from the requisite qualifications for a Welfare Officer. Even assuming that P., was originally appointed as Welfare Officer, there were no service conditions applicable to his appointment which could be said to have continued in his favour, entitling him to permanent tenure. Also, when the Factories Act rules came into operation, P., was no longer in a factory but was in a mine where the rules do not apply to him. Hence, P., is not a Welfare Officer; and protection granted by the Factories Act and rules made thereunder do not apply to him. The appeal is dismissed. (Ref. AIR 1957 Supreme Court on Industrial Law 1950-1978, 2nd Ed. by D.S. Chopra Vol. I, P. 894).

From this supreme Court's judgement, the important conclusions for us appear to be that: (1) a Personnel Officer is different from a Welfare Officer; (2) to seek protection, along with duties performed, the appointee should be officially designated as Welfare Officer; (3) at the time of appointment the service conditions should contain provisions for protection; (4) and finally at the time of termination he should be in such service where the regulations for protection should be relevant and applicable. In spite of the Supreme Court's decision, the case presents points open for interminable arguments. But the decision, does clarify that the Welfare Officer in industry is a statutorily required body with (in some industries and states) protected service conditions, while the Personnel Officer or the Industrial Relations Officer is not.

The question will naturally arise why the rules under the Act contemplate a situation wherein the Labour Welfare Officer is exposed to the risk of his being discharged or dismissed by his employer? Granting that such circumstances could arise, still many other question could be put: "Why, amongst all the other heads of the departments in the factory, the Labour Welfare Officer should be favoured or singled out for such protection as is mentioned above? Can this protection be effective and conducive to his dignity and status in the factory generally, and in the eyes of his colleagues in the other departments? How will the employer take to a Labour Welfare Officer, who is legally protected and whom the employer is not free to discharge or dismiss when he is convinced of the need to take such a step? Suppose a Labour Welfare Officer deserves his services to be terminated, according to the employer. The reasons are properly stated and sent to the Commissioner of Labour. It is possible that due to honest difference of opinion the Commissioner does not approve of the action of the management. This will create a very curious situation of the persons i.e., employer and the Labour Welfare Officer who dislike each other, but are forced to work together. The tenseness of the context is further enhanced by the fact that the employer pays for the services of the unwanted officer whom he hates or dislikes. What employer can look with equanimity on his own position where his money is spent on the work of a person whose very presence is distasteful to him? It is easy to imagine that such a manager will continuously find fault with the Welfare Officer perpetually raising grounds for his dismissal. Neither can such protected Welfare Officer spend peaceful days in the factory, His position is not only "too deep for tears," but too indicrous for laughter.

Welfare Officer

It will be seen that the list of duties given above is quite comprehensive as well as impressive. The duties abound in such cautious phrases "hold consultation," "being to the notice of the factory management," "study and understand," "help and interpret," "watch industrial relations," "advise workers and management," "maintain an impartial attitude," "advise and assist in supervision, etc." "help workers to adjust to working environments," "*encourage* formation of committees," "*suggest* measures for improving standard of living," "*bring to the notice* of the workers their rights and duties, etc." These phrases clearly indicate that the Welfare Officer has very limited executive functions, if he has any at all. His role is to advise, counsel, suggest, watch, study, interpret, bring to the notice but never to take sides. His position is neutral. While the position of all the other heads of `committed' in one way or other in several contexts of work and production, the Labour Welfare Officer definitely belongs to the category of service personnel. While most of his duties are recommendatory, it depends on the management what measure of initiative, resources and authority they give him. The duties suggested by the rules appear to endow the Labour Welfare Officer with no authority whatsoever,—authority understood in the sense of taking decisions involving action. He can perhaps assist the executive officer in taking decisions. But nowhere is it indicated how, in what respect and to what extent he can influence such decisions. For instance, in case of an act of indiscipline by a worker, can he, according to the duties listed above, recommend a course of action, say dismissal? If he does, the union could accuse him of taking sides and being partizan while he is expected to be neutral. On the other hand, if he recommends a mere warning in case where management want to dismiss a worker, the management may look on him as a union man in disguise. The poor Labour Welfare Officer is expected to please and satisfy, and to promote harmonious relation between, labour and management in the factory. Harmonious relation depend on efficient work and adequate wages, proper grievance settlement machinery, human approach off the part both of union officials and workers on the one hand, and a management and of supervisory personnel on the other. Harmonious relations is a balance of human relations resulting from give and take policies. It needs tolerance, equable temper, if not charity, at least a liberal outlook. Peaceful industrial relations depend on a thousand forces, and the Act says nothing, when it says that the Labour Welfare Officer should promote peaceful industrial relations.

Moreover, the Labour Welfare Officer is a paid employee in the service of the management. Psychologically the employer, who is superior in position and powerful too, cannot easily welcome and accept 'advice' from the Welfare Officer. Another factor which makes the position of the Welfare Officer difficult is the fact that the employers have not yet unreservedly accepted labour welfare as a function of management. At least there is a feeling amongst them that too much is required of them in the field of welfare, and that welfare is misused by the workers. There is some argument in this position of the employers. Our workers are mostly drawn from rural areas. They have been poor and largely ignorant and illiterate. Perhaps they lack initiative and co-operative spirit. For several reasons they do not respond satisfactorily by participating in welfare activities. Thus the employer rightly feels that much of welfare work does not produce results. Hence he may be feeling that it is superfluous waste of resources which can be more profitable invested elsewhere. In the Western countries, notably in the United States of America, the workers utilise welfare amenities properly. They possess leadership and initiative, so much so that they are quite capable of managing their own welfare. In India we are in a period of transition. We are witnessing a change over from the old order to the new. In some fields this change over is rapid; in some other fields it is slow. As we have pointed out earlier, human engineering in industry has not kept pace with technological engineering. Hence the experience of frustration and disappointment felt by the labour as well as by the management. As the nation progresses in all walks of life the situation may improve.

Duties

The duties of the Labour Welfare Officer as given in the list could be classified under three heads: those falling under:

1. labour welfare;
2. industrial relations and
3. personnel management.

The three categories of functions are closely related, but are here separated for analysis only.

TABLE-1

Duties Listed Redistributed

Welfare	*Industrial Relations*	*Personnel Management*	*Labour Welfare Industrial Relations & Personnel Management*
1.	2.	3.	4.
7	5	11	8
10	2	13	9
12	4	15	10
5			
14	6		

It is easy to see from the above chart that the duties assigned to the Labour Welfare Officer fall in the three areas of labour welfare, industrial relations and personnel management. It is true, as we have stated earlier that the three areas are not mutually exclusive. If this statement is accepted we may have to accept what follows from this, namely that the Welfare Officer is not an exclusively Labour Welfare Officer, but is also somewhat of a Personnel Officer and an Industrial Relations Officer too. There is a grave defect in the position. The Personnel Officer as well as the Industrial Relations Officer—assuming that these officers exist—are employers' men; though they are expected to be faithful to the principles of their respective disciplines or sciences. But the Labour Welfare Officer is expected to maintain a neutral position; and further, his job is protected to some extent, while those of the Industrial Relations and Personnel Officer are not protected. Thus, one can understand that an unintelligent combination of personnel and industrial relations functions with the functions of the Welfare Officer with protected position and purely advisory duties, easily leads to making the job of the Welfare Officer controversial. The workers look upon him as a management man. The employer thinks he is not such; but wants him to be such. Legal restrictions do not permit him to be such. Thus the Labour Welfare Officer is pitiably plunged into the personnel vortex of conflicting duties.

It should also be stated here that though the welfare functions assigned to the Welfare Officer are fairly comprehensive, though general, the industrial relations and personnel management functions assigned to him are of very limited extent. Thus, recruitment with its manifold duties of man-power estimation, testing, selection, work-assignment, do not figure in the duties listed. Similarly, wage payment, and incentive plans, transfers, merit-rating are also not stated. Again, though some industrial relations functions are indicated, no mention is made of duties arising out of contexts such as conciliation, adjudication and arbitration. Nor is it clear, what part the Labour Welfare Officer—where he is the only officer—should play in collective bargaining process. Since his position is thus magnificently vague, some managements use him to represent them at conciliation, adjudication, arbitration and collective bargaining proceedings. This is another factor which identifies the Welfare Officer with the interests of the employer as against those of the employees. There are several instances where workers have unfortunately felt that the Welfare Officer worked against employee's interests of consequently have physically injured him, and sometimes fatally. On the contrary, there are not wanting illustrations of employers getting rid of the Labour Welfare Officer on the plea that he was not working in the interests of the management, but only promoting labour's interests.

Necessity of Separation of Functions

To conclude, some of the points which make the position of the Labour Welfare Officer controversial. The Labour Welfare Officer is saddled with too many duties. The duties assigned to him also fall in the spheres of industrial relations and personnel management. In the performance of his multifarious duties he is sometimes called upon to support management's cause and sometimes promote labour's interests. The employers generally have not yet unreservedly accepted labour welfare as their responsibility to the extent that legislative provisions require of them. The 'protection' granted to the Labour Welfare Officer Places him in an awkward and unfavourable position vis-a-vis the employer. He is required to be neutral in several important contexts. His functions are purely advisory. These tend to make his role ineffective. How can the position of the Labour Welfare Officer be retrieved or improved? It is clear that if he continues in his position as it is, he is little likely to make his full contribution. The best proposal appears to be to split up and separate the functions of the Labour Welfare Officer, of Industrial Relations Officer and of the Personnel Officer. It is not harmful to combine the jobs of the Industrial Relations and Personnel Officer when such combination is found convenient or desirable. But the functions of the Labour Welfare Officer should not be combined with the duties of any other functionary.

Welfare as well as promotion of industrial relations are also personnel functions. The Personnel Officer should be in overall charge of welfare and industrial relations, in addition to any other personnel functions he may have to fulfil. Welfare and industrial relations thus become divisions of the general personnel department. The Personnel Officer, who is the chief, should be the co-ordinating authority. He should let and lead the Welfare Officer to function fully and satisfactorily in the area of welfare without conflicting with, or impinging on the domain of the Industrial Relations Officer. Nor will he be allowed to treat on the toes of the Personnel Officer. But whenever related and common duties will have to be discussed or performed, the three officers, i.e., the Personnel, the Welfare and the Industrial Relations Officers will meet, exchange views and experiences, outline programmes, evolve policies and implement them so as no conflict anywhere results., The protection given to the Labour Welfare Officer should be removed. The Personnel Officer should assume full responsibility for welfare and industrial relations. The Welfare Officer is accountable to the Personnel Officer. He will no longer be a neutral person in his committee and limited role of Welfare Officer. He is a management man taking care of the welfare programmes in the factory, and if possible outside the workplace too. In his own sphere of welfare he should have executive powers. In conciliation, arbitration adjudication or collective bargaining proceedings the Welfare Officer will not appear and represent any one. It is the Industrial Relations or Personnel Officer who will represent the management at such proceedings. Welfare is a total concept involving a desirable condition of existence of the worker in regard to his physical, emotional, and mental health. A hundred factors combine and contribute to bring about such welfare. The co-operation of all—particularly of the Personnel, Industrial Relations and Welfare Officer, is necessary to bring about such a consummation. The training and qualifications of all the three officers will have to be more or less similar. The job of the Welfare Officer, though lower in the hierarchy of the management structure, is yet not a close one. It should open out stairs and provide stepping stones for the promotion in time into higher level and duties in the hierarchy. Thus a Welfare Officer could be become in time a Personnel Officer in the organization he has served.

12

Problems of Labour Welfare

The labour force in India had hardly any effective organization, and the philanthropists only advocated a humanitarian approach for providing the labour with better living and working conditions. With the advent of industrial revolution in India, the migration of rural population to the urban centres and the industrial belts caused socio-economical problems for thousands of persons having been uprooted from the rural moorings. The new class of industrial workers needed welfare services to be provided to them in their new surroundings, so as to enable them to adopt themselves to changed environs.

The workers, thereafter, started considering the provisions of welfare amenities, either as a matter of right, or as an integral part of service conditions. Out of the total 292 million work force in the country as on March 21. 1985, 117 million were wage earners in the unorganized sectors and another 150 million were self employed workers. The total agricultural labour in the country was 185 million of which 75 million was self-employed, only 24 million were in the organized sector with just 6 million belonging to recognized trade unions with verified membership.

The Sub-Committee of the Parliamentary Consultative Committee appointed by the Ministry of Labour under the chairmanship of Shri Goverdan Das Gupta, to study the problems of unorganized workers in agricultural sector which was spread over a year covering 8 States and over 100 villages revealed that conditions of agricultural workers in the country is dismal and the Government's anti-poverty schemes have made no major impact on them. Besides, there was no uniformity in the minimum wages which varied from as low as Rs. 3 to Rs. 17 per day in some parts of the country and in unirrigated areas work is available only for 60 to 90 days in a year. The Sub-Committee was called for an immediate introduction of a comprehensive Central legislation for agricultural workers to provide a basic framework for their working conditions, wages and social security. The Committee has also recommended strict enforcement of the child Labour (Prohibition and Regulation) Act, 1986, and suitable rehabilitation, educational and welfare of the children involved.

The Union Government has set up an eight Member National Commission on Rural Labour headed by Shri Jeena Bhai Darji, a Gujarat social worker. Shri Suresh Mathur is the secretary of the Commission.

The INTUC Working Committee meeting on March 11, 1987 held at New Delhi, welcomed the said proposal to appoint a National Commission on Rural Labour and ruled out that it will greatly help to focus on the problems of rural labour, particularly the rural poor. The Committee also urged the then Minister of Labour Shri P.A. Sangma to amend the Industrial Disputes Act, 1947, immediately with a view to give effect to the 'check off' system and verification of membership for recognition of Union, as also for the setting up of industrial Relations Commission and other measures agreed to in the Standing Labour Committee and the Indian Labour Conference. The Government convened a tripartite National Labour Conference in September 1982. For the first time in the history of tripartism in India, unanimity was reached in the conference which came out with unanimous conclusions on all issues concerning contents and contours of a new legislation to govern Industrial Relations. The Standing Labour Committee at its meeting held recently on

Sept. 22 and 23, 1986 had endorsed the setting up of an Industrial Relations Commission at the national and State levels.

In view of the recommendations of the Standing Labour Committee a comprehensive Industrial Relations Bill was introduced in Parliament during question hour on August 3, 1987. The proposed legislation would also aim at strengthening the trade union movement by promoting internal leadership and providing for statutory recognized collective bargaining agents at the Unit/Industrial level. This also gave fillip to trade union activities. As welfare became an accepted feature of employment conditions, the State began to intervene in order to widen the scope of applicability of welfare schemes.

Labour Welfare Concept

Labour Welfare is an extention of the term 'welfare' in its application to labour. The value base of the concept of Labour Welfare has behind it a long history through which it has struggled to assume its present form. During the early days of industrialization, optimization of profit was the main concern of employers. The profit oriented employers led them to take maximum work from their employees and pay them as less as possible. Amidst this state of affairs there were men like Robert Owen, who resented this approach of the industrial employers, and who were determined to effect a change in the nature of employer-employee relations. The employers started effecting on humanitarian grounds, improvement in working conditions and hours of work in factories. However, labour welfare services have gradually come to be regarded as normal *first line function* of the industrial society.

The term 'welfare is derived from the French phrase 'welfare' which means "to fare well." The Webster's dictionary defines the term 'welfare' as a state characterized by happiness, well being or prosperity. Thus, in its broader connotation, term welfare refers to a state of living of an individual or a group in a desirable relationship with total environment, economic, and social.

"Welfare" is a broad concept referring to a state of living of an individual or a group of individuals in good health, happiness and comfort, or in a condition of well being and in a desirable relationship with the total environmental-ecological, economic and social. It connotes the state of general well being, happiness, health and comfort. It postulates improved living conditions. Yet in another sense it is aid to the needy and the underprivileged Social welfare is primarily concerned with the solution of various problems of the weaker sections of the society like prevention of destitution, eradication of poverty etc. It aims at social development by such means as social legislation, social reforms, social services, social work, compensatory discrimination, special provisions, social action etc. The object of economic welfare is to promote economic development by increasing production and productivity, and through equitable distribution. Labour welfare is a part of social welfare conceptually and operationally. It covers a broad field and suggests many ideas, meanings and connotations, such as the state of well being, health happiness, satisfaction and the conservation and development of human resources. Welfarism means utilization policies, programmes, schemes and practices of the state agencies and other bodies.

Labour welfare may be viewed as a total concept as a social and economic components. The total concept is a desirable state of existence involving well being. Physical, mental, moral and emotional of the workers These four elements together constitute the structure of welfare, on which its totality is based. The social concept of welfare implies the welfare of man, his family, his dependents and his neighbours. All these aspects are inter-related in a three dimensional approach. The relativity of the concept of welfare implies that welfare is relative in time and place. It is a dynamic and flexible concept, and hence its meaning and content, differ from time to time, region to region, industry to industry, depending upon the value system, level of education, social customs, degree of industrialization and general standards of the socio-economic development of the people.

Labour welfare has both positive and negative aspects. The positive aspect implies the setting up of minimum desirable standards and the provision of facilities like health, food, clothing. Housing, medical assistance, education, insurance, job security, recreation etc. Such facilities enable the worker and his family to lead a good work life, comfortable family life and pleasant social life. On the negative side, labour welfare operates to neutralise the harmful effects of large scale industrialization and urbanization.

Meanings and Inclusions

The expression "Labour Welfare" is one which stands itself to various interpretations, and does not have always the same significance in different countries. The Oxford dictionary defines the expression as "efforts to make life worth living for workmen." To quote R.R. Hopkins "Welfare is fundamentally an attitude of mind on the part of management, influencing the methods by which management activities are undertaken." Obviously, the emphasis here is on the "attitude of mind." In the Encyclopaedia of Social Sciences, the term 'welfare work' has been used to describe the voluntary efforts of an employer to establish, within the existing industrial system, working conditions and sometimes living and cultural conditions of his employees "beyond what is required by law, the customs of industry and the conditions of the market." Arthur James Todd defines welfare work as "anything done for the comfort and improvement intellectual and social of the employees over and above the wages paid, which is not a necessity of the industry, nor required bylaw." E.S. Proud defines welfare work as "voluntary efforts on the part of the employers to improve the existing industrial system and the conditions of employment in their own factories." In the Report II of the ILO Asian Regional Conference, it has been stated that workers' welfare may be understood to mean "such services, facilities and amenities, which may be established outside or in the vicinity of undertakings to enable the persons employed therein to perform their work in healthy and congenial surroundings and to provide them with the amenities conducive to good health and high morals." In its Resolution of 1947, the ILO defined. 'Labour welfare' as "such services, facilities and amenities as adequate canteens, rest and recreation facilities, arrangements for travel to and from work and for the accommodation of workers employed at a distance from their houses, and such other services, amenities and facilities as contribute to improve the conditions under which the workers are employed."

In 1953, the Governing Body of the ILO, considered the scope of labour welfare, and suggested that it was essential to define its scope in view of the fact that "It was a very wide subject, covered a very broad field and was not limited to any one industry or occupation Subsequently, in 1956, the International Labour Conference extended the scope of "labour welfare" to include, inter alia,—

(a) feeding facilities or near the undertaking,

(b) rest and recreation facilities in or near the undertaking (excluding holiday facilities),

(c) transport facilities to and from work where ordinary public transport is inadequate or impracticable."

In India, the concept and scope of 'Labour Welfare' has also undergone a change. In the pre-1947 period, the Labour Investigation Committee (1944-46) includes under "labour welfare activities" anything done for the intellectual, physical, moral and economic betterment of the workers whether by employers, by Government or by other agencies over and above what is laid down by law or what is normally expected as part of the contractual benefits for which the workers may have bargained." Thus, under this definition we may include provision for housing, medical and education facilities, nutrition (including provisions of canteens), facilities for rest and recreation, cooperative societies, day nurseries and creches, provision of sanitary accommodation, holidays with pay, social insurance measures undertaken voluntarily by employers alone or jointly with workers, including sickness and maternity benefits schemes, provident funds, gratuities and pensions etc. The scope and coverage of 'Labour Welfare' has been widening. The Report of the Committee on Labour Welfare (1969), noted that, 'labour welfare' includes "such services facilities and amenities as adequate canteens, rest and recreation facilities, sanitary and medical facilities, arrangements for travel to and from work and for the accommodation of workers employed at a distance from their homes, and such other services, amenities and facilities including social security measures as contribute to improve the conditions under which workers are employed." The whole field of welfare is said to be one "in which much can be done to combat the sense of frustration of the industrial workers, to relieve them of personal and family worries, to improve their health, to afford them means of self-expression, to offer them some sphere in which they can excel others and to help them to a wider conception of life." It promotes the well being of workers in a variety of ways. Realizing the difficulties in giving a precise definition of 'Labour welfare,' the National Commission on Labour has observed that the concept of "Welfare" is necessarily dynamic, bearing a different interpretation from country to country, according to the value system, social institution, degree of industrialization and general level of social and economic development. Even within one country its content may be different from region to region.

Welfare work should thus mean and include any organized agency efforts directed towards improvement of living conditions; social, economic or moral. According to N.M.

Joshi, welfare work "covers all the efforts which employes make for the benefit of their employees over and above the minimum standards of working conditions fixed by the Factories Act and over and above the provisions of the social legislations providing against accident, old age, unemployment and sickness." Thus, the "welfare" is very comprehensive concept. However, it is clear that the scope of welfare activities will become narrower and narrower as more and more of them come to be covered by labour laws and collective agreements, if emphasis continues to be placed on the voluntary nature of welfare work in definitions quoted earlier.

An examination of various definitions of labour welfare reveals that the term has been defined from a board as well as narrow point of view. Considered in its broader connotation, it includes all activities of employers, trade unions, States and other agencies to help workers and their families, to derive greater satisfaction from life by making better home and community life possible. Services designated to create better conditions of work includes suitable provisions regarding controls of heat, light and noise; cleanliness; toilet facilities; canteen; rest rooms, drinking water; lockers; health safety and accident prevention; suitable hours of work; holidays; leave with pay etc. Services that promote better home and family life workers including housing, health, education and recreational measures, clubs, playgrounds, music, libraries, cinemas, cooperatives, welfare centres, employer's counselling, transport etc. Labour Welfare includes social services providing by an employer to his employees over and above what is required to be done legally or in the necessity of industry.

The scope of labour welfarism has been described by writers and institutions of different shades differently. Its limits cannot be rigidly laid down regarding its scope for all industries and for all areas and for all times. It must be administratively viable and essentially, development oriented in outlook. In the final analysis, labour welfare services should include all extra-mural and intra-mural welfare work, statutory and non-statutory welfare activities undertaken by the employers, government, trade unions or other voluntary organizations, and also social security measures which contribute to workers' welfare such as industrial health, safety, insurance, provident fund, gratuity, maternity benefits, workmen's compensations, retirement benefits etc. Any welfare programme, taken in its more comprehensive sense, mentioned above, and as an all embracing phrase, may also be divided into three types: (i) Statutory; (ii) non-statutory; and (iii) mutual statutory welfare. The first type constitutes those provisions of welfare work which depend for their observance on coercive power of the Government. In order to preserve the minimum standard of health and safety of the workers the Government frames certain statutory rules which may prescribe certain obligatory standards to be abided by the employers. They may relate to certain essential working conditions like hours of work, safety, age, sex, light, hygiene and sanitation etc. Such State interference, in providing statutory provisions for workers' welfare, especially for children and women workers is increasing day by day in every country. Non-statutory welfare measures include all those activities within are undertaken by employers for their workers. On the fact of it the idea is apparently philanthropic, but if we go deep into the matter, then, we find that it is a sound investment also, because, the various welfare activities of the employers not only increase the efficiency of the workers, but also reduce the chances of conflicts. Some of the trade unions also undertake voluntary welfare work for the benefit of their members. Mutual statutory welfare refers to social security measures.

The Committee of Experts on Welfare Facilities for Industrial Workers constituted by the ILO in 1963 divided welfare services into the following two categories:

(a) Welfare amenities within the precincts of the establishment (intra-mural): latrines and urinals, washing and bathing facilities, creches, rest shelters and canteens, arrangements for drinking water, arrangement for prevention of fatigue, health services, industrial or occupational safety, administrative arrangements within a plant to look after welfare, uniform and protective clothing, and shift allowances.

(b) Welfare amenities outside establishment (extra-mural) maternity benefits, social insurance measures including gratuity, pension, provident fund and rehabilitation, benevolent funds, medical facilities including programmes for physical fitness and child welfare, educational facilities including adult education, housing amenities, recreational facilities including sports, cultural activities, library and reading room, holiday homes and leave travel concessions, workers' cooperatives including consumers' cooperative stores; fair prices shops and cooperative thrift and credit societies, vocational training for dependents of workers, other programmes for welfare of women, youth and children and transport to, and from the place of work.

The study team appointed by Government of India earlier in 1959 to examine the existing welfare facilities divided these activities into the following three groups:

(a) Welfare within the premises of an establishment; medical aid; creches; canteens; supply of drinking waters; etc.

(b) Welfare outside the establishment: provision for indoor and outdoor recreation, housing, adult education, visual instructions, etc., and

(c) Social security.

Thus, it is clear that the scope of labour welfare activities will become over a period of years narrower and narrower as more and more of them come to be covered by labour laws and collective agreements; if emphasis continues to be placed on the voluntary nature of welfare work in definitions quoted earlier.

Necessity for Labour Welfarism

The aim or object of labour welfare activities is partly philanthropic and partly humanitarian. It is intended to enable the workers to enjoy a better, a fuller and a richer life. It is partly beneficial to improve the efficiency of the workers; and it is directed to develop among them a sense of responsibility and dignity; and thus make them worthy citizens of the nation. Another object of labour welfare is to ensure the future needs and aspirations of the labour. The altruistic motives and purposes which have prompted the adoption of welfare measures have varied from time to time and place to place ranging from paternalistic to maternalistic considerations, and also from ethical to utilitarian directives.

1. The considerations which should prompt employes to provide welfare are neither casual nor altruistic. Some of the early philanthropic and paternalistic employers tried to ameliorate the working and living conditions of their workers by providing various welfare measures, because, unselfish concern for welfare of the latter. This welfare work was drove in a spirit of condescension, and for being good to the employers. In India, in the early years in addition to the paternalistic and philanthropic motives, employers are extremely religious-minded and relatively more concerned about their own well-being after death. Doing good to others in the form of giving alms, during charity, or providing social relief by building *'Dharmshalas'* and *'Sarais'* and *'Aushdhalayas"* feeding the poor and providing drinking water to the thirsty during summer were regarded as the accepted means of being eligible for the blessings after death. Many of the employers in India, and abroad have been prompted in labour welfare work by such consideration.

2. Often the employers have taken recourse to welfare work just to win over their employees' loyalty and to combat trade unionism and to resist socialist ideas. The devotion to welfare work by many American employers during the new deal period could be attributed to their desire to save the workers from trade unionism. It was then thought that,

welfare work by presenting a kind and benevolent picture of the employers and by deeply attracting the workers towards them, would work as a damper to trade unionism and socialism. If the employers, on their own, could provide good working and living conditions, the workers would not turn to hostile socialistic cult of trade unionism.

3. Some employers thought fit to provide labour welfare services to build up a stable labour force, to reduce labour turnover and absenteeism and to promote better industrial relations. Not frequently industries suffering from chronic labour shortage have tried to aùgment their labour force by emphasising welfare measures, and by providing amenities and facilities which the workers would not acquire on their own even with higher wages. The Labour Investigation Committee has emphasized this aspect of welfare work. It is said, "Better housing, co-operative societies, canteens and maternity benefits, provident funds, gratuities and pensions and such other things and bound to create a feeling among the workers that they have a stake in the industry as much as the employer. The present situation under which labour turnover and absenteeism prevail, and the workers are constantly trekking to their village houses in search of social security and recreation will yield place to a new situation in which the working class becomes more satisfied and economically efficient."
4. One of the objects for provision of welfare activities in recent times by certain employers is to save themselves from heavy taxes on surplus profits.
5. The purpose behind provision of welfare amenities some companies is to enhance their image and to create an atmosphere of good-will between labour and management, and also between management and the public.
6. In the present, labour welfare has been conceived by some employers as an incentive and good investment, in particular, to secure, preserve and develop greater efficiency and output from workers. It is thought that such welfare services as canteens where cheap, clean, and balanced food available to workers, improve their physique; education improves their mental efficiency; medical aid and maternity services likewise help them in maintaining better health. The view

is no more true that there is no direct relationship between welfare work on the one hand, and efficiency and productivity on the other. There is certain implied imperceptible *quid pro quo* between investment on labour welfare and returns in the form of increased productivity, although it is not so easy to quantify the additional contribution of welfare measures to the increased productivity. Any how, some studies have shown a positive link between labour welfare and productivity.

7. Some of them took recourse to welfare work, i.e., treating workers as human beings and not as a mere factor of production. The workers as human beings are entitled, as a matter of right, to certain basic amenities in order to lead a decent life.

Thus, the aims and objectives of labour welfare have progressively changed during the last few decades. From the primitive policing and placating philosophy of labour welfare it gradually moved to the era of altruism and paternalism and production targets. True even today there is evidence of humanitarian outlook of some of the employers in many employee welfare programmes, but the present day philosophy in labour welfare is more oriented towards increasing productivity and efficienicy of the working people. An outstanding trend today is that it has become a comprehensive concept relevant to the development of the total human personality embracing physical, mental, social, psychological and spiritual aspect of the employees' well being. In future, it must assume new dimensions in our country as a result of added emphasis on the basic responsibilities of the welfare state and implementation of socialistic directives.

The necessity for labour welfare is felt all the more in our developing country because of its developing economy aimed at rapid economic and social development. As regards the necessity of welfare work in India, it can be easily realized if we look into the conditions of workers in our country.

Often the workers have to work for long hours under unhealthy surroundings and afterwards, have no means to remove the drudgery of their lives Removed from the village community and involuntarily thrown into a strange world of urban areas and uncongenial environment, they are liable to fall easy victims to alcoholic drinks, drugs, gambling and other such demoralising ruinnous practices and habits. Under circumstances it is worth trying to check the evil effects of the industrial revolution which are likely to adversely affect the people crowded in workers colonies. When the workers feel that the employer and the State are interested in his day to day life and would like to make their lot better in every possible way, their tendency to grouse and grumble is likely to be lessened. Labour Welfare plays a vital role in industrial development. It is now an essential part of any labour organization and management, which must attach itself more importance to human good. It increases the productive efficiency of the workers and infuses in them a new spirit of self-realization and consciousness. In India, which has embarked upon a vast programme of industrialization, the need for labour welfare is all the more important. The greatest need of the industry is to increase production and fulfill the target of the Five Year Plans. That can be achieved only by keeping the workers contented, and promotion of welfare activities can go a long way in the direction.

The need of labour welfare was felt by the Royal Commission on Labour as far back as 1931. This need is emphasized by the Constitution of India in the Chapter on Directive Principles of State Policy, and also in the blue prints of Five Year Plans.

Labour Welfare Theories

A theory here means or includes a statement or formulations of principles, assumptions and presumptions which provide rational explanation to labour welfare. To different men various theories seem appropriate. Thus, some seven theories constituting the conceptual framework of labour welfare, have so far mainly been outlined. These include:

1. The Religious Theory of Labour welfare, This has two aspects:
   (a) atonement, and
   (b) investment aspects.
2. The Philanthropic Theory;
3. The Trusteeship Theory;
4. The Police Theory of Labour Welfare;
5. The Placating Theory;
6. The Public Relations Theory;
7. The Functional Theory of Labour welfare.

1. The Religious Theory

This is based on the concept that man is essentially "a religious animal." Even today, many acts of man can be inspired by his religious sentiments and beliefs. The religious feelings sometimes prompt an employer to take up welfare activities in the expectation of future benefit either in this life, or after it. Thus, according to this theory, any good work is considered as "an investment" by which both the benefactor and the beneficiary are rewarded. We come across many trusts and charitable institutions in India which function on the basis of this belief. Another aspect of the religious theory is the atonement aspect. Some people take up welfare work in a spirit of atonement for acts of omissions and commissions divinely forbidden of their sins. Thus, the benevolent acts of welfare are treated either as an investment or an atonement. According to this theory, man is primarily concerned with his own welfare, and only secondarily, with the welfare of others. The religious basis of welfare, however, cannot be rational. It is voluntary and not obligatory. Neither it is universal, nor continuous. Fundamentally, welfare based on charity is not good for the beneficiary in the long run. Nevertheless, though, these services are voluntary, yet sometimes these amount to more than what is required by legal enactments.

2. Philanthropic Theory

This theory is based on man's love for mankind. In Greek' *"philos"* means loving and anthropes' means man. So philanthropic means "loving mankind." It is one man's desire to help his fellow humans by gifts, or through charity. Man is believed to have an instinctive urge by which he strives to remove the suffering of others, and promote their well-being. This crive may be a rather powerful one and may impel him to perform noble sacrifices. When some employers have compassion for their fellowmen, they may undertake labour welfare measures for the benefit of their workers. In fact, the labour welfare movement began in the early years of the industrial revolution with the support of such philanthropists among the employers or otherwise as Robert Owen. In India, Dada Bhai Naoroji, Mahatma Gandhi were some of the eminent philanthropists who strove for the welfare of labour and workers. This theory is thus derived largely from man's love for others, and therefore, cannot but be individualistic. Irregular and occasional philanthropic acts of welfare of a few good men among many not so human may sometimes defeat the very purpose of welfare. All the same the utilization of such philanthropic sentiments on the part of employers and others has worked well for the time being and in select few occasions only.

3. Trusteeship Theory

This is also called the paternalistic theory of labour welfare, according to which "the industrialist or employer holds the total industrial estate, properties, and profits accruing from them in trust." In other words, the employer should hold the industrial assets for himself, for the benefit of his workers and also for society. Workers are like minors they are ignorant because of lack of education, and are not able to look after their own interests. Employers have, therefore, the moral responsibility to look after the interests of their wards, the workers. There is naturally no legal binding; but since it inheres in a moral obligation, it has to be less effective. The main emphasis here is on the idea that employers should provide, out of the funds under their control, for the well being of their workers. Mahatma Gandhi very strongly advocated this Trusteeship Theory. Also, this theory treats "Workers as perpetual minors and industrialists as eternal guardians." The self-reliant growth of the trade union movement is ignored in this theory although it may create a basis of goodwill between labour and management.

4. The Placating Theory

This theory is based on the fact that labour groups are becoming demanding and militant, and are more conscious of their rights and privileges than ever before. Their demand for higher wages and better standards can no longer be ignored. According to this theory, timely and periodical acts of labour welfare can appease and pacify the workers. The welfare programmes are just necessary to pacify by way of friendly gesture. Sincerity may lack in these programmes, though discontent can be bought off for the time being in this manner. Psychologically, this theory is unsound, though it has often been acted upon to secure the workers' co-operation.

5. The Police Theory

This is based on the contention that a minimum standard of welfare is necessary for labourers. Here the assumption is that without policing, that is, without compulsion, employers do not provide even the minimum welfare facilities for workers. Apparently, this theory assumes that man is selfish and so is the employer, he is self-centred, and always tries to achieve his own ends, even at the cost of welfare of the workers. If wealth or authority or both help him to be in an advantageous position, the employer uses it for his own advantage, exploiting those who are unequal in bargain.

According to this theory, the employer-owners and managers of industrial undertakings get many opportunities for the exploitation of workers who must be on road to contract to state. The welfare State has, therefore, to step in to prevent this kind of exploitation and coerce industrialists to offer a minimum standards of welfare to their workers. Such interference is in the interests of the progress and welfare of the State as well. Laws are enacted to compel managements to provide minimum wages, congenial working conditions, reasonable hours of work and social security; and also to provide for policing so that the laws are not observed in breach only. The Police Theory, therefore, leads to,

1. the passing of laws relating to the provision of minimum welfare for workers;
2. periodical supervision to ascertain that these welfare measures are provided and implemented;
3. punishment of employers who evade or disobey these laws.

In this theory, the emphasis is unfortunately placed on fear of punishment of those who disobey law, and not so much on the spirit of welfare which should be the guiding factor. There are some big employers who can but prefer to overlook and hold back welfare programmes which are not required by law, even though they can afford easily to put them into effect. There are others who can on the lawyer's advice find loopholes in the law, and convince factory inspectors that they have duly carried out the legal requirements. These laws, moreover, impose a heavy burden on the government which has to maintain a costly inspectorate to ensure that minimum welfare programmes are implemented in all the industries. However, in a country like India, where working conditions in many places are not at all congenial, and where the majority of workers are illiterate, a certain amount of coercion is essential in the interests of the working population. This commends the police theory as in ensures minimum necessary welfare.

6. Public Relations Theory

This theory provides the basis for an atmosphere of goodwill between labour and management, and also between management and the public. Labour welfare programmes under this theory, work as a sort of advertisement and help an industrialist to build up and promote good and healthy public relations. This theory is based on the assumption that the labour welfare movement may be utilised to improve relations between management and labour. An advertisement or exhibition of labour welfare programme may help an industrialist to project to the public a good image of his company. His sales as well as industrial relations may improve as a result of two-fold benefit to the company. But this kind of programme may also lack in sincerity and continuity. When such a programme looses its advertisement value, it may be neglected by the employer even though it is still useful for the employees. Here, welfare may tend to become a publicity stunt. Nevertheless, these programmes do improve industrial relations.

7. The Functional Theory

This is also called the Efficiency Theory. Here welfare work is used as a means to secure, preserve and develop the efficiency and productivity of labour. It is obvious that if an employer takes good care of his workers they will tend to become more efficient and will thereby step up production. But all this should depend on a healthy collaboration between trade union and development of industry. Any, higher production is of benefit for bot management and labour. The latter will get better wages and, perhaps, a share in the profits. This is the functional aspect of welfare having efficiency as its object which increases productivity. This theory is a reflection of contemporary support for labour welfare. It can work well if both the parties have an identical aim, that is, higher production through better welfare. And this will encourage labour's participation in welfare programmes.

These theories treat labour welfarism as different people look at it. These articulate the rationale behind welfarism. As no two persons think in the same way, a philosopher, a philanthropists, a social worker, a trade unionist and the like must think of labour welfare differently. In each theory there is an aspect of truth. Consistent with the value ethos of a society one theory may be more relevant than the other. But, no one single theory articulates all the justification on reason. Taken together they articulate, rationalise and pragmatise the labour welfarism.

In India, it is said, the industrial system clings largely to the paternalistic approach. Some managements, however, obliged to achieve results through police control. Either way, workers start expecting too much from employers, as a result of which employers provide welfare measures in a somewhat half hearted manner. The trusteeship theory too, can be applied suitably in Indian conditions, though in the longer run, it is better to act on the basis of the functional theory of labour welfare, for it works more effectively by reason of ensuring an intelligent and willing participation of workers.

Labour Welfare and Social Welfare

In fact, labour welfare, the author believes is neither philanthropy, nor charity. It is a system which seeks to up-grade the quality of life of people through appropriate statutory and voluntary mechanisms. It is a method of creating more satisfying working and living conditions for workers employed in industry by increasing workers' sense of involvement in the objectives of the enterprise, and motivating them to lend a willing hard to the development of the country. Conceptually as well as operationally, labour welfare is a part of social welfare which, in term, is closely linked to the concept and role of the state.

Social Welfare: Social welfare programmes aim at enabling the deprived sections of the population to overcome their social, economic or physically handicaps and improve their quality of life. They supplicate the developmental programmes in general in dealing with the problems of poverty and unemployment an are meant in particular to assist the most disadvantaged groups below the poverty line. Especially children from poor families, women, the handicapped, downtrodden and the infirms. Pigou defined it as "that part of general welfare which can be brought directly or indirectly into relation with measuring of money." He, however, recognized the limitation of his definition and said that the elements of welfare were "states of consciousness and probably their relations." According to Willenosky and Labeaux, social welfare alludes to those formally organized and socially sponsored institutions, agencies and programmes which function to maintain or improve the economic conditions, health or inter-personal competence of some parts or all of a population. Social welfare assist the weaker sections, prevents poverty and destitution, and establishes satisfactory conditions of human living. Such an approach to social welfare brings within its fold social reform, social legislation, social services, social action and social work. Considered narrowly, social welfare aims at the well being of people by helping them make better adaptation to the existing social structures. It seeks to raise the human level of life-cultural, economic and psychological. The welfare State is a system of social responsibilities for certain minimum standards of individual and community welfare. Under social welfare sector, preventive, developmental and rehabilitative services are provided to the vulnerable and weaker sections of the society. These services have developed gradually and the inputs steadily through the planned development.

SOCIAL WELFARE IN PLANS

In the First Five Year Plan, a provision of Rs. 4.00 crores was made; and the amount was placed at the disposal of the Central Social Welfare Board, set up in 1953 for encouraging voluntary organizations, especially in the field of women and child welfare. The Second Plan with an approved outlay of Rs. 19 crores witnessed the participation of Central and State Governments in addition to the activities of the Central Social Welfare Board. The scope of social welfare was widened so as to include and promote additional activities for welfare of women and children like welfare extension projects in urban and border areas, condensed courses of education for adult women and socio-economic programmes. In the Third Plan, the State Governments and the voluntary organizations were associated closely in drawing up the Plan with an outlay of Rs. 31 crores. While providing services, efforts were undertaken, in particular, towards sections of the community which needed special care and protection. The Fourth Plan aimed at the consolidation of the initiatives taken in the previous plans. An outlay of Rs. 41 crores was provided for this purpose. One of the major programmes in operation was the Family and Child Welfare Projects in rural areas.

The efforts so far were mainly directed to the provision of some basic curative or ameliorative services. The preventive and developmental aspects which are more effective and economical in the long run did not receive adequate attention. The major thrust in the Fifth Plan with an outlay of Rs. 83 crores was on the expansion of preventive and developmental programmes. During the period child welfare was given the highest priority. To ensure healthy growth and development of children and reduce infant and maternal mortality rates, the scheme of the Integrated Child Development Services (ICDS) was launched on an experimental basis to provide a package of services consisting of supplementary nutrition, immunization, health check-up, referral services, nutrition and health education and non-formal education to children in the age group 0-6 and pregnant and nursing mothers in rural, urban and tribal areas. The programme has been evaluated through various studies which revealed that some of the deficiencies noticed in the early stages have been looked into the coverage of children below 3 years of age, which was found to be low and the provision of services at *Anganwadi* level was reported to be poor, had started improving and there was an increase in the level of preventive health care.

The thrust in the Sixth Plan with an outlay of Rs. 150 crores too was on the child welfare and indigent women. For women in distress and need, diversified schemes of vocational training, self-employment and socio-economic programmes had been given greater importance. During the Sixth Plan, several central programmes had a number of achievements to their credit. These include the sanctioning of additional 869 ICDS projects bringing the total number of projects to 1019; institutional and non-institutional services to 32.000 children in need of care and protection; 4785 condensed and vocational training courses benefitting 1,11.000 women; 3589 socio-economic units covering 47,011 women and disabled persons; continuation of the national institutes for the handicapped; and assistance to 58 voluntary organizations for assisting about 25,000 disabled persons to acquire aids and appliances. In addition, 7,000 creche units covering 1,75.000 children and 344 working women's hostels with a total capacity of 22,150 inmates were functioning by the end of 1984-85. Social Welfare Programmes received further momentum in the State sector as well. A new programme to provide employment to landless labourers has been initiated in Rajasthan, as in other States, under a Central Scheme. Under the programme, the Government provide employment to one member of each landless labourers' family for 100 days a year. In spite of an outlay of Rs. 272 crores on social welfare in the Sixth Plan, there exists certain deficiencies in programme planning and implementation to be remedied in order that the effectiveness of social welfare schemes can be enhanced. Social welfare services in their various facets are preventive, promotive, developmental and rehabilitative in nature. They are designed to enable the targeted sections of society to realize their full potential for growth. The programmes of social welfare are only supplementary in nature, designed as they are to meet certain needs of the most deprived and the vulnerable members of society. The outlay for Central and Centrally sponsored schemes in the social welfare sector in Rs. 799.97 crores. The plan outlay for the States and Union Territories is Rs. 191.87 crores and Rs. 20.52 crores respectively. The Seventh Plan outlay for the states was Rs. 316986 crores while that for Union Territories was Rs. 39 crores.

Concludingly, during the previous plans, welfare services have expanded considerably, particularly in the areas of child, young and women's welfare. Besides a variety of programmes for the economically weaker sections have been introduced by different Ministries at the Centre and also by the State Governments. The administrative machinery for project identification, formulation and implementation, particularly at the State level, should need to be strengthened, taking into account the programme content and coverage. Professionally trained technical manpower, should have to be included at decision making and supervisory levels. Functionaries engaged at different levels in the on going schemes would have to be suitably trained to make them acquire the basic skills required for programme management.

Mostly social welfare programmes by their very nature do not succeed unless the local communities and beneficiaries participate fully and extend their cooperation at all stages of implementation. They should to be involved in identification of local needs and prospective beneficiaries, delivery of services and programme supervision. Welfare Advisory Committees at different levels with representatives from local bodies and other community agencies should be constituted to deliver benefits to the target groups intended.

Labour Welfare and Welfare State

The idea of the welfare State is a response by the western

democracies and by the third world countries to the challenge posed by communism. It is felt that the economic contents of communism might make an appeal, and thus hold sway over the minds of the poor and the weaker sections of those countries. To obviate that possibility of overthrow of democratic system, and to give a lie to the Marxist prediction about the inevitability of class welfare the concept of welfare State is evolved. The plain and obvious purpose is to bring about betterment of the lot of the weaker sections of the community in a smooth and peaceful manner. In earlier years, the welfare plan was set out in the Beveridge Report which laid down the objectives of the welfare State. Those objectives, according to that report, should be a massive attack on the five giant evils-want, disease, ignorance, squalor and idleness. The eradication of these evils has been considered to be the prime requisite for securing social justice. Though the evils enumerated by the Plan are five, a little reflection would show that each one of these evils is a concomitant and natural consequence of poverty. The elimination of poverty, therefore, becomes a question of vital importance in a welfare state. In a welfare State, the community at large recognizes the collective responsibility towards its weaker or less fortunate members and takes definite action to assist them. There was then the political idealism of the view that the welfare State "was one in which social security and social services were the birth right of every citizen, normally without test of means, in which the development of social services are democratically organized to meet the essential needs of the whole community and in which the whole community participates as a matter of course." Another theorist has stated, that "Welfare State," 'is based on two principles: the right to every one to a job and a guaranteed social minimum of health, wealth and leisure.'

The emergence of the concept of welfare state is the legitimate culmination of the democratic process which emphasises the values of equal rights and privileges to all the citizens. A welfare state is "a State in which organized power is deliberately used (through politics and administration) to modify the play of market forces in at least three directions, first, by guaranteeing individuals and families a minimum income irrespective of the market value of their work or their property; second, by narrowing the extent of insecurity by enabling individuals and families to meet certain social contingencies, namely, sickness, old age and unemployment which lead otherwise to individual and family crisis; and third, by ensuring that all citizens without distinction of status or class are offered the best standards available in relation to certain agreed range of social services. Titmuss said, that, "four main categories of services were largely responsible for Britain being described as a welfare state-education, medial care, social security and housing, with a fifth comprising a number of smaller services namely; child care, juvenile delinquency, employment bureau and financial grants to many voluntary agencies." In India, the march towards the establishment of an egalitarian society, the age old feudal system has been abolished. Princes and privy purses were given a fitting burial long back, Bonded labour has also been abolished. For providing necessary infrastructure for rapid economic development with social justice, public sector has been assigned the pivotal role. Freedom of Association has been guaranteed under the country's Constitution. Workers have been given the right to organize and the right to collective bargaining for getting their demand settled. The right of partnership in management has been recognized as incorporated in the Constitution as one of the Directive Principles of the State Policy. There are also number of statutes aimed at safeguarding and promoting the interests of the workers and these statutes are being periodically amended to be in tune with the vast changes over the years. In this context, it is hard to believe that there can still exist a feudal lord in this modern India continuing to treat the worker as mere slaves with utter disregard to the laws of the country.

India is a Sovereign, Socialist, Secular and Democratic Republic. According to Article 38 the State shall strive to promote the welfare of people by securing and protecting as effectively as it may, a social order in which "Justice (Social, economic and political) shall inform all the institutions of the national life." The Forty Fourth Amendment Act, 1978, widened the scope of Article 38, and it is now further provided that, in particular, the State shall strive to minimise the inequalities in income and endeavour to eliminate inequalities in status, facilities in income and endeavour to eliminate inequalities in status, facilities and opportunities, not only amongst individuals, but also amongst groups of people residing in different areas or engaged in different vocations. Article 38 thus sets out, while echoing the words of the Preamble, the objectives of the framers of the Constitution for the establishment of a 'Welfare State.' It enjoys upon the State to promote the welfare of the people by securing and protecting in an effective manner a social order based upon social, economic and political justice. This is clear from the exhortation contained in Article 37 that the Directive Principles shall be fundamental in the governance of the counter, and it shall be the duty of the State to apply those principles in making laws.

So, in a welfare State, all are assured of adequate help in case of need which may be due to illness, old age, physical and mental handicap, or unemployment. State assistance is given as a right, not as a charity, and no stigma of pauperism is attached to the receivers.

Labour Welfare Policy Objectives

Policy is a set course of action which lends direction to activities and programmes and channelises them towards certain accredited objectives. It has its roots in the past and eyes on the future. Administration is a bridge between the policy and programmes; and programmes require resources. Therefore, policy formulation involves determination of objectives, ordering of priorities, estimation and mobilization of resources required and provision for their generation, building administration infrastructure necessary to handle resources and programmes, and a mechanism of evaluation. It is in this light that the author propose to discuss the labour welfare policy in India. For a long time, the labour welfare policy in India was concerned primarily with creating statutory rights including those of labour welfare for workers by creating obligation on employers. It was the Royal Commission on Labour which in its report in 1931 made a comprehensive review of labour scene in India and identified a large number of imbalances then industrial life of the country. The Commission suggested a number of intra-mural welfare measures and said that they were the minimum requirements. It laid great emphasis on industrial housing. It recommended the possibility of making labour both a Federal and a Provincial subject so that welfare programmes could be administered better.

The Government of India Act, 1935, which gave autonomy to province in respect of certain subjects, including labour, proved a milestone in the history of labour welfare. The popular governments that came into offices in 1937, in nine Provinces of British India went all out to improve the welfare and working conditions of industrial labour. The National Planning Committee (1937) also made several recommendations in regard to workers' housing and conditions of work. The independence of India in 1947 added the dimensions of urgency and comprehensiveness to the labour welfare movement. The Industrial Truce Resolution of 1948 declared that production was possible only with the maintenance of good and happy industrial relations. This could be achieved, among other factors, by paying due attention to the welfare of workers. The Plans recognized the importance of industrial labour in fulfilment of plan targets and in creating an economic organization in the country which would best subserve the needs of social justice. The main objective of these plans were 'to bring about welfare of the working class and the country's economic stability and progress.'

Having reviewed the labour welfare policy as it unfolded itself in the past, it is relevant to raise the question in regard to the future policy on the subject. In my opinion, the labour welfare policy should be based on the following four pillars:

(a) promotion of economic development;
(b) harmony with other areas of overall social policy;
(c) administrative feasibility; and
(d) reflection of the dynamics of social change and value structure in the country, and direction to it.

Attempts made by the democratic legislatures with a view to eradicating poverty are to secure economic justice for the citizens. Equality of opportunity to all the citizens to develop their individual personalities, and to participate in the pleasures and happiness of life has been held to be the goal of economic justice.

Ponsion in his book *Social Welfare Policy: Contribution of Theory*, argues that two qualities are essential to the evolution of any real social policy. First, the capacity to feel the misery of others and the wish to help by this the policy becomes social, and second, a sense of reality-by this the assistance becomes a policy. He says that the line of satisfaction, moving from individual needs to those of society at large and that of satisfaction moving from the purely biological to the spiritual needs. The role of administration is very crucial to the achievement of policy goals. One of the most frequent opinion in India is that the leaders talk too piously but accomplies so little, and that we have the best plans but poor results. The transformation of plans into concrete results, and of statements of intentions into tangible action is dependent on the quality of administrative infrastructure and procedures. Welfare policy should be in harmony with the current social values and social structure. Further, it should have the orientation to give direction to the process of social change and the emergence of a new value system which is a dynamic feature of all human groups. The pre-industrial society was characterized by small units that were internally cohesive and otherwise self-sufficient, i.e. joint families, caste-groups, village communities etc. These units gave a high degree of emotional and economic security to their members, the later drew their values and status from the former. However, these units have nearly been breaking under the impact of developmental inputs and are invaded by alien patterns of life. The factory system tends to modify social relationships by making them functionalized recognizes status based on performance and permits individual—to switch from one social group to another.

Socio-Economic Justice and Welfare

Justice—To articulate 'Justice' has always been a vexed question, and has produced diversity in legal thinking throughout the world. The difficulty is further increased, because justice can be used in a wider or more restricted sense. The Greeks used the term in the wider sense in the sense of virtue in general; and Hans Kelson had to say that it is a general term of approval which can be applied at will to whatever phenomenon one choses. Thomas Acquinas says that 'unjust law is no law.' To many justice appears to be roughly synonymous with morality. In the narrower sense, as in the expressions 'course of justice,' 'natural justice,' 'denial of justice,' 'legal justice,' 'moral justice, and 'social justice,' the word 'justice' has a circumscribed meaning limiting it to a purpose or a specified area. The Theorists are far removed from one another as Thomas Acquinas and Salmond subscribed the generally accepted view that, 'justice is the goal which law intends to achieve, and indeed to them it is a logical part of the very notion of law,' Salmond speaks of justice according to law. 'Justice' said Daniel Webster "is the greatest interest of man on the earth." Justice, as Aristotle said, "is the bond of men in society," and 'States without Justice' are as St. Augustine said, "robber bonds." Justice as a force of civic equilibrium presented a much simple problem in ancient society than the modern dynamic world Plato was concerned with a status ridden society; and to him a static condition based upon a nice distribution of appropriate functions represented the most desirable form of equipoise. In contrast, social groupings of today are dynamic not static, and they do not find the ideal equipoise in a condition of mere imperturbability Justice is considered to be the primary goal of a welfare States and the very existence of it rests on the parameters of justice. The greatest contrast, however, between ancient and modern thinking about the social harmony and justice is in the changed conception of individual personality in relation to law. Realizing the difficulty in defining the term 'justice' Justice Mathew says. "I do not think that there is the concept of justice." On the observation of St. Augustine on time "I cannot define it but I know what it is," and Justice opines, "much the same can be said of justice."

Lord Wright while conferring his inability to define the concept of justice, said: *I have not found any satisfactory definition of justice, but what it is, it is the quality of what it is just. And what is just in a particular case is what appears to be just to the just man, in the same way as what is reasonable to the reasonable man.*

Justice with its aforesaid variant and broad uses in the past has in course of time come to acquire in its distributive character a settled meaning of *'Suum Cuique'* to each his due) with a corollary that 'equal should be treated equally.' This distributive justice has come to be known as social justice. But, the concept of social justice itself had its initial vagueness, and it has taken time to crystallise. Untented by the 'perennial fallacy that because something cannot be cut and dried or merely weighed or measured, it does not exist, and undeterred by the dicta of social justice being an inarticulate majore premise which is personal to every court and every judge, emnates from 'fanciful notions of adjudicator, being vague or indeterminate concept defying clear definitions covering all situations, every time, yielding to the convenience of the employees at the cost of the employer next of kin to caprice and humour, trying to create despotism, or with the sermon that it should be based on more solid foundations, social justice had its sway, and in course of time, it has assumed shape and content.

The criticism of controversial nature of the concept and it's variability, advanced by Shri Balkrishna Ayer J. Against social justice appears to be based on the misconception of the very basis and nature of the same. Similarly, Allen is vehemently critical of the concept of social justice when he says that, "I am now sure that those who use the term most glibly do not know very clearly what they man by it. Some mean distribution or redistribution of wealth; some interpret; it is equality of opportunity-a misleading term, since opportunity can never be equal among human beings who have unequal capacities to grasp it. Many, I suspect mean simply that it is unjust that any body should be more fortunate than themselves and the more intelligent mean that it is just." But unconsciously he himself defines it in the end by saying "every effort should be made to mitigate the disparities of human inequality and that no obstacle should be offered, but rather help afforded to practicable opportunities for self improvement." For Spencer, the social justice means each according to desert where desert refers to what is fitting to each person on grounds of status, ability, and finer aspects of labour and mental contribution, while according to Kripotkin, it means each according to his needs. These theories of social justice and Human theory of legal justice were discussed in details by David Miller in his eminent book on social justice and he tested them on sociological perspective dividing the societies into three categories, namely primitive, hierarchical or feudal and market societies. According to him, the pattern of social justice differs with the pattern of the society. David Miller concludes at page 342 that this follows from thesis that 'man holds conceptions of social justice as part of more general views of the societies and that they acquire these views through their experience of living in actual societies with definite structures and embodying particular kinds of inter-personal relationship.

This, it may be said that while economic growth, education and social attitudes have a far-reaching influence on social policy they can exercise their necessarily gradual influence effectively only if law provides a framework of recognized obligation and settle habit with in which they can operate.

To run through the whole gamut of labour welfare legislation, to analyse each one, to pinpoint the lacunose, and to suggest corrective action is by no means an easy task but one well worth attempting. It is in this belief, the present study is planned. .

REFERENCES

A.K. Sen, *Justice from the Common Man,* 1967.

A.C. Pigou; *Economics of Welfare,* London, Macmillan, 1962.

A. Briggs; "*The Welfare State in Historical Perspective,* European Journal of Sociology, Vol. 2, No. 2, 1961.

C.K. Allen, *Aspects of Justice,* (1958), p. 28.

Flyod R. Mecham, *An Inquiry Concerning Justice,* Machingan Law Review (1916), p. 361.

H. Willenosky and C. Labeaux, *Industrial Society and Social Welfare.* Newyork, Russel, Safe foundation, 1918.

Justice K.K. Mathew, *Democracy, Equality and Freedom,* (1978), p. 55.

Kingsley Martin; "*Socialism and Welfare State,* Fabian Tract No. 291 (London) Fabian Publication, 1953.

Labour Party, *The Welfare State,* Discussion pamphlet No. 4; London, 1952.

Lord Wright, *Legal Essays and Addresses* (1939), p. 382.

M. Brose, *The Coming of the Welfare State,* London, 1961.

N.M. Joshi, *Trade Union Movement in India,* 1927.

Plans and Perspective of Social Welfare in India, (1951-61) Government of India, New Delhi, 1963, p. 1.

R.M. Titmuss; *The Welfare State, Images and Realities; The Social Service Review,* March 1963.

Seventh Five Year Plan (1985-90), Vol. II, Government of India, p. 308.

Select Bibliography

A. Briggs (1961), *"The Welfare State in Historical Perspective,* European Journal of Sociology, Vol. 2, No. 2.

A.C. Pigou (1962), *Economics of Welfare,* London, Macmillan.

A.K. Sen, *Justice from the Common Man,* 1967.

Annan, Kofi (1999), *Secretary-General proposes global compact on human rights, Labour, environment, in address to World Economic Forum in Davos.* Address of United Nations Secretary General Kofi Annan to the World Economic Forum in Davos, Switzerland, on 31 January 1999, Press Release SG/SM/6881/Rev. 1. New York, NY, United Nations, 1 Feb.

Barns, Maggie; Forstater, Mayer; Mong, Adrienne; Osgood, Diane; Zadek, Simon, 1997, *Open Trading: Options for effective monitoring of corporate codes of conduct.* London, New Economics Foundations Catholic Institute for International Relations. Mar [for an executive summary see <http//www.oneworld.calvertgroup.com/investor/ind-sri-resolutions.html> (visited 2 June 1999).

Blanpain. Roger, "A general introduction," in Roger Blanpain (ed.): *Multinational enterprises and the social challenges of the 21st century.* Dordrecht, Kluwer.

C.K. Allen (1958), *Aspects of Justice,* p. 28.

Caroll, Archie B. (1996), *Business and society: Ethics and stakeholder management.* Third edition Cincinnati. OH, South-Western College Publishing.

Chote, Robert (1999), "World Bank sets out plans for global code for social policy," in *Financial Times* (London), 22 April, p. 4.

Dickson, Marsha A. (1996), *Socially responsibel consumer behaviour in the appeal marketing system: Preliminary findings from a survey.* Columbus, OH, Ohio, State University (Department of Consumer and Textile Sciences). 18 July.

Diller, Janelle M. Forthcoming. "Social conduct in transactional enterprise operations: The role of the International labour Organization," in Roger Blanpain (ed.): *Multinational enterprises and the social challenges of the 21st century.* Dordrecht, Kluwer.

Ferguson, Clare, (1998). *A receive of UK company codes of conduct.* Report commissioned by the Social development Division, Department for International Development. London, DFID. Aug.

Flyod R. Mecham (1916), *An Inquiry Concerning Justice,* Machingan Law Review, p. 361.

Giri V.V., *Labour Problems in Industry* (1962).

Glassman, James, K. (1999), "Do-good funds that are also doing better," in *International Herald Tribune* (Zurich). 6-7 February, p. 16.

H. Willenosky and C. Labeaux (1918), *Industrial Society and Social Welfare.* Newyork, Russel, Safe foundation.

Haas, Daniel, (1998), *Mit Sozialklauseln gegen Kinderarbeit? Das Beispiel der indischen Teppichproduction.* Berliner Studien zur internationalen Politik. No. 4. Minster, Lit.

Indian Labour Year Book (1983), Government of India.

IRRC (Investor Responsibility Research Center). 1996a *Shareholder action advances worldwide: Investors placed a broader range of topics on more non-US ballots in the 1996 global proxy voting season.* Press release, 29 July. Washington, DC.

Justice K.K. Mathew (1978), *Democracy, Equality and Freedom,* p. 55.

Kellerson, Hillary (1998). "The ILO Declaration of 1998 on

fundamental principles and rights: A challenge for the future," in *International Labour Review* (Geneva), Vol. 137, No. 2, pp. 233-228.

Kingsley Martin (1953), *Socialism and Welfare State,* Fabian Tract No. 291 (London) Fabian Publication.

Kumar, Ritu; Gessese, Nebiyeleul; Konishi, Yasuo (1998), *Responding to global standards: A framework for assessing social and environmental performance of industries—Case study of the textile industry in India, Indonesia and Zimbabwe.* Vienna. United Natices Industrial Development Organization (UNDIO), May.

Labour Party (1952), *The Welfare State,* Discussion pamphlet, No. 4; London.

Lefebvre, Maurica; Singh, Jang B. (1992), "The content and focus of Canadian corporate codes of ethics," in *Journal of Business Ethics* (Dordrecht). Vol. 11, No. 10 (Oct.), pp. 799-808.

Lord Wright (1939), *Legal Essays and Addresses,* p. 382.

M. Brose (1961), *The Coming of the Welfare State,* London.

Mayhew, Nick (1998), "Trouble with the triple bottom line," *Financial Times* (London), 10 August, p. 8.

Murray, Jill (1998), "Corporate codes of conduct and labour standards," in Robert Kyloh (ed.): *Mastering the challenge of globalization: Towards a trade union agenda.* ILO Bureau for workers'; Activities, Working Paper produced under Project INT.97/MO1/ITA ("Information technology, workers' participation and social dialogue"). Geneva, ILO, pp. 45-104.

N.M. Joshi (1927), *Trade Union Movement in India.*

Plans and Perspective of Social Welfare in India, (1951-61) Government of India, New Delhi, 1963, p. 1.

R.M. Titmuss; *The Welfare State, Images and Realities; The Social Service Review,* March 1963.

Ramanujam, G. (1986), *Indian Labour Movement.*

Sajhau, Jean-Paul (1997), *Business ethics in the textile, clothing and footwear (FTC) industries: Codes of Conduct.* Sectoral Activities Programme (Industrial Activities Branch) Working Paper, SAP 260/WP.110. Geneva, ILO.

Saxena, R.C. (1981), *Labour Problems and Social Welfare.*

Sharma A.M. (1981), *Aspects of Labour Welfare and Social Security.*

Stuckelberger, Christoph; Eger, Michel (1996), "A social clause with a TNC: The Migros-Del Monte case," in *Swiss Coalition News* (Bern), No. 7, March, pp. 6-7.

The Payment of Gratuity Act, 1972, Section 4.

UNCTAD (1994), *World investment report: Transnational corporations, employment and the workplace.* New York, NY, United Nations.

United Nations Commission on Sustainable Development. (1999), *Voluntary Initsives and Agreements.* Economic and Social Council, Commission on Sustainable Development, Seventh Session, 19-30 April, Report of the Secretary-General. E/CN 17/1999/12. New York, NY. United Nations, 5 Apr.

United States Department of Labour (1997), *By the sweat and toil of children*—Volume 4: *Consumer lebels and child labour.* Washington. D.C., Bureau of International Labour Affairs.

Varley, Pamela: Mathiasen, Carolya; Vorthers, Meg (eds.) (1998), *The Sweatshop Quandary: Corporate Responsibility on the Global Frontier.* Washington, DC, IRRC.

Index

□□□